Guides to Wines & Top Vineyards

Champagne

2023 edition

Benjamin Lewin MW

Preface

The first part of this guide discusses the region, and explains the character and range of Champagne. The second part profiles the producers. There are detailed profiles of the leading producers, showing how each winemaker interprets the local character, and mini-profiles of other important estates.

In the first part, I address the nature of the wines made today and ask how this has changed, how it's driven by tradition or competition, and how styles may evolve in the future. I show how the wines are related to the terroir and to the types of grape varieties that are grown, and I explain the classification system. For each region, I suggest reference wines that illustrate the character and variety of the area.

In the second part, there's no single definition for what constitutes a top producer. Leading producers range from those who are so prominent as to represent the common public face of an appellation to those who demonstrate an unexpected potential on a tiny scale. The producers profiled in the guide represent the best of both tradition and innovation in wine in the region. In each profile, I have tried to give a sense of the producer's aims for his wines, of the personality and philosophy behind them—to meet the person who makes the wine, as it were, as much as to review the wines themselves.

Each profile gives contact information and details of production, followed by a description of the producer and the range of wines. For major producers (rated from 1 to 4 stars), I suggest reference wines that are a good starting point for understanding the style. Most of the producers welcome visits, although some require appointments: details are in the profiles. Profiles are organized geographically, and each group of profiles is preceded by maps showing the locations of producers to help plan itineraries.

The guide is based on many visits to Champagne over recent years. I owe an enormous debt to the hundreds of producers who cooperated in this venture by engaging in discussion and opening innumerable bottles for tasting. This guide would not have been possible without them.

Benjamin Lewin MW

Contents

Tables

Appellation Maps

Producer Maps

Méthode Champenoise

Take regions where wine production is marginal and full ripeness occurs only occasionally. Most struggle to survive. But the genius of Champagne is to turn weakness into strength by making wine that is acidic and bland as a neutral base for introducing bubbles, with a touch of sweetness to counteract the acidity. The reason why almost all potentially competitive regions have failed to produce anything matching Champagne is that they can actually make reasonable wine: they are simply not marginal enough. You might think that as sparkling wines are far more manipulated than still wines, Champagne would be easier to imitate, but in fact very few alternatives are really competitive in terms of character and quality. Champagne has progressively pushed all other aperitifs into relative insignificance.

The same method is used to produce all quality sparkling wine: performing a second fermentation in the bottle to trap the carbon dioxide that is released *in situ*. This is called Méthode Champenoise, but the term means far more than merely a method for making sparkling wine. The fact that it is banned from use by anyone but the Champagne producers tells you a great deal about their commercial ruthlessness in enforcing their market position. The only term that is allowed for wine made elsewhere by the same methods as in Champagne is Méthode Traditionnelle.

Fermentation to convert sugar into alcohol releases huge volumes of carbon dioxide. There is still controversy about the origin of the idea that you could make sparkling wine by trapping that gas in the bottle. Although Dom Pérignon is often given credit for introducing the second fermentation, in fact his career as cellarmaster at the Abbey of Hautvillers was devoted to trying to stop adventitious fermentation that was occurring in bottled wine and causing the bottles to explode.

At the time, the major production of the region was still a conventional mix of dry red and white wine. Sparkling wine was first made in Champagne in 1695, but it was not until around 1720 (just after Dom Pérignon's era) that it became fashionable, stronger bottles became available that could contain the pressure, and Champagne became the premier sparkling wine. (Today pressure is not usually a problem, but some Champagne houses make visitors wear protective glasses when visiting the caves, just in case a bottle explodes, and every so often you do see a hole in a stack of bottles where one has in fact burst.)

Fermentation in the bottle

The principle of Méthode Champenoise is that the first fermentation—which occurs in exactly the same way as fermentation for any other wine—continues to completion, generating a still *base wine* with low alcohol (10.5-11%). Then a solution called the *liqueur de tirage* containing wine, sugar, and yeast is added, and the bottle is sealed with a crown cap. A second fermentation takes place, bringing alcohol up another per cent, and releasing enough carbon dioxide to create the required pressure of 5-6 atmospheres in the bottle.

The second fermentation leaves a sediment of dead yeast cells. The method of dealing with this goes back to Madame Clicquot Ponsardin, who had taken control of Veuve Clicquot in 1805. The story goes that she was infuriated by the mess the sediment made at the bottom of the bottle. Simply turning the bottles upside down did not work because particles continued to stick to the sides. Experimenting at home, she cut holes in her kitchen table to hold the bottles, and discovered that the sediment would collect in the neck if they were kept inverted and periodically rotated.

It was later discovered that the process works best if the bottles start at an angle of 45°. *Remuage* (riddling in English) became a regular part of production, using a *pupître*, which consists of two boards hinged to form an inverted V; each board contains 60 holes cut at 45°. The bottles are rotated very gradually so that after a period of some weeks they come to a full vertical position.

Dom Pérignon spent most of his career trying to eliminate the bubbles that were spoiling the still wines of the Champagne region, but is remembered as the person who created Champagne. He is credited with developing techniques for producing white wine from black grapes, harvesting under cool conditions to preserve freshness, and introducing the idea of blending lots from different areas to make more complex wine.

Pressing

Fermentation (usually in tank)
produces 11% alcohol base wine

Assemblage
30-40 lots from current vintage
plus 25% reserve wines

Second fermentation in bottle
creates 5-6 bars pressure
and increases alcohol to 12.5%

Aging on lees
15 months (non vintage)
36 months (vintage)

Remuage (riddling)
1 week (gyropalette)
3 months (manually)

Disgorgement

Add dosage (sugar)

Champagne is made by a conventional alcoholic fermentation, a second fermentation in the bottle, extended lees aging, disgorgement, and the addition of dosage. Aging lasts more than 18 months for nonvintage and more than three years for vintage Champagne.

The romantic view of Champagne production is that a skilled remueur (or riddler) can turn several hundred bottles a day, adjusting the angle by tiny increments. Almost all tours of caves in Champagne take you past rows of pupîtres, but the fact is that today the process is largely mechanized. A machine called the gyropalette is used for virtually all Méthode Champenoise

At the start of the twentieth century, Champagne house cellars were full of pupîtres for riddling.

production. Holding bottles in a crate, it follows a program for rotating them en masse until they are vertical. It takes days, compared with weeks for conventional riddling. Less romantic, but more practical—and more economical.

How does the quality compare? "It's absolutely clear gyropalettes give better results than riddling by hand. I did not want to believe it, but the inventor of the machine visited and gave me a machine to test. After 6 months I looked and I could not see a difference between gyropalettes and hand riddling. So I took sample bottles to a lab to measure turbidity, and the machine was doing a better job. I decided I must not be nostalgic, I should take the best of modern technology," says Bruno Paillard, whose modern facility on the outskirts of Reims is full of gyropalettes. "Gyropalettes have the advantage of being able to go from absolutely horizontal to absolutely vertical. Quality depends on how you use the machine: you can rush the process through in as little as four days, or spend a week to get it perfect."

Except for a few holdouts who believe in the old methods, gyropalettes have taken over everywhere. There is a curious reversal for some of the prestige cuvées in which a house may use gyropalettes for everything except its very top wines. The houses like to say that these were produced with individual attention, but the fact is that riddling by hand is less reliable than gyropalettes. While gyropalettes can give quality at a variety of levels—basically depending on how quickly the program completes the process—the sad reality is that, at their best, they produce the most consistent results. If the issue were really about quality, as opposed to marketing, gyropalettes would be used for the top cuvées, but then this is Champagne...

Most riddling in Champagne or elsewhere is now performed by gyro-palettes.

Disgorgement and Dosage

Once the sediment has collected in the neck it has to be disgorged. This is the most amazing part of the process. The necks of the inverted bottles are dipped into a refrigerated bath. The sediment in the neck becomes frozen. The bottle is turned upright, the cap is taken off, and voila!—the internal pressure ejects the sediment. *Dégorgement à la glace,* to give the process its full name, was invented in the late nineteenth century. The original concept is the basis for more automated machinery today.

(An old manual technique called dégorgement à la volée—flying disgorgement—is sometimes used, when the bottle is turned upside down without stirring up the lees, the cork is taken off, and the bottle is returned to vertical in the same moment. It requires great skill and is used by some artisans and occasionally for large bottles.)

After the second fermentation, the wine should be completely dry, but the natural high acidity of Champagne generally needs to be counteracted by some sweetness. The style of Champagne is determined by a topping-up process that follows disgorgement. A small amount of wine is added to compensate for material that was lost when the sediment was ejected. This is done by using a solution called the *liqueur d'expédition,* more commonly called the *dosage,* which consists of sugar dissolved in wine. Then a new cork is put on.

Champagnes (and other sparkling wines) are labeled according to the amount of sugar in the dosage:

- A wine without any added sugar is called Brut Nature or sometimes Zero Dosage.

- A wine with less than 6 g/l of sugar can be called Extra Brut.

- Brut (by far the most common label) can have from 0 to 12 g/l (so a Champagne with less than 6 g/l dosage can labeled either as Brut or Extra Brut).

- In addition, there are various levels of sweetness in the Sec category (although Sec means "dry," a Sec or Demi-Sec Champagne is actually sweet).

However, perception of sweetness depends a great deal on the balance between the level of sugar and the acidity (sweetness is less evident at high acidity, or put another way, a wine with higher acidity may require higher dosage).

The machine for dégorgement à la glace was invented in 1884.

Méthode Champenoise is the highest quality method for making sparkling wine because the second fermentation that generates the bubbles occurs in the very bottle that you will open. There's a slight exception for very small bottles (splits) and for bottles larger than magnums, where riddling and disgorgement may not be practical: usually the Champagne is produced in a normal bottle, but is then transferred into smaller or larger bottles. This *transvasage* involves emptying the bottles into a vat, which is then used to fill the smaller or larger bottles, but although

Modern equipment uses the old principle of dégorgement, but is completely automated.

all this is done under pressure, it's difficult to avoid some loss of gas. Bottles and magnums are therefore the way to enjoy sparkling wine under optimal conditions.

The unique characteristic of sparkling wine is its mousse—the fine froth of bubbles that forms on the surface when it is poured. Once the initial rush has died down, the bubbles help to propel aromas out of the glass, contribute to the sense of acidity, and give the wine its characteristic prickle. Smaller bubbles are usually considered to be better, as they give an impression of finer texture. The 20 million bubbles in every bottle are not just for show.

The Grapes of Champagne

Sparkling wine was originally produced from black grapes. Lack of color was made possible when methods were developed early in the eighteenth century for gentle pressing that allowed juice to be obtained by running it straight off with minimal skin contact. Before then, most Champagne was probably rosé. This was one of Dom Pérignon's accomplishments.

It's uncertain exactly what grape varieties were used in Dom Pérignon's time, but Pinot Noir and Pinot Gris, known locally as Fromenteau, were major varieties. Juice from white grapes began to be included only in the second half of the eighteenth century, first becoming common in the region around

The Major Grape Varieties

Chardonnay brings freshness and elegance. It is most concentrated on the Côte de Blancs.

Pinot Noir brings density and structure. It is most concentrated in the north on the Montagne de Reims, in the valley of the Aÿ to the east of Épernay, and in the south, on the Côte des Bar.

Pinot Meunier is closely related to Pinot Noir, and brings more forward fruits, but is less refined. It is the most durable variety, and is concentrated in the Vallée de la Marne, because it resists Spring frosts best.

Avize, which became known as the Côte des Blancs. Before phylloxera arrived, no less than 80 different grape varieties were growing in the Champagne region. The replanting caused by phylloxera focused on the varieties that are dominant today.

When the first appellation rules were defined in 1919, Champagne was limited to seven varieties. Only three are important today: one white variety, Chardonnay, and two black varieties, Pinot Noir and Pinot Meunier. The other varieties remain legal, but now are grown only in tiny quantities. The main change in the varieties from the nineteenth century is the disappearance of Pinot Gris.

Most Champagne is made from a blend of varieties, but a Blanc de Blancs comes exclusively from Chardonnay, and a Blanc de Noirs comes exclusively from black varieties (usually only Pinot Noir). Differences in styles are due to many factors, among which grape varieties are only part, but in general a Blanc de Noirs is likely to have a slightly fuller body, while a Blanc de Blancs has a greater sense of precision and minerality. Sometimes lower pressure (5 bar instead of 6 bar) is used to give a creamier expression for Blanc de Blancs.

Aside from Blanc de Blancs or Blanc de Noirs, most Champagne is a blend of all three grape varieties. Chardonnay and Pinot Noir are held in distinctly higher esteem than Pinot Meunier, but Pinot Meunier has the practical advantage that it flowers later than Pinot Noir, so it is less susceptible to Spring frosts. "Pinot Meunier is the most rustic cépage in Champagne, but it's the only one that resists difficult conditions," says Rodolphe Péters of Champagne Pierre Péters. The warming trend has made this less of a factor, and the proportion of Pinot Meunier has been declining: it was the most important variety in the vineyards in the 1950s, when it was 45% of all plantings, but today it is only 32%. Pinot Noir is now the most widely planted variety at 39%, and Chardonnay is 29%.

A variant of Pinot Noir, Pinot Meunier takes its name from the white flour-like appearance of the underneath of its leaves (Meunier is French for miller). It brings more forward fruits and aromas, which help the wine when it is young: perfect for nonvintage Champagne. "We do consider Pinot Meunier as essential in the blend. It's all a matter of selecting the terroir and using the proper proportion. On average we have a third of each cépage. It's true that Pinot Meunier will mature a little quicker than Pinot Noir or Chardonnay and won't last

Gentle pressing is achieved in Champagne by the traditional basket press, in which the lid comes down onto the mass of grapes, and the juice comes out between the wooden slats. Courtesy CIVC.

as long, but it helps create more harmony and balance," says Jean-Marc Lallier-Deutz at Champagne Deutz. But it tends to bring an element of coarseness with aging, which is why it is often excluded from vintage Champagne.

Until the past decade, Pinot Meunier was relegated to obscurity: part of the blend, but rarely discussed. More recently, some producers in the Vallée de la Marne have been making cuvées specifically from Pinot Meunier (technically these can be described as Blanc de Noirs or Blanc de Meunier), and even occasionally producing vintage cuvées. While these are not likely to change the general perception of Pinot Meunier, some are very fine and show an unexpected ability to age.

Types of Champagne

All Champagne, even a Blanc de Noirs, should be a pale golden color. Except, of course, for rosé. This can be a bit of a trick: most rosé Champagne is made simply by adding a little red wine to the (white) base wine. This is illegal as a means of producing rosé for all wines in the E.U. except for Champagne; and, indeed, proposals to legalize it for still wine production led

The Champagne Label
Nonvintage and *Vintage* are distinguished only by the fact that vintage states the year whereas nonvintage does not.
All labels carry an indication of dosage: *Dry Styles*   *Brut Nature* (or *Zero Dosage*) has no added sugar.   *Extra Brut* has dosage less than 6 g/l.   *Brut* has less than 12 g/l.
Sweet Styles   *Extra Sec* (12-17 g/l), *Sec* (17-32 g/l), *Demi-Sec* (32-50 g/l), or *Doux* (more than 50 g/l) are all rare today.
Blanc de Blancs comes exclusively from Chardonnay.   *Blanc de Noirs* comes only from black varieties, usually Pinot Noir, but Pinot Meunier is allowed.
Grand Cru means that the grapes come only from the 17 villages classified as grand cru.   *Premier Cru* means that the grapes come only from premier cru villages.

to a great outcry about loss of quality. The method of production means that rosé Champagne does not necessary come from black grapes; because the color is provided by the small percentage of red wine, the rest can include Chardonnay.

Everywhere wine is produced in France, the winemaker is the key person. (Even though sometimes in Bordeaux one is driven to think about the marketing manager...) But in Champagne, the cellarmaster (*chef de cave* in French) is king: he is in charge of blending, and the wine is a neutral basis for him to work his skill. The crucial fact is that Champagne is all about blending, by assemblage from different years, different locations, and different grape varieties.

Nonvintage Champagne

The vast majority of Champagne is nonvintage, meaning that base wines from recent years are blended before the second fermentation. Each Champagne house prides itself upon maintaining consistency of style by blending, and it's the nonvintage Champagne that best displays its skill. The blend may include as many as 30-40 different cuvées, coming from different parts of the region; possibly only perfume blending has the same complexity.

A major factor in maintaining quality and consistency is the use of reserve wines. Some producers establish reserve wines by setting aside part of each vintage to be kept (under inert conditions) for later use, some keep their

Reference Wines for Champagne Styles	
Zero Dosage	Ayala, Zero Dosage Laurent-Perrier, Ultra Brut
Extra Brut	Jacquesson Larmandier Bernier
Brut	Bollinger Bruno Paillard Deutz
Blanc de Blancs	Pierre Gimonnet Pierre Péters, L'Esprit De Sousa Ruinart Tarlant
Blanc de Noirs	Egly Ouriet Philipponnat
Rosé d'Assemblage Rosé de Saignée	Billecart-Salmon Laurent-Perrier
Pinot Meunier	Chartogne-Taillet, Les Barres Egly Ouriet, Les Vignes de Vrigny Tarlant, La Vigne d'Or Demière, Lysandre Dehours, Terre de Meunier Bérêche, Rive Gauche

reserves as a blend of older vintages, and some maintain what is called a perpetual reserve, or solera, replenished each year by adding wine from the latest vintage to replace what is withdrawn.

A typical nonvintage Champagne probably contains up to three quarters of wine from the most recent vintage (sometimes called the *base year*), a fair proportion from the previous couple of vintages, and smaller amounts of reserve wine from older vintages. The proportion and age of the reserve is often a measure of quality. Reserve wines aren't necessarily any better in quality than the current vintage; the significance is more that their different characters provide the basis for blending.

Using reserve wines evens out vintage variation, and allows sub par vintages to be absorbed. But the disadvantage is that you do not see the maximum quality in nonvintage wines when vintages are good. Ann de Keyser at Nicolas Feuillatte was quite honest about it: "Reserve wines may be used to increase or decrease quality depending on the current vintage." As Dominic Demarville, cellarmaster of Veuve Clicquot, explains, using all the wine in a good year would compromise quality in lesser vintages because there would be no high quality reserve wines. "It's a delicate balance," he says.

Most producers accept the model of "blend, baby, blend," but a handful go another way. "The concept of nonvintage, of being completely consistent, began to frustrate us," says Jean-Hervé Chiquet at Champagne Jacquesson. "In 1998 we were still making a classic blend, we were working on the 1997, and it was very good but it would be impossible to reproduce in another year. So we made another blend. But afterwards we realized that we'd made a wine that wasn't as good. So we decided we should make the best wine (each year) and we identified it by the number of the cuvée." Now each numbered release consists of an assemblage from a base year supplemented by the assemblages from the previous two years. There's more sense of variation between releases, without going to the extremes of representing a single vintage.

Some producers, such as Pierre Moncuit, make what are effectively undeclared vintages by not using any reserve wine. There's something of a trend at smaller producers to break out of the straightjacket of consistency and to allow more annual variation in nonvintage wines; some producers now indicate the year of the base wine on the back label. But large houses are still committed to the consistency of the brand.

Vintage Champagne

Vintage Champagne typically is made only in the better years, 3-4 times per decade historically, 5-6 times more recently. Here variation is expected to reflect the character of the year, as seen through the prism of house style. Vintage Champagnes are also blended, of course, but the blend is only between vineyard sources and grape varieties. Whereas nonvintage Champagne is intended for consumption soon after release, vintage Champagne is intended to support some aging in the bottle.

Another significant feature of vintage Champagne is that it spends longer before disgorgement. The rules require nonvintage Champagne to rest on its lees for 15 months before it is disgorged; for vintage Champagne the period is increased to three years. Many producers age their wines—especially prestige cuvées—for longer than the minimum.

The process of aging is completely different before and after disgorgement. While the wine is on the lees, it is in a reductive environment (effectively oxygen is excluded) and it picks up flavor and richness due to the process of *autolysis*, as the dead yeast cells break down to release material that protects the wine against oxidation and aging, giving a fresh flavor. After disgorgement, the environment is oxidative, and the major factor influencing development is a process called the Maillard reaction, which involves interactions between sugar and amino acids that were released by autolysis. This is what gives Champagne those biscuity notes of toast and brioche as it ages.

As a rough working rule, the longer a Champagne has spent before disgorgement, the longer it will age interestingly after disgorgement. But the basic moral is that if you like Champagne in a relatively fresh style, you should drink it soon after disgorgement, whereas if you prefer some toast and brioche, you should wait, perhaps a year for a nonvintage Champagne and three years for a vintage.

The objectives in producing nonvintage Champagne are somewhat opposed to those for vintage: nonvintage Champagne relies upon assemblage to even out vintage variation, whereas vintage Champagne is intended at least in part to highlight the character of the year. Because vintage Champagne is produced only in the best years, the grapes are likely to be riper at the outset. A longer period before disgorgement increases richness; and the tendency to exclude Pinot Meunier increases refinement.

So a vintage Champagne should be finer, more precise, and should show more complexity because it can be aged longer than nonvintage. Indeed, one of the criteria for making a vintage Champagne is that it should have aging potential. But maintaining house style is still a paramount concern: vintage variation is allowed to go only so far. "Many people making vintage Champagne are too shy, they make it like a sort of super nonvintage," says cellarmaster Richard Geoffroy at Dom Pérignon.

The Champagne Region

Champagne's beginnings as a wine-producing region were not propitious. The word "Champagne" was used in the fourteenth century to describe the poor area around Reims used for pasture and growing cereals. Until the sixteenth century, the wines of the region were lumped together with those produced around Paris as "wines of France." By 1600, the wines of Reims and Épernay had their own identity and were known as "Champagne."

The areas considered to produce the best wines were to the east of Reims (devoted to red wines) and Aÿ (specializing in white wines). Like Burgundy, the best areas were defined by the monks: in the twelfth and thirteenth cen-

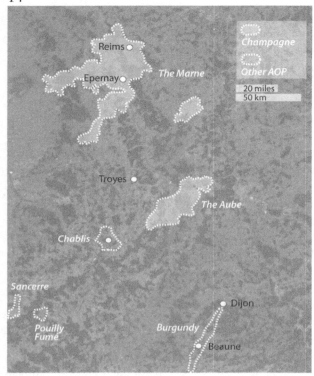

The vineyards of Champagne are the most northern in France. The major vineyards extend from Reims and Épernay, but Champagne also includes the Aube, which is farther south.

turies, the Abbaye of Saint-Nicaise in Reims went on a buying spree of top vineyards.

Although sparkling wine was being produced by the early eighteenth century, it was a long time before it became the major product of the region. Until the nineteenth century, the wine was light (9-10% alcohol) and not highly sparkling (1.5-2 atmospheres). At the start of the nineteenth century cheap red wine was 90% of production, and by 1850 it was still almost 75%. A dramatic transition took place in the twentieth century, when cheap wine production collapsed before the first world war. This left sparkling wine as the major product.

Where exactly Champagne comes from is not quite as simple a question as it might appear. Defining the area of Champagne has always been controversial. Reims and Épernay define the heart of the region, a little less than a hundred miles to the east and north of Paris. But 50 miles to the south, beyond the city of Troyes, is the region of the Aube, where the vineyards were regarded historically as belonging to Champagne.

Champagne Ayala was one of the Maisons sacked in the riots of 1911. The stock and the building were destroyed. Ayala unusually had an insurance policy and was rebuilt (but the insurance company was bankrupted).

In fact, the Aube is closer to Chablis than it is to Reims. The justification for its inclusion was basically that this allows Champagne to cover the entire administrative region of Champagne-Ardennes, as defined after the Revolution. So the Aube was included for administrative convenience, whereas geography might have made it more logical for it to be part of Burgundy.

Tension between the Marne and the Aube came to a head in 1907 when a commission established to define the limits of Champagne excluded the Aube. In 1911, as the rules came into effect, riots culminated in some of the major Champagne houses being sacked. The Aube remained excluded until the limits of Champagne were redefined in 1927. The conflict at this time was that the Aube had a large amount of Gamay, which was considered unsuitable for Champagne. However, the Aube was readmitted to Champagne on condition that the Gamay would be removed over the next twenty years. (In fact it was well into the 1950s before all the Gamay was gone.)

Terroir and Grape Varieties

The classic regions around Reims and Épernay account for three quarters of the vineyards. The key to understanding the terroir of Champagne is chalk: the best vineyards have thin topsoil on a subsoil of chalk beds. The limestone is friable, and acts like a sponge to absorb the rain. The most pronounced outcrops of chalk are found around Reims, and south of Épernay, with a

The terroir throughout Champagne is based on chalk. Courtesy CIVC.

small stretch also running along the river in the Vallée de la Marne west of Épernay.

The chalk is evident in occasional cliff faces, and more dramatically in the cellars that have been excavated under Reims and Épernay, where there are a couple of hundred of kilometers of underground galleries. Farther south, at Vertus, the chalk is much softer. Pinot Noir and Chardonnay are concentrated on the chalk outcrops.

Most vineyards are on slopes, but the incline is not the determinative factor. "In Champagne you don't have the same logic of position on the slope as in Burgundy. Quality depends on the depth of soil above the chalk. Some of my best vineyards are flat," says Charles-Henry Fourny at Veuve Fourny in Vertus. The other major factor is exposure, with angles varying from south- to east-facing.

The Champagne area is quite spread out. It's often described as extending around Reims, but it's easier to think of it as a fan extending from Epernay, with the principal regions formed by blades to the north (Montagne de Reims), South (Côte de Blancs), and west (Vallée de Marne). The differences between the major areas have more to do with the lie of the land and climatic exposure than soil. Going back to the period when Champagne really was a marginal climate, Pinot Noir was planted on the warmest, south-facing slopes, whereas Chardonnay was planted on east-facing slopes.

- The forest of the Montagne de Reims separates Reims from Épernay, and around its circumference are the vineyards named after it.

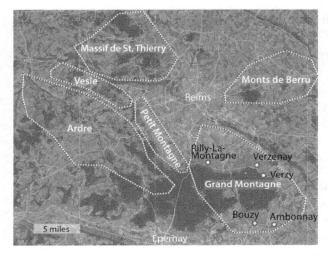

The region around Reims is a monoculture of vines all the way to Epernay, except for the forest of the Montagne de Reims. It is divided into five subareas.

Vineyards are on the slopes running down from the forest. Historically this area was well regarded for red wine; today it has a high concentration of Pinot Noir in the villages facing south, and produces the most full-bodied sparkling wines. At the northern edge, the turn of land means the vineyards face north and there is more Chardonnay. The Petit Montagne to the west has lower elevations, and is less well-known than the Grand Montagne in the southeastern quadrant, which has a concentration of grand cru villages.

- Lying just to the south of Épernay, the Côte des Blancs has a long series of east-facing slopes, running from Chouilly to Le-Mesnil-sur-Oger, that are protected from the wind and from Spring frosts, allowing the vines to mature slowly. It concentrates on Chardonnay and is known for its finesse. As a rough working rule, the wines become more saline and mineral going south. Many of the best-known individual sites in Champagne are on the Côte des Blancs. Along the Côte, there are variations in terroir between chalk and clay, and in exposure to the sun reflecting the exact lay of the land.

- The Vallée de la Marne runs along the river to the west. There is a high concentration of Pinot Meunier because later bud break and earlier ripening make it more resistant to the frosts typically associated with the valley. (This may change with global warming.) There's a difference in exposition, of course, between the north and south banks, with more tendency for vineyards to face north from the south bank, but the land turns enough that there is no fixed rule. The soils here have more clay.

- The area at the eastern end of the Vallée de la Marne, running west to east around Épernay, is sometimes called the Grand Vallée. To the immediate west, Dizy and Cumières are not really considered part of the Vallée de la Marne proper. To the east, Aÿ is an important grand cru village, together with Mareuil-sur-Aÿ just a little farther along the river. Around Épernay, Pinot Noir is king.

The view that blending from all three major areas gives the best quality and complexity goes back to Dom Pérignon, and most large houses source grapes from all over the area. The grapes are usually taken to small, isolated buildings that are press houses in each area, and after pressing, the juice is transported to the winery.

Going farther south, there's a disjoint when you go all the way down to the Aube, where along the Côte des Bar the wines become somewhat richer. The subsoil here is mostly a Kimmeridgian clay, which is more like Chablis and Sancerre than the vineyards in the Marne, and the surface is very stony. (The vineyards of the Côte des Bar are actually nearer to Chablis than they are to Epernay.) It's also a little warmer—harvest is usually a bit earlier—and the focus is on Pinot Noir. There are no premier or grand cru villages.

The villages of the Côte des Blancs are nestled into a monoculture of vines on the hillsides.

The Côte des Bar has extremely stony Kimmeridgian terroir.

Until relatively recently, the Côte des Bar was the region that could not speak its name. Major houses would not even admit they purchased grapes here. Today there are several growers making wines specifically from this region. Bernard Dumont of Champagne R. Dumont describes the situation: "We grow grapes on the same soils as the growers in Chablis. There they produce white wine from white grapes, and here we produce white wine from red grapes."

The Champagne region also has an AOP for still wines, called Coteaux Champenois. Most Coteaux Champenois is red, and the wines are usually single varietals, most often Pinot Noir. The best known is the Pinot Noir from Bouzy. There are also Pinot Meuniers and a little Coteaux Champenois Blanc from Chardonnay. Although some houses, especially around Bouzy or Aÿ, have always produced a little still wine, it has never been much of a focus, but it's possible this may change with global warming. Bollinger makes a still red Pinot Noir, La Côte aux Enfants (which sells at a higher price than the Champagne), and Roederer is doing trials with still wines.

Grand Crus and Premier Crus

Because Champagne is usually blended, you rarely see individual sources indicated, but in fact Champagne has a classification system for vineyards dating from the end of the nineteenth century (first suggested unofficially in 1895 when the magazine Le Vigneron Champenois picked out 13 villages as

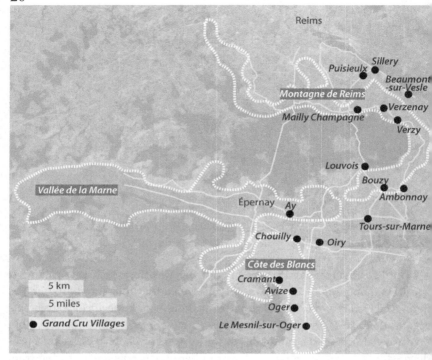

The 17 Grand Cru villages are located in the core of the Champagne region, mostly in the Montagne de Reims and the Côte des Blancs.

the best). The formal system of *échelle des crus* was established in 1911. Every village has a rating from 80% to 100%. (Originally some villages were classified lower, but the minimum climbed to 80% in modern times.)

Villages classified at 100% are called grand crus, and villages rated between 90% and 99% are premier crus. Until a few years ago, the rating determined the price paid for all grapes from each village: whatever base price was set for the vintage would be pro-rated according to the village's position on the scale. The major problem with the échelle des crus was that the whole village was classified at the same level; there was no distinction for quality of grapes or individual sites. Imagine if all Vosne Romanée was classified at one level: no Romanée Conti, no premier crus, no separate village wine, all just one level. The échelle des crus was abolished in 2010, but the distinction between premier and grand crus remains.

The Best Known Villages
Montagne de Reims

Facing full south, *Bouzy* is one of the warmest spots in the Montagne de Reims. Largely planted with Pinot Noir, it is well known for producing still red wine as well as Champagne.

Its neighbor *Ambonnay* has vineyards facing southeast as well as east, with a little more chalk than Bouzy, but the same focus on Pinot Noir.

Verzy and *Verzenay* have vineyards turning around to north-facing, but are dominated by Pinot Noir, giving strong wines, more powerful in Verzenay, more tension in Verzy.

Villers-Marmery is an anomaly where Chardonnay predominates, giving Blanc de Blancs that are fleshier and more overtly powerful than those of the Côte des Blancs.

Sillery was regarded as one of the top villages (together with Aÿ) in the nineteenth century. Vineyards are on slopes facing northeast. There is more Chardonnay than Pinot Noir. It's known for steely Chardonnay that takes a long time to come around, which makes about a third of Ruinart's Dom Ruinart prestige cuvée.

Tours-sur-Marne has an ambiguous location, poised between Montagne de Reims (with which it's usually affiliated) and the Grand Vallée. Pinot Noir predominates on south-facing slopes. Originally it was a grand cru for red, but a premier cru for white grapes. Laurent-Perrier is located here.

Côte des Blancs

At the very start of the Côte des Blancs, *Chouilly* has a richer, less mineral style than the villages to its south. *Oiry* counts as part of the Côte des Blancs, although it's farther east, with vineyards that are the flat ends of the slopes in Chouilly, Cramant, and Avize.

Cramant and *Avize* were the first villages to be classified as grand crus on the Côte des Blancs. They share a mixture of soils varying between chalk and clay.

Oger is riper than the villages to its north, with vineyards where the sun is trapped in an amphitheater.

Le Mesnil-sur-Oger is famous for the minerality and austerity it brings to Champagne. The wines have the greatest sense of tension on the Côte des Blancs. Le Mesnil is its most famous producer, with steely wines that take years to open.

Grand Vallée

Aÿ is famous for Pinot Noir and provides the best combination of power and elegance in the region.

Mareuil-sur-Aÿ is nominally a premier cru, but many people think it should be a grand cru. The best vineyards, such as Clos des Goisses, overlook the river.

Reference Wines for Important Villages		
Montagne de Reims		
Ambonnay	Éric Rodez	Blanc de Noirs
Bouzy	Paul Bara	Grand Rosé de Bouzy
Mailly	Champagne Mailly	Grand Cru Blanc de Noirs
Trépail	David Léclapart	L'Amateur
Verzy & Verzenay	Jean Lallement	Brut Réserve
Sillery	Françoise Secondé	Blanc de Noirs, La Loge
Côte des Blancs		
Cuis	Pierre Gimonnet	Blanc de Blancs
Cramant	Diebolt Vallois	Fleur de Passion
Avise	Agrapart	Vénus
Oger	Jean Milan	Blanc de Blancs
Le Mesnil-sur-Oger	Pierre Péters	Les Chetillons
Vertus	Larmandier-Bernier	Terre de Vertus
	Veuve Fourny	Vertus Brut Nature
Grand Vallée		
Aÿ	Gatinois	Grand Cru Aÿ Tradition
Mareuil-sur-Aÿ	Philipponnat	Mareuil-sur-Aÿ
Vallée de la Marne		
Oeuilly	Tarlant	Cuvée Louis
Côte des Bar		
Urville	Drappier	Brut Nature

These reference vines are nonvintage whenever possible so as to showcase the origin rather than the vintage.

Today there is more discrimination. "The pricing of the grapes is not linked to classification any more, it's a free market, we have private contracts with growers, with prices that are linked to the prices indicated by the CIVC. Everything is handled by parcel," explains Jean-Marc Lallier-Deutz. As Hervé Deschamps, cellarmaster at Perrier-Jouët, says, "There are 180 tanks for base wine from 70 villages for our nonvintage. It's very important to understand that each tank is different. If you have twenty tanks for one village they are all different, they are not the same. They differ in the slopes, the grapes, the time of harvest."

Given wide variations in terroir between vineyards within the same village (and in the efforts of individual growers), it's certainly not true that all grand cru vineyards are better than all premier cru vineyards. The classification was a blunt tool indeed. The échelle des crus may have become irrelevant, but "the most common question I am asked is whether the grapes come from grand cru or premier cru villages," says Jean-Marc Lallier-Deutz. Individual crus are not identified on the label, but the terms Grand Cru and Premier Cru can be used if all the grapes come from the same class of village, indicating that the producer regards the Champagne as of higher quality.

The Expansion of Champagne

Champagne is bursting at the seams. The (potential) expansion of the vineyards is a continuing controversy. Under pressure to increase production, in 2003 the producers asked INAO to reclassify the area, this of course being a euphemism for increasing the approved area, which has reopened the controversy about where Champagne should really be made.

Champagne has contracted and expanded according to the rhythm of the day. Before phylloxera, there were 60,000 hectares of vineyards; by 1919 there were only 12,000 ha. When the Champagne production zone was defined in 1927, 40,000 hectares of vineyards were included in 407 villages. Responding to a decline in the market, this was reduced to 34,000 ha in 302 villages in 1951. Only 11,000 ha were used for Champagne production in the 1950s, but since then the vineyards have expanded steadily to fill the entire allotted area of the AOP. Today there are just over 33,000 ha.

INAO has been reviewing the areas where grapes can be grown and wine can be made. A leak to the press revealed that the proposal was to include 40 new villages and to remove two existing villages. Detailed examination of vineyards in these villages is still continuing, and no one knows yet exactly which plots will be included in the Champagne AOP. The original plan was to make decisions by 2017, but this has been put back, so it will be a while before the first new vineyards are planted.

The rationale for the reclassification is that there was much less knowledge about conditions for viticulture when the original limits were defined, and historical accidents influenced the outcome—such as the mayor of a village seeing no point in being included in the AOC. (When the vineyards were classified in 1927, grain, dairy, and cattle farming were more profitable than Champagne, and many landowners were aristocrats who were not interested in wine production.) Most of the proposed new areas lie close to or within the existing areas, the two outstanding exceptions being a large expansion around Troyes and also just below Château-Thierry.

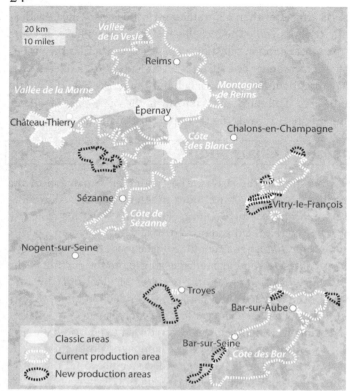

The Champagne production zone has 319 communes extending over 300,000 ha, and includes 33,000 ha of vineyards. Proposed new production areas include 40 extra communes, but vineyards have not yet been classified.

The question is whether this is more than a ploy to increase production at the expense of quality. The precedents are not good: most expansions of the vineyards of classic wine regions have been associated with dilution of character. There seems to be some skepticism about the potential new villages at top producers. Will you buy grapes from the new villages, I asked Jean-Pierre Mareigner, cellarmaster at Champagne Gosset? "No—perhaps in a hundred years, but not now. We work essentially with grand cru and premier cru in the traditional villages. The new areas will be unplanted land which hasn't had vines before; we look for the typicity of established vines."

Understanding the character of the vineyard is the main issue. "When we taste for assemblage we have a long history of the parcel, but if we work with

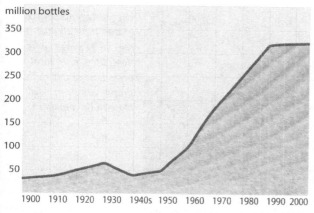

million bottles

Champagne production doubled in the first half of the twentieth century, and in the second half increased almost ten fold.

wine from vines that are only a few years old, we have no history to guide us," explains Jean-Marc Lallier-Deutz. The view is more positive at the largest Champagne houses, which feel more need for a wider supply of grapes in order to expand.

Vineyards are planted at high density, typically 9-10,000 vines per hectare. This is usually associated with quality: in regions such a Burgundy and Bordeaux, this is the planting density of top vineyards. A proposal to allow planting at lower density was first made in 1986, and various systems have been tried on a trial basis since then. It remains highly controversial, with proponents arguing it will allow modernization, such as better use of tractors, and respond to climate change by giving better resistance to drought, and those against arguing that it will reduce quality. From 2023, the minimum planting density has been reduced from 8,000 to 5,000 vines/ha.

The major controversy in Champagne should be the extraordinary yields, but almost no one ever mentions this. The exponential growth in Champagne production in the past fifty years has partly been due to an increase in the vineyard area, but equally due to a tripling of the yields. Yields are calculated in an unusual way in Champagne. Elsewhere in France, the limits are in terms of the amount of wine that can be produced from a given area, as hectoliters per hectare. But in Champagne they are calculated as the kilograms of grapes harvested per hectare. This is a moving target, set each year with a primary agenda that regards market demand as a more significant factor than quality of grapes.

A great deal of misinformation is put out in an attempt to make yields appear lower than they really are. They are usually actually around 14,000 kg/hl, but with a restriction that only some of the harvest can be used for

Large Maisons source grapes from all over the region; to preserve freshness, they have local press houses where the grapes can be pressed close to the vineyard.

producing wine for current consumption; the rest, however, can be used to make reserve wines for future use. While this may serve its purpose for manipulating supply and demand, in terms of quality it's the total yield that matters.

Converting to a more conventional measure, 14,000 kg/hl corresponds to a whopping 89 hl/ha, equivalent to table wine, and about double the usual limit for quality wine. The only relief is that pressing is divided into two stages: the first pressing, called the cuvée, is used by most producers, and a second, smaller pressing, called the taille, is usually not used.

The Champenoise defend their extraordinary yields by arguing that they need to make a neutral base wine: they are not looking for the same level of ripeness or flavor development that would be appropriate for a still wine, so higher yields are in order. This may be true up to a point, but does it really extend all the way to the dizzy heights of 89 hl/ha? Because Champagne is extensively blended, it's hard to directly assess the effects of lower yields.

Occasionally you get a chance to taste a Vieilles Vignes Champagne, where the vines are old enough that yields are significantly reduced. There's distinctly more concentration on the palate, to the point at which you can see what would be gained if only they would reduce yields in Champagne. I think it's very probable that if harvests were limited to, say, 10,000 kg/ha, there'd be a noticeable all-round improvement in quality. Of course, whether the consumer would want to pay for this is another matter.

Champagne today tastes richer than it did ten or twenty years ago; you might think an impression of more softness and even sweetness represents an increase in dosage, but actually it's the other way round; dosage has been declining to compensate for the extra ripeness of the grapes. (Although the grapes harvested in Champagne would be regarded as seriously unripe by the standards of still wine production in, for example, Burgundy.)

The fact that chaptalization is still often needed indicates that the region remains marginal for wine production. This is a major factor in its success. If Champagne reaches a point in at which chaptalization is no longer necessary, it will be on the verge of succumbing to the same problem as its would-be rivals where adequate ripeness prevents success. (Should this happen, the long history of Anglo-French rivalry comes to the fore in suggesting southern England as a possible location for future Champagne production. Indeed, Taittinger and Roederer are already hedging their bets by plantings vineyards there.)

Growers and Houses

Many of the characteristics of Champagne are intrinsic to its production: the focus on nonvintage is a means to compensate for the vicissitudes of annual variation in a marginal climate, assemblage reflects the inconsistency between different areas each year, and the use of dosage compensates for the difficulty of getting to other regions' standard of ripeness. But some are an indirect consequence of the organization of Champagne, in particular the dichotomy between grape growing and wine production.

The Avenue de Champagne in Épernay is lined with major Champagne Houses. This was the private residence of Perrier-Jouët.

Major Houses	
LVMH	Moët & Chandon
	Mercier
	Ruinart
	Montaudon
	Veuve Clicquot
	Krug
	Dom Pérignon
Lanson-BCC	Lanson
	Maison Burtin
	Besserat de Bellefon
	Boizel
	Chanoine
	Philipponnat
	De Venoge
	Alexandre Bonnet
Vranken-Pommery	Vranken-Pommery
	Charles Lafitte
	Heidsieck Monopole
	Bissinger
Laurent-Perrier	Laurent-Perrier
	De Castellane
	Salon-Delamotte
	Lemoine
Pernod-Ricard	Mumm
	Perrier-Jouët

Small Houses

AR Lenoble
Brice
Bruno Paillard
Cattier
Chaudron
Comtes de Dampierre
Cristian Senez
Cuperly
Edouard Brun
Gardet
Gremillet
Henri Abelé
Henri Giraud
Jacquesson
Jacquinot & Fils
Janisson & Fils
J. de Telmont
Lallier
Leclerc Briant
Lombard
Louis
Massing
Louis de Sacy
Moutard
Diligent
Pierre Mignon
Soutiran
Veuve Cheurlin

Pie chart: Major Groups, Small Houses, Medium Houses, Others

Medium Houses

Louis Roederer + Deutz
Taittinger + Irroy
Bollinger + Ayala
Piper Heidsieck + Charles Heidsieck
Thienot + Canard-Duchêne + Joseph Perrier + Marie Stuart
N. Gueusquin
Martel + Charles de Cazanove
Billecart-Salmon
Duval Leroy
Pol Roger
Henriot
Malard
Mansard Baillet
Gosset
Charles Mignon.
Janisson & Fils
Barons de Rothschild
+ indicates houses under same ownership

Two thirds of Champagne is produced by the major houses of the large groups plus the medium houses.

The leading Champagne houses produce two thirds of all Champagne, accounting for three quarters of its value, and 80% of all exports. But they own only 3,000 ha out of the 33,000 ha in Champagne; the other 30,000 ha are owned by some 16,000 growers. And individual vineyard holdings tend to be very small; those 33,000 ha are broken up into 276,000 individual parcels. Fewer than 2,000 growers make their own wine; most production comes from 140 cooperatives and 320 Champagne houses. The extremely fragmented nature of the holdings makes it difficult to be organic: there are only 600 ha of organic vines and 200 ha of biodynamic vines in all Champagne.

Because the major Champagne houses own relatively few vineyards, they must buy most of their

Codes for Champagne Producers

RM (Récoltant-Manipulant) uses only estate grapes. (There is an exception allowing purchase of red wine to make rosé.) Also known as grower-Champagnes or boutique-Champagnes (because they are small).

NM (Négociant-Manipulant) can use both purchased grapes and estate grapes. The mix varies with the house. The houses are usually larger, and include the Grand Marques that produce most Champagne.

CM (Coopérative-Manipulant) is a cooperative, producing the Champagne under its own label, from grapes supplied by its members.

RC (Récoltant-Coopérateur) is a member of a cooperative who puts his own label on wine produced by the coop.

ND (Négociant-Distributeur) means the wine was made by an unknown producer, and merely purchased and labeled by its nominal producer.

grapes. Roederer and Bollinger, in the exceptional situation of owning enough vineyards to supply most of their grapes, are much envied by other producers. Power in the inevitable clashes between growers and producers oscillates according to the state of the economy.

When times are good, the growers have the whip hand, and it's dangerous for producers to turn away grapes, even if quality is not up to their standard. When times are bad, the growers may be squeezed on price.

This makes for a tug of war when the CIVC decides on the yield limits each year: growers need to maximize returns, but the houses will not want more than they believe is supported by the current market. The situation reduces interest in single vineyard wines: when parcels are tiny, and the producer may not even own them, it is hard to commit to a single vineyard cuvée.

It's a common impression that Champagne is all grand Maisons, with snazzy tasting rooms where degustations are conducted by PR people. This is certainly true of the producers on the Avenue de Champagne in Épernay, where the Maisons are very grand indeed, or in the center of Reims, for example. But although this may account for the majority of Champagne production, it's a small proportion of the number of houses, many of which are (relatively) small.

Visiting boutique houses in the villages, you get quite a different impression of passionate producers, often very conscious of their family history, and somewhat akin to Burgundy in their general attitude; this is where most of the driving force comes from for recognizing terroirs in individual cuvées.

Top Grower Champagnes

Montagne de Reims

Egly Ouriet	Ambonnay
Éric Rodez	Ambonnay
Paul Bara	Bouzy
Vilmart et Cie	Rilly-La-Montagne
Chartogne-Taillet	Merfy

Côte des Blancs

Agrapart et Fils	Avize
Jacques Selosse	Avize
Vazart-Coquart	Chouilly
Bonnaire	Cramant
Pierre Gimonnet et Fils	Cuis
Pierre Péters	Le Mesnil-sur-Oger
Pierre Moncuit	Le Mesnil-sur-Oger
Larmandier-Bernier	Vertus

Grand Vallée

Gosset-Brabant	Aÿ
Geoffroy	Aÿ
Henri Goutorbe	Aÿ

Vallée de la Marne

A. R. Lenoble	Damery
Tarlant	Oeuilly

That's why the list of reference wines for villages (page 22) focuses mostly on smaller growers; by contrast, the diversity of sources, coupled with the larger scale of production, leads large houses to focus more on consistency, which is why they dominate the list of reference wines for styles (page 11).

Champagne production has become steadily more concentrated in the hands of a small number of owners. The bigger fish are continuing to gobble up the smaller ones at a fairly steady pace. Well over half of all production comes from five major groups and another quarter from a small number of large houses. These are the Grand Marques. (Grand Marque was defined by a group of major houses who formed an association, later disbanded, but now is more loosely used to indicate major houses with significant international representation.)

Grand Marque carries no implication of quality. As large producers, the Grand Marques rely on a mix of grapes from their own vineyards and purchases from growers (in most cases a majority of the latter); they are the leading houses in the group that is described as Négociant-Manipulants, in-

Miles of caves have been hollowed out from the chalk underneath the Champagne houses.

dicated by NM on the label, which means the house is entitled to use purchased grapes.

Every bottle of Champagne carries a discrete mark on the label indicating the character of the producer. At the other extreme from NM is the Récoltant-Manipulant, indicated by RM on the label. This describes a grower who vinifies wine only from estate grapes. These are the so-called Boutique or Grower Champagnes. They are relatively small, with holdings typically ranging up to about 30 ha. (Basically they are smaller than the small houses listed on page 28). Indeed, any size increase is limited by the fact that it's all but impossible to buy vineyards, and of course purchasing grapes would mean losing the RM status.

With it impossible to expand because of the cost of land, there is a trend for growers either to add a negociant activity or simply move to NM status. "It is the new philosophy. RM is finished. It's now NM....If I want a hectare in Le Mesnil sur Oger, it is €2 million. It is very expensive. I prefer to buy the grapes," says Frédéric Savart of Champagne Savart in Écueil. The number of growers with RM status dropped from 2,015 in 2011 to 1,766 in 2018, because it's just not economic to function at a level of producing the average 20,000 bottles a year.

In fact, the only way to obtain vineyards is to buy a Champagne house that owns them. LVMH have been playing this game with some success. They purchased Pommery in 1991, and then sold it to Vranken in 2002, but without its 300 ha of vineyards, which were kept in the LVMH portfolio. Even more swiftly, LVMH purchased Montaudon in 2008 and then sold it in 201(to the Champagne Alliance cooperative—but without its vineyards or con tracts to purchase grapes. "For some years there has been a war for grapes i Champagne. There is a gigantic super power. Unfortunately the panzer divi sions of M. Arnault [LVMH] have won the war," a smaller produce comments. In fact, LVMH have more or less amalgamated their vineyar holdings; each of its houses may have some vineyards that it uses tradition ally, but also can source grapes from the LVMH holdings as a whole.

A general critique of large houses would be naïve, but there is a certai skepticism about producing Champagne on such a vast scale. On the on hand, the large houses do maintain remarkable consistency in spite of th scale of production, but on the other, the question is what the wine repre sents: place, vintage, or production process? By contrast, a grower' vineyards are usually concentrated in one area of Champagne, which helps t bring character to the wine. Where there is a house style, it owes as much t the taste of the grower as to the perceptions of the marketing department. I' be inclined to say that grower Champagnes are usually more interesting– even if you don't always entirely like the choices that have been made.

CM describes a Cave Coopérative, producing wine from grapes harveste by its members. Nicolas Feuillatte is the most prominent example, develope in 1987 as its marque by the Centre Viticole federation of cooperatives. A impressive facility, with all the latest equipment, this is the very model of modern cooperative, and one of the most successful in France. Champagn Jacquart (which now also owns Montaudon) was acquired in 1998 as it principal marque by Alliance Champagne, another major cooperative group.

Although coops have become less important in France as a whole, an generally are of lower importance in more prestigious areas, Champagne i an exception in which they retain a major (even a growing) place, accountin today for more than a third of the harvest. This is another consequence of th system in which there are many growers with parcels that are too small t justify producing finished wine.

Finished Champagne sold from cooperatives falls into two categories About half is sold under the cooperative label, and is marked CM. The othe half goes under the RC category, which indicates a grower who sticks his ow label on wine produced by a cooperative to which he belongs. This is unlikel to be of high quality. "Out of 5,000 growers, 4,000 make the same wine at cooperative under a different label; only 1,000 are really independent," say Bruno Paillard.

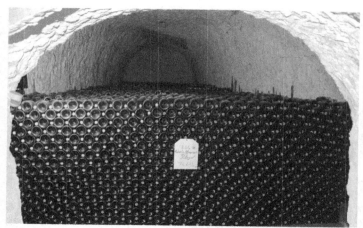

Before disgorgement, Champagne is stored flat. Thin layers of wood are usually included every few rows, which gave rise to the name "sur latte."

What you do not want to see on a label is ND, which stands for Négoci-ant-Distributeur. This means the finished wine (bubbles and all) was produced by someone else, and was simply purchased by the final owner, who disgorged it and put his own label on it. This is known pejoratively as the trade *sur latte*. Reports that it had been banned as of 2004 appear to have been exaggerated, as producers say today that it is perfectly legal. Some restrictions have been introduced, including a requirement that the label says *distribué par* rather than *elaboré par*, but it is a rare consumer who might spot this on a bottle.

The deceptive thing is that a major house may sell both its own wine and sur latte wine under the same label, and you would really have to look at the small print to see whether it's their own wine or something they picked up in the market to bulk out sales. Is this fraudulent or is it fraudulent? I have been unable to find producers who will admit to the practice, but there is some-thing of a feeling that it serves a useful purpose in establishing market prices.

Styles of Champagne

"At the time of my parents, Champagne was not wine, it was for parties," says Charles-Henry Fourny, describing a general change over the past gen-eration from treating Champagne as an aperitif then to regarding it now as a wine that can accompany a meal. A generation ago, the base wine of Cham-pagne was thin and acidic, and only the dosage turned it into an acceptable

Most Champagnes are produced exclusively in stainless steel. Quantities for major brands can be very large. The tank halls at Nicolas Feuillatte are among the largest in Champagne.

drink. Today base wines are much richer—in the admittedly rich year of 2018 you could almost enjoy them in their own right—and Champagne correspondingly has greater density. Dosage for Brut Champagne often used to be at the limit of 12g, but today it's usually much closer to the level of Extra Brut.

Dosage is not a simple issue: it's more about balancing acidity than creating a perception of sweetness. In fact, three factors go into determining the balance of the wine: the acidity of the grapes at harvest; whether malolactic fermentation is performed; and how much sugar is included in the dosage.

The perception among producers is that global warming has produced higher potential alcohol and lower acidity at harvest. This is certainly the trend, but the actual change measured by the CIVC is still quite small. Perhaps the producers have been compensating for climate change by harvesting relatively earlier. It's a prime objective in Champagne to harvest early enough to retain high acidity in the grapes. "We used to harvest in October and we were caught between lack of maturity and development of botrytis. Now we harvest in September, the days are longer, there are fewer disease problems, and we get perfectly ripe berries. We can harvest up to 11% alcohol, so chaptalization is often still necessary," says Rodolphe Péters.

A major stylistic issue is whether to perform malolactic fermentation (MLF). This reduces acidity (by converting the sharp malic acid to the softer lactic acid), but it also makes wine generally creamier. The old school of thought was that malolactic fermentation was more appropriate for nonvintage Champagne, but that retaining higher acidity was better for the ageability of vintage. That seems to have been replaced by a view that malolactic fermentation generally produces a better balanced wine, and it has become the rule rather than the exception, with less distinction made between non-vintage and vintage.

"It reduces sharpness of the acid and gives better lines to the wine, a final touch on the finish of minerality, salt, citrus, between zest and fruit," says Rodolphe Péters. "If you block MLF you'd better be sure to have good storage because the wine will need to be kept longer before release," says Jean-Marc Lallier-Deutz. It may also need more dosage. "Without dosage malic acid can be very aggressive," says cellarmaster Hervé Deschamps at Perrier-Jouët. Most Champagne houses today have a general policy, either to perform or to block malolactic fermentation (the majority perform it). This may be changing with global warming. "We do less and less malolactic fermentation with the warmer vintages," says Delphine Colin at Champagne Colin in Vertus.

While it's true that excess dosage can be a means to cover up other problems, producers refute any simplistic idea that less dosage is always better. "Dosage is not to give sweetness, but to keep the same taste and to reduce acidity, it's the last touch of the chef to increase flavor," is how Hervé Deschamps describes his approach. "If you believe you can use dosage to counter natural austerity, it doesn't work. If you add high dosage you get an artificial *sucrosité* at the end," says Jean-Hervé Chiquet at Jacquesson.

Viewing dosage as part of the means by which consistency of style is maintained across vintages, most producers have reduced it over the past ten or twenty years in response to their sense that the grapes are riper. Bringing dosage down started as an attempt to keep style constant in the face of warmer vintages, but then producers discovered it gave more precision in the fruits, they realized that too much dosage can muddy the style, and reducing dosage changed from a means to an end.

There is more to maintaining consistency than simply getting the blend right. Deutz cellarmaster Michel Davesne says, "Over thirty years the dosage has gone down, we have reduced it because there is less acidity. And I think the consumer prefers a lower dosage." Dominique Garreta confirms the trend at Taittinger: "Globally over the range dosage is 9 g/l, decreased from 11-12 g/l a few years ago. We changed dosage because the grapes have changed." Vintage Champagne tends to have lower dosage, because it comes from riper years.

Dosage is not necessarily fixed for a cuvée, but may be different when the same wine is disgorged more than once, at different times. Because a wine gains in richness with time on the lees, later disgorgements may have less dosage than earlier disgorgements. Jean-Marc Lallier-Deutz explains the approach at Deutz: "We dose on the basis of tasting. But Classic starts with 9.5 to 10 g/l when we begin disgorging, and later disgorgement will go down to 9 g/l, and then with the new cuvée back up."

When Dom Pérignon is first released, the dosage tends to be around 7 g/l. When it is re-released 12 years later, the dosage is significantly less; and then is reduced again for the next re-release at 18 years. "The later releases are more mature, so there is less dosage, it's that simple," says cellarmaster Richard Geoffroy.

Today, by far the most common style of Champagne is Brut. The Brut classification covers a multitude of sins: anything from 0 to 12 g/l dosage. Although Extra Brut can be used to describe wines below 6 g/l, it is not necessarily always used, because for some cuvées around the limit, the producer wants to maintain flexibility to go over or under the limit depending on annual conditions. Producers also think some consumers react against the name of Extra Brut, so there is now a surprising amount of Brut Champagne that is below 6 g/l dosage. "We use 4.5 g/l dosage in the vintage wines. The wines are still labeled Brut, but we are asking ourselves if we should change the label to Extra Brut," Charles Philipponnat says, describing his policy of having reduced dosage since he took over at Philipponnat.

Dates of Disgorgement

The issue of disgorgement dates is a hot topic in Champagne. With non-vintage Champagne, production is a more or less continuous process, and there is an assumption that the wine is disgorged, and the dosage is adjusted, so that it is ready to drink when released: for practical purposes this means within a year or so of purchase.

With vintage Champagne, the date of disgorgement is more significant. A vintage Champagne usually becomes available between four and five years after the vintage, but will not necessarily all be disgorged at that point: some may be kept back to be disgorged later. It will gain increased complexity from longer time in the bottle before disgorgement, but the aromas and flavors are different from those developing after disgorgement, when oxidative aging replaces the initial freshness with notes of nuts, toast, and brioche.

The reductive character of the lees keeps the wine fresh while it ages before disgorgement, and the slow dissolution of the yeast cells adds weight to the wine. "The beauty of lees aging is that it is not passive, there is an active aging. The lees are swallowed up to give more viscosity, more intensity. We believe that this element of active maturation is part of winemaking as much as terroir," says Richard Geoffroy. So there may be a huge difference in flavor between a 1990 Champagne disgorged in 1996 and the same wine disgorged in 2006. Which you prefer depends whether you value freshness or maturity.

The view in Champagne is increasingly coming around to the position that the wine is best enjoyed soon after disgorgement. This was the logic behind the creation of Bollinger's R.D. cuvée: R.D. stands for recently disgorged: a great vintage is kept on the lees for a protracted period—the current release in 2016 was the 2002.

Other houses have followed suit. Dom Pérignon has taken the principal to its logical extreme. Late releases were originally called Oenothèques, but now have been renamed Plenitudes, to reflect the belief that aging is not a linear process, that there are certain discontinuous points in time where the wine reaches a stage of additional complexity that merits disgorgement (P2 after about 12 years, and P3 after about 18 years).

It's controversial in Champagne whether disgorgement dates should be stated on the bottle. In the case of nonvintage, this would protect the consumer against bottles that have been left for too long in the distribution chain. (The same issue arises with other quality wines that don't have a vintage, such as Sherry). With vintage wines, because they may be disgorged at different times after the vintage, and because there's more of a tendency to age them before consumption, it's more a matter of indicating style.

Some Champagne houses now indicate disgorgement dates on the back label. Bruno Paillard was the first, but until recently was followed by relatively few others. "I started putting disgorgement dates on bottles in 1983; for more than twenty years I was the only one to do it," Bruno says. Why did you do this, I asked? "Like everyone I saw variations in bottles with no explanation. You could guess but you should have the information."

Some houses are putting codes on the back label that can be scanned by a smart phone to give the date of disgorgement as well as other information. Some are moving more towards a code that can be read by the trade, but not necessarily by the consumer.

The objections to stating the date of disgorgement are ostensibly that it may be misleading. "It's not very relevant because the pattern of aging after

disgorgement is very different for each wine. If we put dates on, some con
sumers will look at the label and say, it's too old; others might say it's to
young," explains Jean-Pierre Mareigner, cellarmaster at Gosset. At Tait
tinger, Dominique Garreta is forthright: "For us it's a nonsense to put
disgorgement date on the label for several reasons. Putting a date on any
thing you eat or drink means an expiration date for the consumer, so thi
would lead to a total misunderstanding. Let's be honest, most of the brand
that print disgorgement dates don't age very well."

Personally I think Bruno's position is irrefutable, but it seems likely to b
some time yet before information becomes widely available, although there i
a definite trend towards more openness, including stating the assemblag
(base wine and reserve wine vintages and proportions) and dosage.

Zero Dosage

There is something of a trend to produce Brut Nature, or Zero Dosage, a
the current fashion calls it, with absolutely no additional sugar. Zero dosag
wine has a tendency to austerity, but the best zero dosage Champagnes ar
not merely the same wine as the Brut without dosage. Some producers dis
tinguish the zero dosage by giving longer time on the lees to pick up extr
richness to compensate for the lack of dosage. Champagne Ayala, after bein
acquired by Bollinger in 2005, has made a specialty of low dosage; its zer
dosage has an extra year before disgorgement. Some producers make zer
dosage specifically from parcels that achieve greater ripeness.

"The trend for zero dosage is nothing new to us," says Anne-Laur
Domenichini at Laurent-Perrier. "Veuve Laurent Perrier created the first no
dosage Champagne—Grand Vin Sans Sucre—around 1881, at the request c
British customers. It was withdrawn around the first world war as it wasn't t
the taste of the French. Bernard de Nonancourt reintroduced it in 1988 whe
nouvelle cuisine started the trend for sauces without cream. He called it th
naked Champagne."

Today Laurent-Perrier's Ultra Brut comes from an equal blend of Pino
Noir and Chardonnay chosen for high ripeness and low acidity; in fact, it
not made in years that aren't sufficiently ripe. Indeed, I am not sure I woul
peg this as zero dosage in a blind tasting, because the fruits are so ripe. "Thi
is not the nonvintage with no dosage, but is its own wine," Anne-Laure says.

But there are skeptics. "It's very amusing to disgorge a wine and drink i
in the Nature style, but zero dosage is a bit like a chair with three legs—it
missing something. An Extra Brut is always more interesting than a Nature-

it brings out the fruits better. Zero dosage usually has 1 g/l sugar anyway because it's made by using indigenous yeast and they never ferment absolutely dry," says Rodolphe Péters.

And it may not be so simple as deciding to go for the zero style at disgorgement. "I believe zero dosage Champagne is a global project, meaning that it starts in the vineyard when you select your grapes with the idea that there won't be any dosage. There are in fact very few Champagne houses that respect this concern. There are few really great zero dosage Champagnes," says Dominique Garreta at Taittinger. A side issue is that, because the aging of Champagne depends on sugar (for the Maillard reaction), there's a question as to whether zero dosage wines will have aging capacity.

My own opinion is that you see the purity of fruits more directly with zero dosage; but this means they need to be absolutely top quality. Otherwise the acidity can be somewhat brutal. A direct comparison of zero dosage with Brut at Philipponnat (the same wine with a few months difference in disgorgement) shows that the zero dosage is less generous, less broad, but more precise. The main point is that the difference is not just a matter of the sweetness level, but the whole flavor spectrum is shifted from stone to citrus. Zero dosage champagnes—and even Extra Brut at lower dosage levels—move away from the overt fruitiness of Brut Champagne towards a more savory flavor spectrum. (It is especially important not to have zero dosage Champagne at too cool a temperature as this can really suppress flavor and make it seem almost brutal.) However, as producers have gained more experience with zero dosage, the style has become less austere, and recently I have had many with an evident degree of ripeness that would make them hard to identify as zero dosage in a blind tasting.

Generally, I would be more inclined to have zero dosage with a meal and Brut or Extra Brut as an aperitif. I often prefer Extra Brut to Brut, because going into the Brut range tends to muddy impressions. But there are really no rules: there are Brut Champagnes at the level of, say, 9 g/l dosage which appear drier on the palate than some Extra Bruts. It's all in the balance: dosage is a key tool in compensating for vintage variation.

Rosé Champagne

If nonvintage, vintage, and single vineyards all represent different types of Champagne, rosé is a further style. A relatively recent innovation in Champagne, it is in a sense a reversal of the success in eliminating color in the eighteenth century. Introduced by a handful of houses around forty years ago, the idea was to introduce a style that was more expensive than nonvintage Brut but less than the prestige cuvées. Production has increased sharply in the past few years.

Rosé can be made in either of two ways. Most is *rosé d'assemblage*, made by blending 10-20% red wine into the base wine. The alternative is *rosé saignée*, in which the color comes directly from macerating Pinot Noir (or Pinot Meunier) for anywhere from 6-72 hours before the juice is pressed off the skins. Some producers prefer the term 'rosé de maceration.'

For still wine, a rosé must be made from black grapes, but because the color in rosé d'assemblage Champagne can come from blending in red wine, any grape variety can be used for the major part. The rosé character should add something, but too often in Champagne it dampens down the flavor profile. The reason may partly be that addition of red wine reduces the sense of liveliness. My complaint with many rosés is that the red wine seems to stand aside. It softens and rounds out the Champagne without adding any character or really integrating into the wine.

As this is a Champagne and not a still wine, you are not looking for overt red fruit character; indeed that would detract from the sense of Champagne. At its best, there should be something of that sense of the elegance and precision of fine Pinot Noir coming from the structure of the wine, perhaps a slightly fuller impression of a Blanc de Noirs.

Many Champagne producers regard rosé not exactly as a frivolity, but as something they produce because fashion has created a demand, rather than because the wine offers something distinctively interesting. "There is too much rosé in Champagne. If you taste blind in black glasses, you can't tell it's rosé. Why should you pay extra money if you can't taste any difference?" asks Jean-Baptiste Geoffroy of Champagne Geoffroy. He does not believe in rosé d'assemblage. "The problem with assemblage is that when you mix two colors you get complete blending of the colors, but not of the flavors."

You can make great rosé by either method. Billecart-Salmon is best known for its rosés, which have an unusual elegance and character. "It's a secret," says cellarmaster François Domi when asked what's special about Billecart's rosés, but later he relents and explains that it's the quality and character of the red wine. When asked about the total production of rosé, he says that's *really* secret, but admits that it's somewhat more than is usual at most Champagne houses.

"We search for a rosé Champagne but not a Champagne rosé," is how François puts it. "In the rosé we balance the power of Pinot Noir with the

Chardonnay. We look for elegance and delicacy, it should be discrete and not too heavy. Red wine is about 10%. The color of the red wine is obtained before fermentation. There shouldn't be too much tannin, enough to stabilize the color but not more. If the red isn't good, you cannot make rosé. If you served this in black glasses, it would be important not to be able to tell, the rosé should have the aroma and taste of Champagne, not red wine." Here the rosé indeed has the delicacy and elegance of top Champagne.

Another house well known for its rosé is Laurent-Perrier, one of the leaders in introducing rosé in 1968. The Laurent-Perrier rosé comes exclusively from Pinot Noir, mostly from Grand Cru; it is a *rosé saignée,* and has an impression of the earthy quality of Pinot Noir, almost a faint tannic texture.

Any difference between rosé saignée and rosé d'assemblage may be partly intrinsic, but choice of technique may also reflect a difference in objectives, and that may in part be why saignée rosés sometimes seem to be more structured. As rosé Champagne has become more important, there's been something of a movement to make rosés by saignée instead of assemblage.

Single Vineyard Champagnes

It is both a strength and a weakness that Champagne has only a single appellation. It gives instant recognition to anything that says Champagne on the label, but it makes it more difficult to distinguish wines that come from particular areas. The only official distinctions are the marks of premier or grand cru (very general) and the styles (Blanc de Blancs and Blanc de Noirs).

Producers are conscious of the differences between villages, but this is more in the context of using them to increase complexity and balance in the blend than to represent the differences in individual cuvées. It's a reasonable question whether and how differences between individual villages might be reflected in finished Champagne given the extent of manipulation during production. There are relatively few Champagnes representing individual villages through which the question might be examined, and it's probably fair to say that there is little chance of villages developing reputations for particular styles, equivalent to communes in Burgundy, for example, because the style of the individual house is more important.

You never used to hear people talk about terroir in Champagne except in the context of the superiority of premier and grand cru vineyards, but now it is increasingly common, especially at grower houses, to find cuvées representing individual vineyards or types of terroir. Insights into the potential for

Krug's Clos du Mesnil is one of the most famous single vineyards. Its 1.8 ha are nestled under the village of Mesnil-sur-Oger, protected by walls dating from 1698.

single vineyard Champagnes come from some exceptional producers who make a point of them.

At the head of this group is Champagne Jacques Selosse. A person of strong opinions, Anselme Selosse takes his marching orders from Burgundy, where he learned oenology. "When I saw Romanée Conti, it was a revelation. The vines come from selection massale and are the same as with the other slopes. The exposure is the same. The water is the same. So it must be the soil."

Dosage is very low or zero to allow the terroir to express itself in the Selosse single vineyard wines, and this is part of a general movement. There's a correlation between low dosage and production of single vineyard wines: producers who want to show origins often feel that lower dosage is important. "We want to have Champagne that really tastes of where it comes from, that's why we make single vineyard Champagnes. The aim is to make dosage invisible, we want to taste the wine, the most we ever use is 3-4 g/l" says Sophie Larmandier of Larmandier-Bernier. "You see the terroir better with lower dosage," says Jean-Sébastien Fleury.

Anselme Selosse defies conventional wisdom in another respect: oak. Extensive use of oak for fermentation and aging leads to a more oxidative style than common. Generally, there is little oak in Champagne. Base wines are made and held in stainless steel until the second fermentation is started in bottle. Krug and Bollinger are unusual in fermenting in (old) barriques; they feel this adds richness and depth to the wine, and makes for longer aging. More recently there's been a move towards maturing wines in barriques, mostly for special cuvées.

There is some skepticism about single vineyard Champagnes, not so much as to whether they reflect significant differences, but as to whether they make the most complex wines. "Elegance is more difficult to obtain than concentration. Our top parcel is like Puligny for still wine, but for balance it needs to be blended. That's the key about single vineyards. It's not necessarily the case that a plot making a wonderful still wine will by itself make the most complex Champagne," says Didier Gimonnet, explaining why he has been resisting calls to make a single vineyard wine from the parcel. Gimonnet has in fact just produced its first single village wines, a break with the past when the blend was always between grand cru for structure and premier cru for freshness.

There's a concern about the effects of taking out the best wines. "Because people wanted to produce great quantities they blended more, so everything became more the same—and the growers are reacting against that, they want to express authenticity. But it's less complex, the best balance comes from blending. Of course there are exceptions but it's very rare. And of course the more you take off the best terroirs the more you decrease the quality of your blend. That's why philosophically I'm against single vineyard wines," Didier explains.

But the trend to make Champagne from single vineyards is certainly strengthening. Since plots are small, there is a tendency for the single vineyard wines to be either Blanc de Blancs or Blanc de Noirs and to represent single vintages. Interestingly, there is also a movement in precisely the opposite direction, with some producers now making wines directly from their 'perpétuelle reserve," by drawing out some wine for bottling, and replacing it from the current vintage. The wine is therefore a blend from many vintages, albeit weighted towards the more recent. It eliminates the effect of vintage even more effectively than traditional blending.

Prestige Cuvées

Special cuvées are at the peak of Champagne. What makes them special? Well, first, of course, since we are in Champagne, the price: anything from double the price of a regular Champagne to ten times or more. Technically they usually represent long disgorgements, longer than three years and up to ten years. With the notable exception of Krug, they almost always exclude

The oldest bottles still awaiting disgorgement at Salon come from the great 1928 vintage.

Pinot Meunier. They rarely represent single vineyards, so the principle of assemblage remains intact. Anywhere else you would look to old vines or reduced yields as an important part of the special character, but those features are rarely mentioned in Champagne. What makes the grapes special remains somewhat undefined.

Most prestige cuvées are vintage, but there is something of a recent trend to make special nonvintage cuvées at a price level going into the vintage range. Prestige cuvées usually come from grand and premier crus, but the brand name is more important to the consumer than the source of grapes. Of course, it is generally true of Champagne that reputation of the brand is emphasized over vintage or source.

The best known special cuvées, if only because they are the most widely available, are Moët's Dom Pérignon and Roederer's Cristal. These are really

Wine for some prestige Champagnes is vinified in oak. Quantities can be very small: a few barriques account for the entire production of Bollinger Vieilles Vignes Françaises.

brands in themselves. Most large houses now have an equivalent high-end cuvée. And then there are the houses that produce nothing but special cuvées: Krug and Salon, which interestingly take quite different approaches to top quality. Neither is independent any longer.

Krug was family-owned until the house was sold to LVMH in 1999, although Henri Krug continued to run it. Today the family feeling has been replaced by a more corporate atmosphere, but the wines remain extraordinary. The Grand Cuvée is a Brut nonvintage that outshines most vintage Champagnes, and unusually for this level includes Pinot Meunier.

Salon is a smaller operation, acquired by Laurent-Perrier in 1988, now run in conjunction with its neighbor Champagne Delamotte, and still focusing on a single Blanc de Blancs produced from Mesnil-sur-Oger only in top vintages (37 times in the twentieth century, five years so far in the twenty-first). The objectives of its founder were to produce a vin de garde; he thought Le Mesnil had the appropriate austerity, and this remains one of the tightest and longest lived Champagnes.

Crémant

Champagne is the most important (and best) sparkling wine produced in France. Sparkling wine is about 5% of all French wine production, and Champagne accounts for about two thirds of the 30 million cases produced each year in France. It accounts for about 10% of the world volume of sparkling wine, but 30% of the value. Champagne is the only region where sparkling wine is the main product; elsewhere, it is distinctly second-best to still wine.

The next quality level is crémant, made in the same way as Champagne, but coming from other areas. This accounts for about 20% of sparkling wine. It is no surprise that it also comes mostly from cool northern regions: Alsace, the Loire, and Burgundy. Grape varieties depend on the region of origin. The Loire also produces a lot

Crémant usually has the same pressure as Champagne and forms a similar mousse when poured. Courtesy Cave de Lugny.

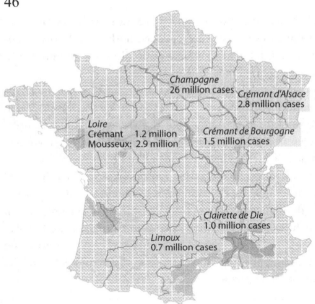

Sparkling wine production is concentrated in the North. Outside of Champagne, it is divided between Crémant (made by Méthode Champenoise) and Mousseux (which has lower pressure and is not made by Méthode Champenoise).

of sparkling wine in the lower category of Mousseux, made by second fermentation in bulk. In the south, some regions produce alternative types of sparkling wine. The traditional wines of Clairette de Die and Blanquette de Limoux are made by bottling the wine before the first fermentation has finished, so the pressure is much lower. This was probably the very first method used to make sparkling wine.

The distinction between Champagne and Crémant is no longer a matter of method of production, but simply comes down to place of origin (and the grape varieties that are allowed in each place). The formal classification of sparkling wines in France is determined by the pressure of carbon dioxide in the bottle, the method of production, and, of course, the place of origin. Originally the pressure was a major distinction, with Champagne above 5 bars (usually it is around 6 bars), Crémant above 3 bars, and Pétillant between 2.5 and 1 bar. Mousseux is a general term that describes all sparkling wine with a pressure of more than 3 atmospheres of carbon dioxide, but it carries the implication that the wine did not achieve the higher status of Crémant

Crémant is made by Méthode Champenoise: by performing the second fermentation in the bottle. Today it is usually technically similar to Champagne, with the same pressure. The original areas for Crémant were Burgundy and the Loire. Most of the other Crémant appellations were cre-

Reference Wines for Crémant & Pétillant	
Crémant de Bourgogne	Domaine de la Vougeraie
Crémant d'Alsace	Albert Boxler
Crémant de Loire	Château de l'Eperonnière
Crémant de Jura	André et Mireille Tissot, Indigène
Blanquette & Crémant de Limoux	Domaine Antech
Saumur Mousseux	Thierry Germain, Bulles de Roche
Anjou Pétillant	Domaine Richou
Touraine Pétillant	François Pinon
Vin de France	Couly-Dutheil (Chinon)

ated after 1985, in a quid pro quo that allowed additional regions to use the term Crémant in return for abandoning Méthode Champenoise as a description, so Crémant now states Méthode Traditionnelle. Like Champagne, the major regions for Crémant production have cool climates, but the grape varieties tend to be more exotic. This can be a problem, as the aromatics may clash with the neutrality that is required from the base wine.

Crémant de Bourgogne would be the obvious challenger since it comes from the same grapes as Champagne, but the fact is that sparkling wine in Burgundy is very much an also-ran, made mostly from grapes that simply aren't good enough to make still wine. Something of the same problem is found in the Loire, where grapes are selected for dry, sweet, or sparkling wines depending on vintage conditions, and much sparkling wine is used to absorb grapes that didn't quite make it. The other problem in the Loire is that the aromatics of Chenin Blanc do not fit gracefully into the spectrum of sparkling wine. The flavor profile is flatter than Champagne. The Loire is the largest producer of sparkling wine after Champagne, with 2-3 times more Mousseux than Crémant.

Vouvray makes both Crémant and Pétillant. Although Pétillant is sometimes disdained as having less fizz, purists consider that it shows off the character of Chenin better, because varietal character is less obvious under a full mousse. "I make a Pétillant (not a méthode traditionelle) because I don't like too much pressure," said François Pinon in Vouvray. Purists also feel that Pétillant is harder to produce, as it shows up any problems with the grapes more directly.

Limoux is another place where the tradition is for Pétillant. Blanquette de Limoux is one of the last holdouts for the Méthode Ancestrale, in which wine is bottled before the first fermentation has completed, creating a low pressure of bubbles. The traditional grape here is Mauzac, and at its best this gives a light sparkling wine with an impression of apples, but it can tend to be a bit sour or bitter. Moving into the modern era, there is now a Crémant de Limoux, which includes Chardonnay and Chenin Blanc as well as Mauzac; this is smoother and creamier than Blanquette.

Alsace is the largest producer of Crémant, which can come from Riesling, any of the Pinots, Auxerrois, and Chardonnay, although by and large Riesling is too valuable to include. So the varietal composition can be more similar to Champagne than you might expect. In spite of the similarity of climate, however, the Crémant tends to have a softer, more perfumed impression. A rosé can come only from Pinot Noir (whatever would happen if they introduced such a regulation in Champagne...)

Champagne's unique advantage lies in picking grapes very early specifically with sparkling wine in mind; elsewhere they would not really be considered ripe. It's conceivable that other regions in the cool north could make high quality sparkling wine, but so far they have failed to use varieties sufficiently challenged by marginal conditions. (The problem outside of France is often that the region is not sufficiently marginal: as a rough rule of thumb, if you can make good still wine, conditions may not be marginal enough to make the highest quality sparkling wine.) So Champagne reigns supreme.

Vintages

There are no official figures for how many houses produce a vintage Champagne each year, but global warming has seen a trend for vintage Champagnes to be produced more often—five or six or even more times per decade at the present. One measure of the year is whether the great prestige cuvées—Dom Pérignon, Cristal, Salon, Krug—are made. Totaling the number released each year gives a rough rating of vintages as 1 to 4 star. By that measure there was universal enthusiasm for 2002, 1996, 1995, and 1990, and minimal enthusiasm for 2005, 2003, 2001, and 1994. Remember that it's about five years before a vintage is released and can be assessed in bottle. Because vintage Champagne is intended for aging, and some wines are re-released as late disgorgements many years later, older vintages are of more than usual interest.

There is not much vintage Champagne from 2009-2011; 2008 was the urrent release for most houses, and is now being superseded by 2012. Those ouses who released 2009s often did so before the 2008s were released. The est year of the decade was 2002, which is regarded as exceptional right cross the range. The 2004 vintage is somewhat in the same style, but not uite as intense. Before that, 1996 was the exceptional vintage of the mid ineties, although the decade started with the outstanding 1990.

Year	Rating	Description
2019	***	Weather extremes of frost in Spring and heatwaves in summer, plus problems with mildew, reduced yields by about 20% compared to 2018. Good conditions in late August and September improved matters for harvest, and there should be vintage Champagnes.
2018	***	Enthusiasm for the vintage goes so far as for some producers to describe it as the vintage of the century. Very early harvest with high yields and higher ripeness levels than usual, so style of vintage releases is likely to be on richer side.
2017		"The most challenging vintage of my career," says Gilles Descôtes at Bollinger. Warm, wet conditions in August forced early picking in order to avoid botrytis. Unlikely to be many vintage releases.
2016	**	Low yields as everywhere in France but decent quality.
2015	***	Small berries at harvest may make high alcohol an issue, and should be a rich vintage.
2014	**	Good year for quality and quantity; producers expect to make vintage wines better than 2013 or 2012.
2013		Small crop size, but rescued by Indian summer and late harvest. Good acidity means vintage wines may have longevity. Not as good as 2012.
2012	*	Poor growing season rescued by warm August and dry September. All varieties did equally well and vintage Champagnes are good.
2011		An average year with high yields and some problems with maturity.
2010		Very variable, little vintage wine. Rot reduced size of crop.
2009	*	Variable with few vintage wines. There is a tendency for the wines to be a little too heavy, and they will mature early.
2008	**	Generally a vintage year. Wines on the austere side, in fact some producers considered releasing them after the richer 2009s as they need more time and will age longer.
2007		Good year for Chardonnay, with Blanc de Blancs from the vintage, but otherwise a light year.
2006	*	Rainy August was disappointing, but harvest rescued by hot September. Some good vintage wines.
2005	*	A bit on the warm side. Overall an average year but quite a few vintage wines.

2004	**	A very good year, similar style, not quite as good as 2002; better than 2005 with more vintage wines.
2003	*	Too hot to achieve the elegance and acidity needed for longevity.
2002	***	Regarded as the top year of the century so far, equally successful for Chardonnay and Pinot Noir.
2001		Universally unsuccessful due to very high rainfall.
2000	**	Above average with many vintage wines. Soft and attractive, but not long-lived.
1999	**	A workmanlike year above average, but acidity is on the low side, so for consumption relatively soon.
1998	**	Hot growing season gave wines that were soft and attractive when young, but not for long aging.
1997	*	A decent year but overshadowed by 1996.
1996	***	The best vintage of the decade after 1990; combination of refreshing acidity and ripeness gave wines that aged well until recent problems with oxidation.
1995	***	The first really good vintage year since 1990. A top vintage for the Chardonnays of the Côte des Blancs.
1994		Rain was a problem in all vintages between 1990 and 1995, but this was the worst.
1993	*	Seemed less ripe than 1992 at harvest, but vintage wines more or less comparable
1992	*	A passable year felt to be the only one really suitable for vintage between 1990 and 1995.
1991		Generally a disappointing year.
1990	***	One of the great vintages of the century, combining ripeness with good acidity. This is a classic.

Visiting the Region

"If Reims is the capital of the Grand Maisons, Aÿ is the capital of the vignerons," says Christian Gosset of Gosset-Brabant in Aÿ. There are really several separate foci for visiting Champagne.

Way to the south (nearer Chablis than Reims) is the Côte des Bar. However, the Route Touristique de Champagne runs more through fields of sunflowers and past granaries, with vineyards well out of sight on the hills to the side. There are more growers than houses here, and it's not a major tourist attraction, although Champagne Drappier is worth visiting.

Reims is almost exclusively Grands Maisons: Krug, Roederer, Veuve Clicquot, Taittinger, Lanson, Piper Heidsieck, Charles Heidsieck, Henriot, Mumm, Ruinart, Pommery and others all have their headquarters here. Now that the tram system has been completed, Reims is not the disaster for the visitor that it is used to be. All the houses accept visits, although some require or prefer appointments: visits tend to be conducted by professional guides. Cellars are often old and extensive, at the large houses a visit may include a propaganda movie, and often enough now there is a charge for tasting. The underground chalk *crayère* cellars are one of the major tourist attractions of Reims: Taittinger, Ruinart, and Veuve Clicquot have the most extensive cellars. Remember that even at houses where visits are professionally organized, the lunch hour is sacrosanct in France, and tasting rooms are usually closed between 12:00 and 2:00 p.m.

The atmosphere is similar on the Avenue de Champagne in Épernay, where there is a sequence of major houses including Moet & Chandon, Perrier-Jouët, Pol Roger, Mercier, with others such as Cazanove, Gosset, and Alfred Gratien close by. The houses are close enough that you can walk between them. (In fact, there is a very long tunnel underground between the cellars of Moët & Chandon at one end of the Avenue and Mercier at the other end.)

Épernay is the obvious base for visiting the regions where there are major concentrations of grower-producers: Aÿ (not much more distant than a suburb of Épernay) and surrounding villages to the east; and the villages of the Côte des Blancs to the south. Within 30 minutes you can drive to the farthest points out to the east or south. These houses are much smaller, visits tend to be more personal, and you are likely to meet with the owner or cellarmaster (very often the same person). Because they may well be involved in actually making the wine, it is a good idea to make

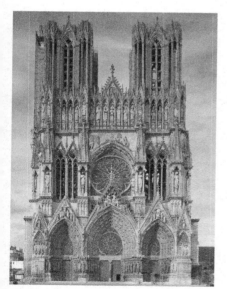

Champagne houses are found all around Reims; the cathedral marks the center, and is one of the major tourist attractions of France.

The Avenue de Champagne in Epernay is a mile-long stretch of famous Champagne houses.

an appointment in advance to be sure there will be someone available.

Unlike other wines, do not swirl Champagne before tasting: this releases carbon dioxide which obscures the aromas of the wine. The etiquette of tasting assumes that you will spit; producers will be surprised if you drink it all. Tasting rooms are usually equipped with spittoons. Most Champagne houses are geared to sell wine directly. English is spoken almost universally.

Maps

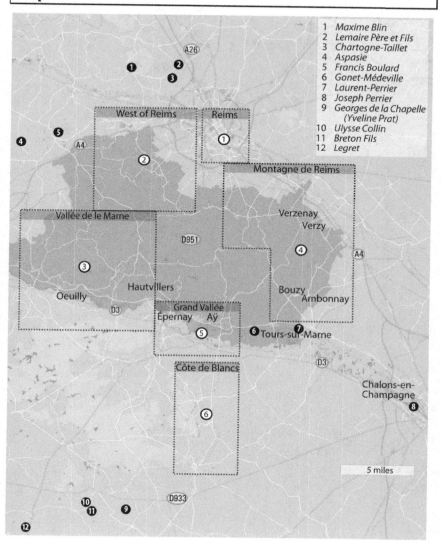

1. Maxime Blin
2. Lemaire Père et Fils
3. Chartogne-Taillet
4. Aspasie
5. Francis Boulard
6. Gonet-Médeville
7. Laurent-Perrier
8. Joseph Perrier
9. Georges de la Chapelle
   (Yveline Prat)
10. Ulysse Collin
11. Breton Fils
12. Legret

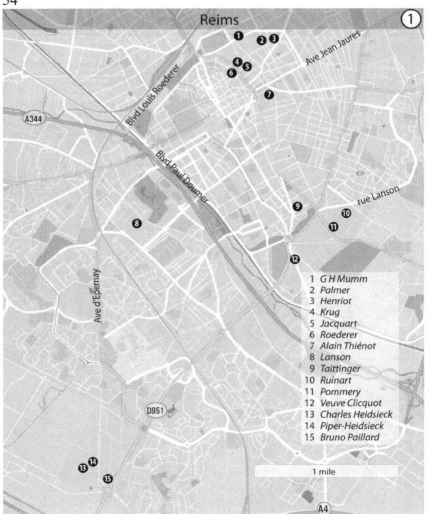

Reims ①

1 G H Mumm
2 Palmer
3 Henriot
4 Krug
5 Jacquart
6 Roederer
7 Alain Thiénot
8 Lanson
9 Taittinger
10 Ruinart
11 Pommery
12 Veuve Clicquot
13 Charles Heidsieck
14 Piper-Heidsieck
15 Bruno Paillard

1 mile

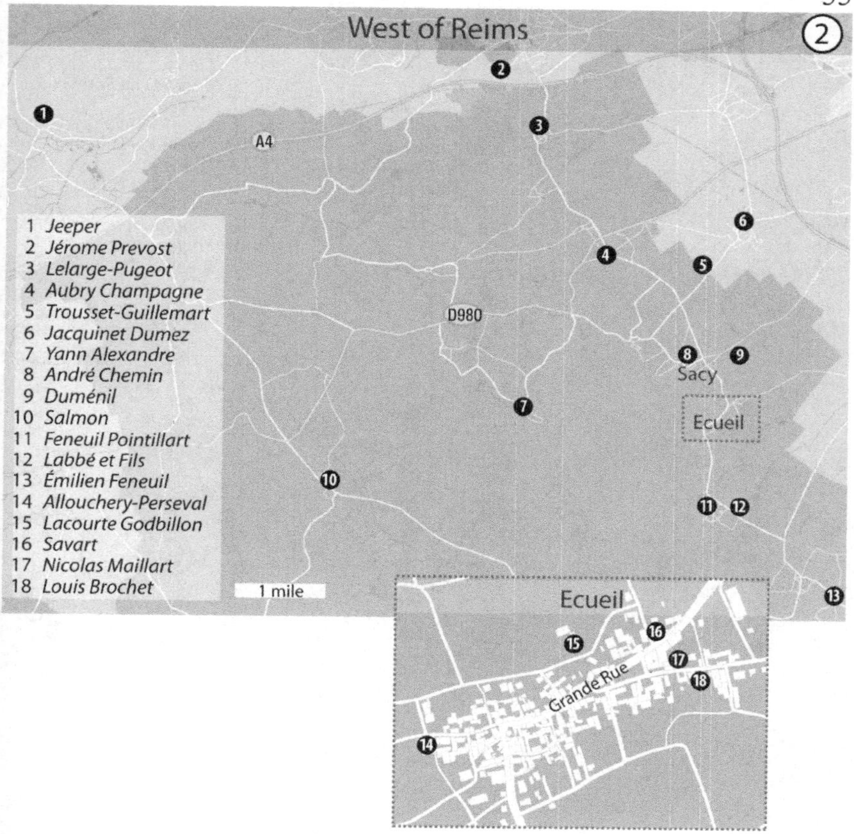

West of Reims

1 Jeeper
2 Jérome Prevost
3 Lelarge-Pugeot
4 Aubry Champagne
5 Trousset-Guillemart
6 Jacquinet Dumez
7 Yann Alexandre
8 André Chemin
9 Duménil
10 Salmon
11 Feneuil Pointillart
12 Labbé et Fils
13 Émilien Feneuil
14 Allouchery-Perseval
15 Lacourte Godbillon
16 Savart
17 Nicolas Maillart
18 Louis Brochet

A4

D980

Sacy

Ecueil

1 mile

Ecueil

Grande Rue

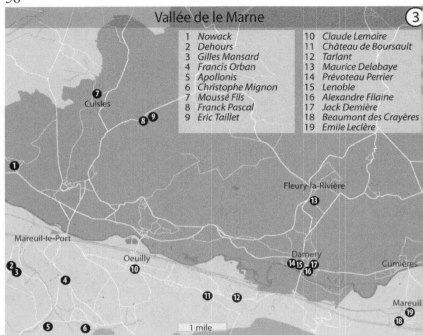

Vallée de le Marne ③

1 Nowack
2 Dehours
3 Gilles Mansard
4 Francis Orban
5 Apollonis
6 Christophe Mignon
7 Moussé Fils
8 Franck Pascal
9 Eric Taillet
10 Claude Lemaire
11 Château de Boursault
12 Tarlant
13 Maurice Delabaye
14 Prévoteau Perrier
15 Lenoble
16 Alexandre Filaine
17 Jack Demière
18 Beaumont des Crayères
19 Emile Leclère

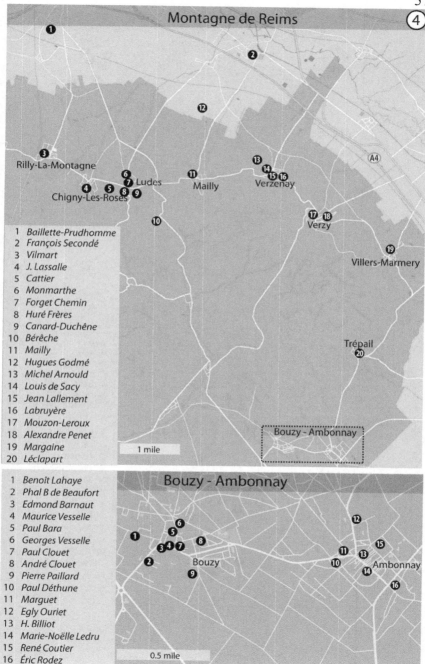

Montagne de Reims

④

Rilly-La-Montagne

Ludes
Chigny-Les-Roses
Mailly
Verzenay

Verzy

Villers-Marmery

Trépail

A4

Bouzy - Ambonnay

1 mile

1 Baillette-Prudhomme
2 François Secondé
3 Vilmart
4 J. Lassalle
5 Cattier
6 Monmarthe
7 Forget Chemin
8 Huré Frères
9 Canard-Duchêne
10 Bérêche
11 Mailly
12 Hugues Godmé
13 Michel Arnould
14 Louis de Sacy
15 Jean Lallement
16 Labruyère
17 Mouzon-Leroux
18 Alexandre Penet
19 Margaine
20 Léclapart

Bouzy - Ambonnay

Bouzy
Ambonnay

0.5 mile

1 Benoît Lahaye
2 Phal B de Beaufort
3 Edmond Barnaut
4 Maurice Vesselle
5 Paul Bara
6 Georges Vesselle
7 Paul Clouet
8 André Clouet
9 Pierre Paillard
10 Paul Déthune
11 Marguet
12 Egly Ouriet
13 H. Billiot
14 Marie-Noëlle Ledru
15 René Coutier
16 Éric Rodez

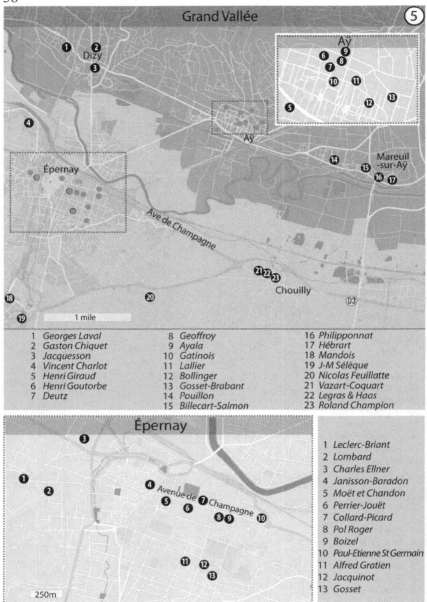

Grand Vallée

Dizy
Aÿ

Mareuil
-sur-Aÿ

Épernay

Ave de Champagne

Chouilly

1 mile

1 Georges Laval	8 Geoffroy	16 Philipponnat
2 Gaston Chiquet	9 Ayala	17 Hébrart
3 Jacquesson	10 Gatinois	18 Mandois
4 Vincent Charlot	11 Lallier	19 J-M Sélèque
5 Henri Giraud	12 Bollinger	20 Nicolas Feuillatte
6 Henri Goutorbe	13 Gosset-Brabant	21 Vazart-Coquart
7 Deutz	14 Pouillon	22 Legras & Haas
	15 Billecart-Salmon	23 Roland Champion

Épernay

Avenue de Champagne

250m

1 Leclerc-Briant
2 Lombard
3 Charles Ellner
4 Janisson-Baradon
5 Moët et Chandon
6 Perrier-Jouët
7 Collard-Picard
8 Pol Roger
9 Boizel
10 Paul-Etienne St Germain
11 Alfred Gratien
12 Jacquinot
13 Gosset

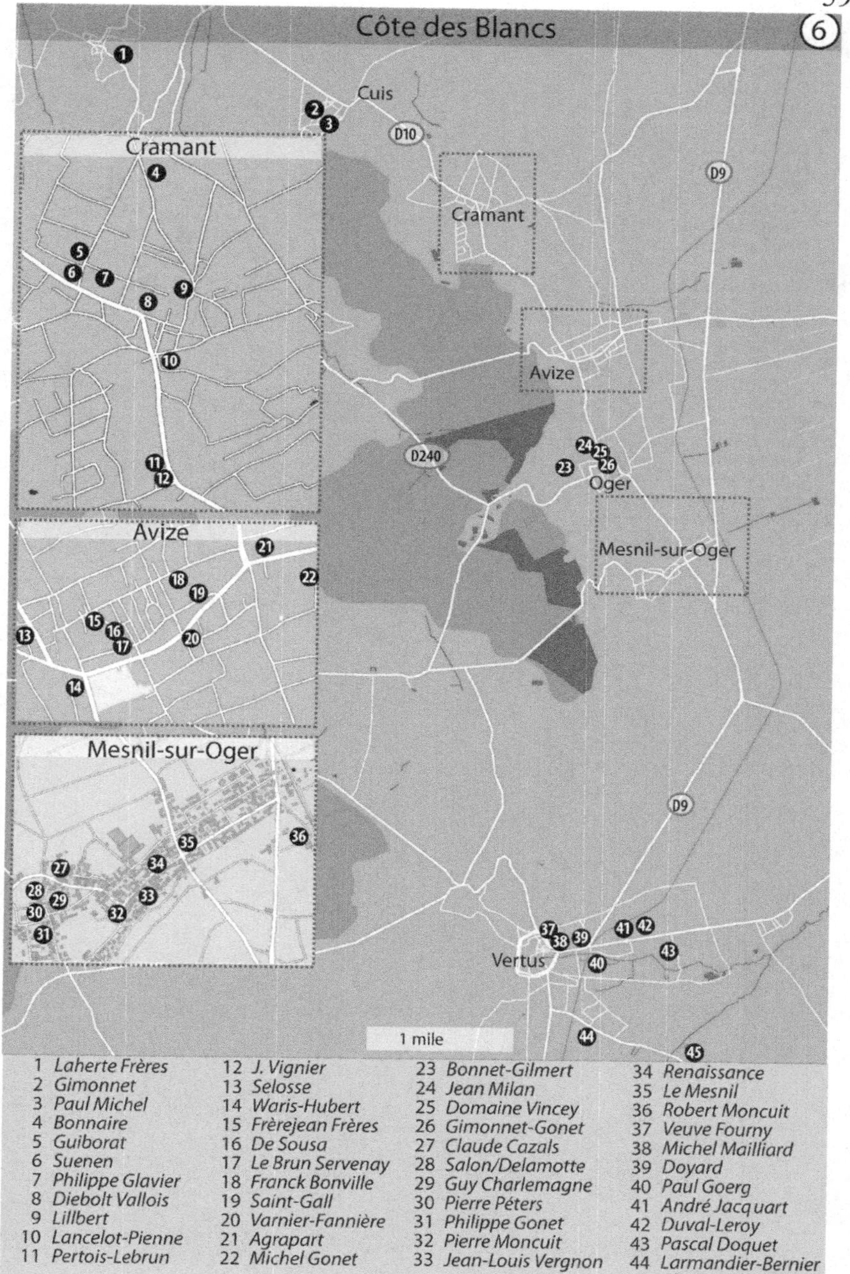

Côte des Blancs

Cramant

Cuis

D10

D9

1 Laherte Frères

2 Gimonnet
3 Paul Michel

4 Bonnaire

Cramant

5 Guiborat
6 Suenen
7 Philippe Glavier
8 Diebolt Vallois
9 Lillbert
10 Lancelot-Pienne

11 Pertois-Lebrun
12 J. Vignier

Avize

21 Agrapart
18 Franck Bonville
19 Saint-Gall
22 Michel Gonet
15 Frèrejean Frères
16 De Sousa
17 Le Brun Servenay
20 Varnier-Fannière
13 Selosse
14 Waris-Hubert

Avize

D240

24 Jean Milan
25 Domaine Vincey
26 Gimonnet-Gonet
23 Bonnet-Gilmert

Oger

Mesnil-sur-Oger

Mesnil-sur-Oger

35 Le Mesnil
36 Robert Moncuit
34 Renaissance
27 Claude Cazals
28 Salon/Delamotte
29 Guy Charlemagne
33 Jean-Louis Vergnon
32 Pierre Moncuit
30 Pierre Péters
31 Philippe Gonet

D9

37 Veuve Fourny
38 Michel Mailliard
39 Doyard
41 André Jacquart
42 Duval-Leroy
43 Pascal Doquet
40 Paul Goerg

Vertus

44 Larmandier-Bernier

45 Champagne Colin

1 mile

1	Laherte Frères	12	J. Vignier	23	Bonnet-Gilmert	34	Renaissance
2	Gimonnet	13	Selosse	24	Jean Milan	35	Le Mesnil
3	Paul Michel	14	Waris-Hubert	25	Domaine Vincey	36	Robert Moncuit
4	Bonnaire	15	Frèrejean Frères	26	Gimonnet-Gonet	37	Veuve Fourny
5	Guiborat	16	De Sousa	27	Claude Cazals	38	Michel Mailliard
6	Suenen	17	Le Brun Servenay	28	Salon/Delamotte	39	Doyard
7	Philippe Glavier	18	Franck Bonville	29	Guy Charlemagne	40	Paul Goerg
8	Diebolt Vallois	19	Saint-Gall	30	Pierre Péters	41	André Jacquart
9	Lillbert	20	Varnier-Fannière	31	Philippe Gonet	42	Duval-Leroy
10	Lancelot-Pienne	21	Agrapart	32	Pierre Moncuit	43	Pascal Doquet
11	Pertois-Lebrun	22	Michel Gonet	33	Jean-Louis Vergnon	44	Larmandier-Bernier
						45	Champagne Colin

60

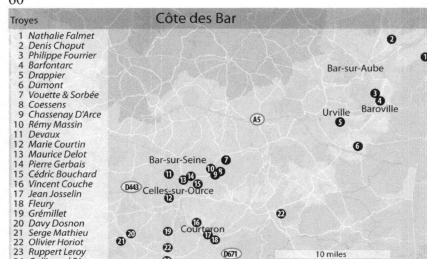

Côte des Bar

Troyes

1 *Nathalie Falmet*
2 *Denis Chaput*
3 *Philippe Fourrier*
4 *Barfontarc*
5 *Drappier*
6 *Dumont*
7 *Vouette & Sorbée*
8 *Coessens*
9 *Chassenay D'Arce*
10 *Rémy Massin*
11 *Devaux*
12 *Marie Courtin*
13 *Maurice Delot*
14 *Pierre Gerbais*
15 *Cédric Bouchard*
16 *Vincent Couche*
17 *Jean Josselin*
18 *Fleury*
19 *Grémillet*
20 *Davy Dosnon*
21 *Serge Mathieu*
22 *Olivier Horiot*
23 *Ruppert Leroy*
24 *Gallimard Père*

Profiles of Houses

Ratings	
****	Sui generis, standing out above everything else in the appellation
***	Excellent producers defining the very best of the appellation
**	Top producers whose wines typify the appellation
*	Very good producers making wines of character that rarely disappoint

Symbols for Producers

- Address
- Phone
- Owner/winemaker/contact
- Email
- Website
- Area
- Reference wines
- Grower Champagne (R.M.)
- Champagne House (N.M.)
- Cooperative (C.M. or R.C.)
- Conventional viticulture
- Sustainable viticulture
- Organic
- Organic (Certified)
- Biodynamic
- Biodynamic (Certified)
- Natural Wine
- Wine with No Sulfur
- Vegan Wine

- Tasting room with especially warm welcome
- Tastings/visits possible
- By appointment only
- Charge for tasting
  (free if no symbol)
  $ - nominal, $$ - moderate, $$$ - expensive
- No visits
- Sales directly at producer
- No direct sales
- Winery with accommodation

ha=estate vineyards
bottles=annual production

Profiles of Leading Estates

Champagne Agrapart et Fils ★★

57 Avenue Jean-Jaurès, 51190 Avize	📞 +33 3 26 57 51 38
@ *info@celuga.fr*	👤 *Pascal Agrapart*
🌐 *www.champagne-agrapart.com*	*[map p. 59]*
🚫🍷🍇 *12 ha; 100,000 btl*	*Terroir*

Agrapart was founded by Pascal Agrapart's grandfather and is still very much a family domain. Pascal's father started to commercialize the Champagne in the sixties and seventies; Pascal built the domain up from 3 ha to 12 ha. "We wouldn't grow beyond, say, 15 ha and be able to continue as we like to consider ourselves true artisans," says Nathalie Agrapart. Vineyards include more than 70 individual parcels, mostly Chardonnay Grand Cru with some Premier Cru on the Côte de Blancs, and a little Pinot Noir on the Montagne de Reims. "We are specialists in Chardonnay, we just have some small plots with Pinot Noir," says Nathalie.

The artisan nature of the operation becomes clear going around the cellars, set around a charming courtyard off the street, and somewhat larger than they appear, as they go down for three levels. The top level is for vinification, the second level is full of pupîtres, and the third is for stockage. There are two old presses, where the juice runs out directly into an underground vat. Riddling is all manual, and there's no transvasage, remuage is done manually up to jeroboams. Vinification is stainless steel or in barrique, depending on the cuvée. Disgorgement is not done by the usual automated machinery, but individually by Pascal: his son dips the inverted bottle into the freezing mixture and quickly turns them back up, then Pascal snips off the cork with a pair of pliers, sticks the end of the pliers into the neck to release the foam, and sniffs to check all is well, before the bottle is passed on for dosage and bottling.

There are seven cuvées. Only two are based on assemblage from different parcels; the majority are single-vineyard wines or represent specific terroirs. Only one is Brut, the rest are Extra Brut or Brut Nature. Pascal thinks a lot about his cuvées. "The idea in my head was..." he tends to explain with a gesture, as he introduces each cuvée. The only conventional blend is the 7 Crus Brut, an assemblage of premier crus from seven villages. Terroir is a Blanc de Blancs assembled from several grand crus; then there are Blanc de Blancs representing specific terroirs. "We have vineyards very close to the Maison and make three completely different wines." Mineral comes from very calcareous plots in Avize and Cramant. "In the same village you can find different terroirs, clay or calcareous, different depths of soil. My idea is to reflect those differences by selecting vineyards that show the mineral side." Avizoise is a vintage that comes from the oldest vines (60 years) from soils with more clay in Avize. "Mineral has the verticality, Avizoise has more volume and breadth." Exp. 12 is a Brut Nature from Avize. "This is nothing but Champagne. No dosage, no sugar at all. The liqueur comes from another vintage. So it's all Champagne."

The range gives a terrific expression of different terroirs through the prism of Chardonnay. An extremely fine sense of texture runs through all cuvées. Flavors in the citrus spectrum are subtle, and deepen going from the vins d'assemblage to the single-vineyard wines, but all cuvées have that impression of refinement and delicacy, giving a sense that a finely coiled spring is waiting to develop. The Extra Brut style allows purity of fruits to shine through.

Champagne Yann Alexandre   *

8, chemin des Jardins, 51390 Courmas	📞 *+33 6 81 03 81 79*
@ *champagneyannalexandre@orange.fr*	👤 *Séverine Alexandre*
🌐 *www.champagneyannalexandre.fr*	*[map p. 55]*
📅 €€ 🏭 🍇 ℃ *6 ha; 30,000 btl*	🍾 *Roche Mère*

The domain has a typical history for a small estate, starting eight generations ago by growing grapes, then moving into producing base wines that were sold to negociants, and finally in 1966 starting to bottle Champagne under their own label. Yann took over from his father in 1999. Vineyards are in 30 separate parcels in nine different villages, with a concentration of 14 parcels in the home village of Cormas. Typically for the Petite Montagne de Reims, Pinot Meunier dominates: plantings are 55% Pinot Meunier, 30% Chardonnay, and 15% Pinot Noir. Vinification depends on the cuvée and the year, but nonvintage wines usually age in stainless steel, while vintage cuvées see at least some oak. Malolactic fermentation varies, although there's an increasing tendency to block it.

Brut Noir and Roche Mère Brut Nature both have 45% Pinot Meunier, with Brut Noir aging on lees for 4-5 years and the Brut Nature aging for 6 years. There's only a slight increase in weight going from Brut Nature to Brut Noir and very little change in the sense of ripeness. Coming from premier cru vineyards, the Grande Réserve Brut has Pinot Meunier reduced to 20%, and ages for 7 years on the lees. Blanche Terres Rosé de Blancs is 92% Chardonnay plus the 8% red wine to make rosé and really tastes like Blanc de Blancs with eyes closed. Vintage cuvées include an Extra Brut (60% Chardonnay and 40% Pinot Noir) and a Blanc de Blancs. There are also occasional cuvées called Les Ephémères, produced in amounts as small as 1,000 bottles, representing parcels or unusual assemblages. The house style favors a mid weight elegant palate with flavors poised between stone fruits an citrus, although the vintage Blanc de Blancs has more of an overt acid presence.

Champagne Ayala   **

2 boulevard du Nord, BP 6, 51160 Aÿ	📞 *+33 3 26 55 15 44*
@ *contact@champagne-ayala.fr*	👤 *Philippe-Alexandre Bernatchez*
🌐 *www.champagne-ayala.fr*	*[map p. 58]*
📅 €€ 🏭 🏠 ℃ *19 ha; 900,000 btl*	🍾 *Brut Majeur*
Owner: Champagne Bollinger	

Founded in 1860 by Edmond de Ayala (of Spanish descent) when he obtained the Château de Aÿ and vineyards as dowry, the house of Ayala was one of the original Grand Marques. Known for its (relatively) drier style, in its heyday in the 1920s Ayala was producing a million bottles annually. By late twentieth century, its reputation had slipped; in 2001 it was purchased by the Frey Group, who then sold it in 2005 to the Bollinger family (but Frey kept the old stock and the vineyards).

There has been considerable investment, including a new cuverie. "Today there is a young team, the youngest in Champagne," they say proudly. Run independently, Ayala is being repositioned as a Chardonnay-driven brand. Wines that do not correspond to this style have been dropped, and the line focuses on the Majeur nonvintage (Brut, Rosé, and Natur), the Blanc de Blancs vintage, and the Perle d'Ayala prestige cuvée. Nonvintage is typically 40% Chardonnay, 40% Pinot Noir, and 20% Pinot Meunier; Perle d'Ayala is 80% Chardonnay with 20% Pinot Noir.

Returning to Ayala's roots, dosage is always low, the highest being 7 g/l in the Brut and rosé. This is something of a move to distinguish itself from Bollinger. "Bollinger is driven by Pinot Noir and oak, Ayala is Chardonnay-driven in stainless steel," says marketing manager Laurence Alamanos.

The house has made something of a stir with its zero dosage (the Majeur Natur). House style is crisp and sassy, emphasizing clean lines and purity of fruits, showing at its peak with the saline minerality of the Brut Nature, which is the real thing so far as zero dosage goes: you see the fruits, the whole fruits, and nothing but the fruits. You would be hard put to identify it as based on the same wine as the Brut Majeur, although it's the same blend given one year longer aging on the lees. The elegant Brut Majeur tastes more like Extra Brut, the richness of the fruits makes the vintage Blanc de Blancs less obviously mineral, Perle d'Ayala is rounder and fuller, and the softness of the 8% red wine in the rosé pushes minerality into the background.

Champagne Paul Bara   *

4 rue Yvonnet, 51150 Bouzy	📞 +33 3 26 57 00 50
@ info@champagnepaulbara.fr	👤 Stéphanie Ducloux
🌐 www.champagnepaulbara.com	[map p. 57]
😃 🏭 🍇 🕰 11 ha; 100,000 btl	Special Club

Started in 1833, the house is still in hands of same family. Originally the Baras were growers, then they joined the cooperative in Bouzy, but after the second world war, Paul Bara started to bottle his own Champagne. Today his daughter Chantale is the cellarmaster. The domain is located in some gracious old buildings around a courtyard on the road through Bouzy. The vineyards, only Pinot Noir and Chardonnay, and many with old vines, are all in Bouzy grand cru, and have been have been in the family for a long time. Do they ever buy any more? "Oh no, it's too complicated."

There are seven different cuvées plus a red Bouzy. Everything is Brut: Chantale did some trials with zero dosage and wasn't satisfied. The blends are dominated by Pinot Noir (70-90%). Most cuvées have moderate dosage of 8 g/l, but the Special Club (a vintage cuvée presented in a special bottle that is shared by a club of 28 growers) has 6 g/l dosage. Wines are vinified in stainless steel, and all go through malolactic fermentation, except for a new cuvée, Anunciade, starting with the 2004 vintage, which is a Blanc de Noirs matured in barriques and without any MLF. The style is light and elegant, showing well with the Brut Réserve, becoming just a touch deeper on the Special Club, softened by the rosé (a rosé d'assemblage made with 10% of the Bouzy red), then with added density from the vintage.

Champagne Bérêche et Fils   *

33 rue Craon de Ludes, 51500 Ludes	📞 +33 3 26 61 13 28
@ contact@equinoxes.fr	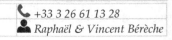 👤 Raphaël & Vincent Bérêche

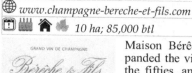

| www.champagne-bereche-et-fils.com | [map p. 57] |
| 10 ha; 85,000 btl | Le Cran |

Maison Bérêche was founded in 1847 as a grower, expanded the vineyards and started producing Champagne in the fifties, and has risen greatly in reputation since winemaker Raphaël and vineyard manager Vincent started working with their father in 2004. Somewhat spread out, vineyards are mostly on the Montagne de Reims, but with some parcels in the Vallée de le Marne.

Originally an RM (récoltant-manipulant or grower-producer), Bérêche has become an NM (négociant-manipulant) in order to be able to purchase grapes from three growers for the Brut Réserve; all the other cuvées have exclusively estate grapes. Under the separate negociant label of Raphaël et Vincent Bérêche, there's a series of cuvées called Crus Sélectionnés to represent different terroirs.

Vinification has been moving towards using oak, and barriques or tonneaux now account for about three quarters. Malolactic fermentation does not occur. The second fermentation occurs under cork rather than capsule in the belief that this creates a finer Champagne through more oxygenation. The wines show the lack of malolactic fermentation in their acid backbone, which combined with moderate dosage can give a slightly austere impression. The nonvintage Brut Réserve is a good representation of the house style, but the single vineyard cuvées Les Beaux Regards and Le Cran convey a smoother impression; the Campania Remensis Extra Brut rosé is an elegant example of rosé.

Champagne Billecart Salmon   ***

40, rue Carnot, 51160 Mareuil-sur-Aÿ	+33 3 26 52 60 22
billecart@champagne-billecart.fr	Mathieu Roland-Billecart
www.champagne-billecart.fr	[map p. 58]
50 ha; 2,000,000 btl	Brut Rosé

Presently in the seventh generation under François Roland Billecart, the family sold a minority interest (45%) to the Frey Group in 2005. Mathieu Roland-Billecart gave up his career in the City of London to take over the house in 2018. The house was founded in 1818 by two families who had been in the village since the sixteenth century. The original vineyards were lost in 1925, but later partly restored; today estate grapes provide about a quarter of the supply, which comes from all over the region.

Cellarmaster François Domi uses prolonged fermentation at low temperature with the philosophy that, "We are not looking for expression, we are looking for discretion." There is no set policy about malolactic fermentation, which depends on the acidity of the year. A small proportion of the vintage Champagne is vinified in old fûts. "There are no rules" is the most frequent expression here, "Everything depends on the year."

The range includes nine cuvées, extending from the nonvintage Extra Brut, Brut, Blanc de Blancs, and Rosé to the vintage, the named vintage cuvées, Nicolas François and Elisabeth Salmon (rosé), and the single vineyard Clos Saint Hilaire. In addition, the range has now been widened by the Vintage line (intended to make vintage wine more accessible) and the Sous Bois (using barriques to achieve broader flavors). The fame of the Maison is based on the elegance of its rosés. The Brut Rosé vintage adds an integrated smoothness to the flavor spectrum of the Brut nonvintage, and the Elisabeth Salmon vintage offers seamless layers of flavor.

Champagne Bollinger ***

16 rue Jules-Lobet, BP 4, 51160 Aÿ	📞 *+33 3 26 53 33 66*
@ *contact@champagne-bollinger.fr*	👤 *Charles-Armand de Belenet*
🌐 *www.champagne-bollinger.com*	*[map p. 58]*
📅 ⚒ 🏠 ⌛ *174 ha; 2,500,000 btl*	🍾 *La Grand Année*

Still controlled by the original family, Bollinger is the most important of the Champagne houses remaining in private hands. It is the most traditional of houses, but that is not to say stultified. It is known for using barriques (3,000 of them) for vinification, using corks rather than crown caps for the first bottling, and storing Reserve wines in magnums. All this contributes to a recognizable intensity of style. An exceptionally high proportion of grapes (almost three quarters) come from Bollinger's own vineyards.

Until recently there was no rosé, because it was not regarded as serious enough, but the house succumbed to market pressure and introduced one in 2008. The nonvintage is called the Special Cuvée, and the vintage has been called Grand Année since 2004. The Vieilles Vignes Françaises is a Blanc de Noirs from two small plots of ungrafted vines behind the Maison. The most recent cuvée, introduced in 2020, is a nonvintage Blanc de Noirs, PN VZ, which comes from the commune of Verzenay. PN VZ 15 has a base of 2015 vintage, with wines dating back to 2009.

Pinot Noir is the dominant grape, more than 60% in the Special Cuvée and Grand Année. Bollinger are sceptical about Pinot Meunier; cellarmaster Gilles Descôtes says, "It is more rustic and does not age as well. This does not matter for nonvintage (where it is limited to 15%), but is an issue for vintage." Bollinger introduced the idea of re-releasing old vintages by holding them on the lees for several extra years until disgorgement, as indicated in the name of the prestige R.D. cuvée (Recently Disgorged). Whether nonvintage or vintage, the style is dry, toasty, and muscular, in a full bodied style.

Bollinger expanded into the Loire by buying Maison Langlois-Chateau in 1973, and more recently acquired Château de Thauvenay (2016) and Domaine Hubert Brochard (2022) in Sancerre. Bollinger made its first foray outside France in 2021 by buying Ponzi Vineyards in Oregon (which produces Pinot Noir and Chardonnay, but not sparkling wine).

Champagne Bonnaire *

120 Rue Épernay, 51530 Cramant	📞 *+33 3 26 57 50 85*
@ *contact@bonnaire.com*	👤 *Jean-Étienne Bonnaire*
🌐 *www.bonnaire.com*	*[map p. 59]*
📅 ⚒ 🍇 ⌛ *22 ha; 200,000 btl*	🍾 *Blanc de Blancs*

The domain was founded by Fernand Bouquemont in 1932; his grandson Jean-Louis Bonnaire ran the domain for fifty years until his death in 2015. Jean-Louis's wife, Marie-Thérèse Clouet-Bonnaire, owns Champagne Paul Clouet (see profile) in Bouzy. Jean-Louis made the wine there, and today his son Jean-Étienne makes the wine for both domains in a modern building on the side of Cramant. His other son,

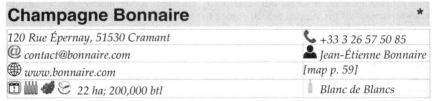

Jean-Emmanuel, manages the commercial side. The ranges are different, except that Brut and rosé are the same for both houses.

Most of the Bonnaire vineyards are in Cramant, with some elsewhere on the Côtes des Blancs, planted with Chardonnay, and there are also some in the Vallée de la Marne growing Pinot Noir and Pinot Meunier. Wines are aged in stainless steel— "my father put in stainless steel because he liked freshness," Jean-Emmanuel says. All the grapes from outside the Côte des Blancs go into Cuvée Tradition, which is 50% Chardonnay, 30% Pinot Noir, and 20% Pinot Meunier; it's softer and broader than the rest of the range. Except for Tradition and rosé, all the cuvées are Blanc de Blancs.

There's a transition to the Blanc de Blancs where the style is fresh and more tinged towards citrus. The nonvintage has the characteristic minerality of the Côte des Blanc. The vintage Cramant is smoother with a greater sense of ripeness. Vers Sacrum vintage is aged under natural cork instead of crown caps, and shows greater fruit concentration. Variance is barrel fermented and aged in oak with full malolactic fermentation, showing an intense palate on the edge of salinity. (Its source is being restricted to a single vineyard in Cramant.) Vintage wines have a great capacity to age. The original disgorgements of the 1995 and the 1980 are still full of flavor today, showing a creamy palate with stone fruits and honeyed impressions. The rosé (shared with Clouet) also has a citric edge.

Champagne Chartogne-Taillet   *

37-39 Grande Rue, 51220 Merfy	📞 +33 3 26 03 10 17
@ chartogne.taillet@wanadoo.fr	👤 Alexandre Chartogne
🌐 www.chartogne-taillet.com	[map p. 53]
	🍾 Beaux Sens

Vines have been grown in Merfy since the Roman era. Located just to the north of Reims, more or less at the edge of the Montagne de Reims, the estate dates from 1683. Vineyard consists of fourteen separate parcels, including three with ungrafted vines. The Maison is located in the center of Merfy, and is the only grower-producer in the village. Alexandre Chartogne has been the winemaker since 2006; he is a protégé of Anselm Selosse.

Sainte Anne is the only nonvintage cuvée, but gives a good sense of the house style, although broader than the individual cuvées. The rosé is the only general blend. All the other cuvées come from specific terroirs or parcels. The vintage comes from Les Couarres while Fiacre comes from two neighboring plots; both are made in stainless steel. Heuretebise Blanc de Blancs is a natural wine, fermented in stainless steel with no filtration and is a little fuller than the single-vineyard wines. Beaux Sens is the smoothest, Les Barres is more forceful, coming from Pinot Meunier from ungrafted vines that predate phylloxera, and Les Orizeaux is vinified in oak barriques and conveys a sense of precision.

All fermentation uses natural yeast, and malolactic is spontaneous—"usually the wine goes through malolactic fermentation in the Spring when the cellars warm up," says Alexander. "I don't want to interfere too much with the wine." The style gives an impression of precision with a savory edge, aided by moderate or zero dosage Beaux Sens, Les Barres, and Orizeaux are all labeled as Extra Brut): the overall impression is that the fruits are allowed to speak for themselves.

68

Champagne Deutz ✸✸

16, rue Jeanson, Bp 9, 51160 Aÿ	☎ +33 3 26 56 94 00
@ *contact@champagne-deutz.com*	🏆 *Fabrice Rosset*
⊕ *www.champagne-deutz.com*	*[map p. 58]*
📅 ⚒ 🏠 ♺ *46 ha; 2,500,000 btl*	🍾 *Brut Classic*
Owner: Champagne Louis Roederer	

Founded in 1838, Deutz remained under family contro until it was sold in 1983 to the Rouzaud family who ow Roederer. Estate vineyards account for about 20% of sup ply, and the rest comes from vineyards within a 30 kn radius of the Maison. "We concentrate at Deutz in develop ing a strong purity, finesse, and elegance—no wood barrels no fermentation in wood," says Jean-Marc Lallier-Deutz To maintain freshness, reserve wines come from the pas couple of years, and form a high proportion of the Bru Classic, which accounts for around 80% of production. Malolactic fermentation i routine, and dosage is usually around 9 g/l. "The Deutz style is already clean and mineral; with less dosage or no MLF, the wines would be too aggressive, too aus tere," explains Jean-Marc.

The hallmark of the house style for me is a certain sense of texture on the palate suggestive of long time on the lees, which counterpoises the typical freshness. Thi shows clearly in the Brut Classic, and is accompanied by just a touch more density and power in the vintage Blanc de Blancs. It becomes a backdrop to a style that i more delicate and precise in the Armour de Deutz (a Blanc de Blancs); and then witl the richness of the spectacular William Deutz the texture is superficially less obviou because of sheer fruit concentration. The vintage rosé is elegant, showing the re finement and purity of Pinot Noir (until 2006 it was 100% Pinot Noir; since then a little Chardonnay has been included).

Dom Pérignon ✸✸✸✸

Champagne Moët et Chandon, 20 Avenue de Champagne, 51333 Épernay	☎ +33 3 26 51 20 00
@ *contact@moet.fr*	
⊕ *www.domperignon.com*	
📅 ⚒ 🏠	*1190 ha; 5,500,000 btl* *Owner: Champagne Moët et Chandon*

Dom Pérignon is undoubtedly the best known prestige cu vée in Champagne, and an altogether different quality leve from Moët & Chandon (see profile), where it started as a late disgorgement (in 1936) from the fabled 1921 vintage Since 1947 it has been produced separately. Regarded a: Moët's prestige cuvée until relatively recently, it has be come an independent brand, with production around 5-(million bottles (which would place it among the top Cham pagne houses by size, albeit dwarfed by Moët' production). Vineyard sources are grand crus from Moët' holdings, with some premier cru from around the abbey at Hautvillers, which Moë now owns.

There are three releases for each vintage of Dom Pérignon. The first is a minimum 8 years after the vintage; subsequently there are two Plenitudes (originally called Oenothèques), P2 disgorged after at least 12 years, and P3 after at least 18 years. "All vintages are meant to give P2 and P3, it's built into the criteria," says cellarmaster Richard Geoffroy. Longevity seems to be unaltered by time before disgorgement (at least for the first release and P2); typically I would say each lasts about 20 years. The assemblage contains only Pinot Noir and Chardonnay, with up to 60% of either, depending on vintage. Since 1959 there has also been a rosé. Dom Pérignon is created in more years than you might expect, with seven vintages in the 1990s.

Champagne Drappier ★★

Rue des Vignes 10200 Urville	📞 +33 3 25 27 40 15
@ info@champagne-drappier.com	👤 Michel Drappier
🌐 www.champagne-drappier.com	[map p. 60]
📅 €€ 🏭 🏠 ▨ ∅ 60 ha; 1,700,000 btl	Carte d'Or

Occupying the center of Urville in the Côte des Bar, southeast of Troyes, Drappier is the most important Champagne house in the Aube. Founded in 1808, this family house is now in its eighth generation, led by Michel Drappier, helped by his daughter Charlene and son Hugo. Michel's inquisitive approach gives it a lively air. "My father is very experimental and is always trying things," says Charlene Drappier. As a result, each cuvée has its own character.

The southern location results in a dominance of Pinot Noir. In fact, Drappier led the region in replanting Pinot Noir in the 1930s. The estate vineyards are all around Urville, but there is an equal area of vineyards under contract throughout the rest of the Champagne region. The most important vineyard is Grande Sendrée, a misspelling that represents its origin in a large fire in 1836 that covered the area with ashes and led to the vineyard being planted.

Wines are mostly fermented in stainless steel, everything goes through malolactic, but barriques are used for partial maturation of the top cuvées. The best single word to describe the style would be flavorful, but each cuvée in the range expresses its own personality. The regular Brut cuvée, the Carte d'Or, is 80% Pinot Noir, and is fresh and lively. A focus on low dosage sees an unusual rosé that is a 100% Pinot Noir produced by saignée with zero dosage, and this trend is combined with an emphasis on low sulfur in a Blanc de Noirs Brut Natur that is bottled with no sulfur. Cuvée Charles de Gaulle is dominated by Pinot Noir and shows a muscular character. The vintage Grande Sendrée is 55% Pinot Noir and 45% Chardonnay; it is not so much overtly rich as simply filled with flavor.

Millésime Exception is the most different. "The idea is the vintage not the terroir. It has to reflect the weather of one season, and is chosen from lots in the cellars, not by picking—the other cuvées are chosen in the vineyard—but for Millésime we choose those wines that are an especially good reflection of the vintage," says Michel. Quattuor includes forgotten white varieties (with a quarter each of Arbanne, Petit Meslier, Pinot Blanc, and Chardonnay). "I wanted to make a new Blanc de Blancs with no Chardonnay. I planned to have one third each of Arbane, Blanc, and Petit Meslier, but the blend was too vegetal. At the last minute we decided to add Chardonnay, which gives balance and makes it all come together."

Michel is in a constant quest to understand and control every aspect of his wine. The liqueur d'expédition is produced in house and matured for 15-20 years in oak vats and glass demi-johns—"we probably have 25 types of liqueur," Michel says. Drappier specializes in large formats, with sizes up to 30 liters matured in the bottle; a new shape of bottle was introduced with a narrower neck to reduce oxidative exposure; there've been experiments in maturing wines under the sea. It's all go.

Champagne Duval-Leroy   *

69 Avenue de Bammental, BP 37, 51130 Vertus	📞 +33 3 26 52 10 75
@ champagne@duval-leroy.com	👤 Louis Duval-Leroy
🌐 www.duval-leroy.com	[map p. 59]
🔲 €€ 🏭 🍇 🕰 200 ha; 2,000,000 btl	Blanc de Blancs

A residential avenue in Vertus leads out of town to some grand Champagne Maisons including Duval-Leroy, which was founded here in 1859 by the Duval and Leroy families, one a winegrower and the other a wine merchant. It has remained family owned, and is now in the sixth generation under Carol Duval and her three sons. It's a very large enterprise with a huge courtyard leading to a vast warehouse for the grape reception center, the laboratory to one side, and the winery underground. The modern winery was mostly built in 1991. There's also another facility at Châlons-en-Champagne.

Estate vineyards provide 40% of the grapes, coming mostly from the Côte de Blancs, but there are also vineyards in all the other areas, with five pressing centers. All the juice comes to Vertus for vinification, mostly in a hall with endless stainless steel tanks, but the top cuvées are vinified in barriques. One feature of vinification is that no products of animal origin are used. Nonvintage wine is aged for three years, and everything is aged longer than the requirements.

There are about twelve cuvées: "The objective is to have one for every taste;" some are made in very small amounts. Fleur de Champagne is the principal Brut, a blend of 70% Chardonnay and 30% Pinot Noir coming from premier cru vineyards. There are two Blanc de Blanc vintage releases, the Grand Cru, which is a Brut, and a Brut Nature, which shows similar density to the vintage Brut but has greater purity and precision to the fruits. Femme de Champagne is a prestige cuvée, made in top years since 1990. Clos des Bouveries is a historic vineyard of the house, an east-facing parcel of 3.5 ha at Vertus with flinty soil. It ripens early and is always the first vineyard to harvest. The grapes used to go in the blend, but since 2002, there has been a separate cuvée every vintage from half of the grapes. It is vinified in barriques. "We want to make it every year to demonstrate the effect of vintage, this plot is like a little laboratory for us."

The mark of the house is the lovely acid/fruit balance, with palates showing a mix of stone and citrus fruits, followed by a delicious acid catch at the end. This is accentuated in the Blanc de Blanc cuvées, which are the major strength of the house.

Champagne Egly Ouriet   **

15 rue de Trépail, 51150 Ambonnay	📞 +33 3 26 57 00 70
@ contact@egly-ouriet.fr	👤 Francis Egly
	[map p. 57]
🚫 🏭 🍇 🕰 15 ha; 140,000 btl	Blanc de Noirs

Founded in Ambonnay in 1930, this boutique house focuses on black varieties and today is run by Francis Egly, the fourth generation, who is known for being difficult to contact, if not actually reclusive. "That's Francis," others growers say, when you comment on his idiosyncratic manner.

Most of the vineyards (8 ha) are in Ambonnay; all are grand cru except for a 2 ha plot of premier cru Pinot Meunier in Vrigny. The emphasis in the vineyards is on controlling yields, with a strong green harvest, so yields are about half of the typical level for Champagne. This results in greater levels of ripeness.

Wines are fermented and matured on the lees in a mixture of oak barriques and tanks; there is no fixed policy about malolactic fermentation; and aging after the second fermentation is longer than usual, typically almost four years for the Brut Tradition. The ripeness of the grapes allows dosage to be kept low, typically less than 3 g/l (although the wines are labeled Brut).

Three quarters of plantings are Pinot Noir. The plot of old (40 year) Pinot Meunier in Vrigny is used for an unusual monovarietal cuvée, Les Vignes de Vrigny. This is an interesting wine, but less refined than the Blanc de Noirs or the Brut Tradition (70% Pinot Noir and 30% Chardonnay).

Dominated by Pinot Noir, the house style is relatively weighty and oxidative, developing classic toast and brioche fairly soon after disgorgement, showing well in the Grand Ambonnay vintage cuvée. Egly-Ouriet is also known for producing a still red Pinot Noir from Ambonnay.

Champagne Fleury ⁎⁎

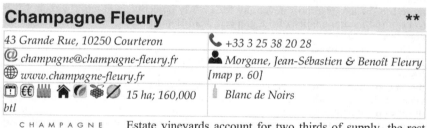

43 Grande Rue, 10250 Courteron	📞 +33 3 25 38 20 28
@ champagne@champagne-fleury.fr	👤 Morgane, Jean-Sébastien & Benoît Fleury
🌐 www.champagne-fleury.fr	[map p. 60]
🔲 €€ ⚒ 🏠 🌿 🐝 ⊘ 15 ha; 160,000 btl	🍾 Blanc de Noirs

Estate vineyards account for two thirds of supply, the rest coming from two of the neighbors who went biodynamic. "They asked my father if he would buy the grapes, so we became a buyer in 1997." There's lots of experimentation here—"every year is different"—says Jean-Sébastien. There's a real attempt to decrease dosage, aided by longer maturation of 4-5 years for nonvintage, 7 years for vintage. "You see the terroir better." Vinification in wood has been introduced for the top cuvées. "I split the lot into two equal parts, and during fermentation I could see the difference in flavor, then during élevage the extra purity of wood becomes clear."

The style is rich, almost powerful, with the full force of Pinot Noir (85% of plantings) showing on the Blanc de Noirs. With the Brut Nature, which is the same wine as the Brut, but without any dosage, the main effect of the lack of dosage is that acidity becomes more evident, but there is the same impression of a rich style. Nates Blanches started in 2009, and is 100% Pinot Blanc, vinified entirely in oak as a Brut Nature. Sonate #9, presently nonvintage but about to become vintage, has no sulfur. "The idea was to follow biodynamics into vinification." Jean-Sébastien feels it has extra refinement. The wines are distinctive in style and a good representation of the character of the Côte des Bar.

Champagne Geoffroy   *

4 rue Jeanson, 51160 Aÿ	📞 *+33 3 26 55 32 31*
@ *info@champagne-geoffroy.com*	👤 *Jean-Baptiste Geoffroy*
🌐 *www.champagne-geoffroy.com*	*[map p. 58]*
🔲 🏭 🍇 ☕ *15 ha; 110,000 btl*	*Expression Brut*

"We are in Aÿ to taste wine from Cumières. We do not have any vineyards in Aÿ, almost all are in Cumières and almost all are premier cru," says Jean-Baptiste Geoffroy. The family was involved in wine in Cumières since the seventeenth century, and his father, René, stopped selling grapes in the 1970s to keep the entire production to make Champagne. "I was a bit concerned that moving would upset my father, but we had three separate premises in Cumières, so everything always had to be moved around." Since Jean-Baptiste bought the new facility in Aÿ in 2006, everything has been in one place, enabling gravity-feed winemaking.

After trying a modern press, Jean-Baptiste went back to the old vertical press. "It gives the best juice with less oxidation." Vinification is in enamel tanks—"I don't like stainless steel, I think it gives too much reduction"—and various sizes of wood ranging from foudres to barriques. Wood is used for about 40%, starting with fermentation. "I never put a finished wine in oak, I put juice, because I want it to have more life." There is almost never any MLF. "My objective is to work without MLF to keep the natural acidity of the grapes," Jean-Baptiste says, but occasionally a lot goes through MLF.

The flagship cuvée, about 60% of production, is Expression. The blend has a changed by using more Chardonnay to get more elegance. Dosage varies. "My philosophy is to adjust dosage for each cuvée and for each year." The cuvée I tasted at the Maison had 5g, but the previous release had 8g. The wine is light and attractive, very much an aperitif style. "It should bring immediate pleasure." Pureté is a zero dosage cuvée from the same grapes, but ages for one to two years longer, depending on the base year, to get compensating richness. It shows a touch of maturity balanced by some austerity at the end. "This is really a demonstration of the quality of my grapes."

The vintage Empreinte (the blend changes each year but is about 75% Pinot Noir) is mostly vinified in oak. "You have my philosophy of oak in this Champagne, to get a touch of oxidation." A richer underlying impression is counterbalanced by low dosage. Volupté is a Blanc de Blancs, and shows an intriguing combination of richness on the palate and saline minerality on the finish. Les Houtrants is an unusual cuvée, coming from five varieties (including Petit Meslier and Arbin) which Jean-Baptiste planted intermingled in 2004. "I don't want anything to interfere with terroir," he says, "so it is zero dosage and there is no oak." It's so full of flavor it would be difficult to identify it as zero dosage. Only made in exceptional years, Terre comes from the oldest vines, ages for 10 years, and has dosage of 2-4 g; vinified in 100% oak, it is smooth and full bodied, creamy and austere at the same time. There are two rosés. Rosé de Saignée is the more conventional, softer with the austerity of the house style pushed into the background. Blanc de Rose is made by comacerating equal amounts of Pinot Noir and Chardonnay grapes and is more delicate with a great sense of tension. The house style, except for Expression, tends towards savory.

Champagne Pierre Gimonnet et Fils ✶✶

rue de La République, 51530 Cuis	📞 +33 3 26 59 78 70
📧 info@champagne-gimonnet.com	👤 Didier Gimonnet
🌐 www.champagne-gimonnet.com	[map p. 59]
😊 €€ ⛏ 🍷 🌿 30 ha; 250,000 btl	🍾 Cuis Premier Cru

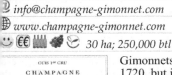

Gimonnets have been in the village of Cuis since at least 1720, but it was Didier Gimonnet's grandfather who created the Maison after he began to vinify his own wine in the 1920s. He had a variety of crops, and sold white wine to the bistros, as well as a few bottles of Champagne; and he kept ows until 1959. "It was my father who gave a real identity to our wine when he egan to vinify parcel by parcel in stainless steel, and to make rational blends," says)idier, who runs the domain today with his brother Olivier. "We are engineering raduates and for us everything must be rational," he adds.

The focus here is on Blanc de Blancs, with different cuvées representing assem-lages of parcels in different proportions. The house philosophy is to blend grand rus for structure with premier crus for freshness. The two nonvintage cuvées are the Cuis premier cru, which plays on delicacy, and the Oger grand cru, which is fuller han the usual Gimonnet style. Responding to market demand, there is also a Rosé Les Blancs, which is 90% Chardonnay. Gastronome is a lighter vintage style. Fleu-on is the principal vintage wine. Oenophile is a zero dosage version of the same vine (it's labeled Extra Brut). Special Club is a Vieilles Vignes bottling, and shows ncreased purity and precision. Except for Oenophile, all the wines have low dosage, sually 6.5 g/l. The house style tends to freshness and lightness, with filigree acidity: iry and delicate is how Didier describes it.

Champagne Henri Giraud ✶

'1 boulevard Charles de Gaulle, BP 26, 51160 Aÿ	📞 +33 3 26 55 18 55
📧 contact@champagne-giraud.com	👤 Julien Decelle
🌐 www.champagne-giraud.com	[map p. 58]
🎁 €€€ ⛏ 🏠 🌿 9 ha; 250,000 btl	🍾 Esprit Nature

The family has been growing grapes in Aÿ since the seventeenth century; Claude Giraud, who took over in 1983, is the twelfth generation. All the estate vineyards are in Aÿ, spread among 35 separate plots. Henri Giraud is generally regarded as a grower Champagne, but in fact since 1975 has been registered also as a negociant. About half of production is the Esprit range, which comes from grapes sourced from local vineyards. The other half comes only from estate vineyards. A small House, Henri Giraud was not well nown until recently, because until the 1990s most of the production was sold di-ectly to private clients in France and Italy.

Harvest is always late to give the grapes maximum ripeness. Wines for the Esprit ange are fermented in stainless steel, but wines from the estate grapes are fermented n barriques (sourced from the Argonne forest). There is always full malolactic fer-nentation. Wines are matured in barriques before second fermentation. A "solera" system is used for holding reserve wines. In addition to the oak, concrete eggs are now also being used.

As Claude Giraud is quick to explain to visitors, the introductory Esprit Natur range is not a zero dosage, but is a Brut. In fact, it has around 7-8 g/l dosage, which is typical for the Giraud cuvées. The style is fresher and more direct in Esprit broader and richer in Grand Cru Fût de Chêne (vinified in oak), even more intense in Dame Jane, which contains some Pinot Noir from very old vines, and showing the finesse of Aÿ in Grand Blanc de Craie. Refined minerality shows across the range An emphasis on Pinot Noir (most cuvées are 70-80% Pinot Noir) adds a sense of power to the palate. Blending across vintages is emphasized in the name of the MV10 cuvée, as MV stands for the multivintage basis of the reserve solera.

Champagne Gosset ★★

12 rue Godart Roger, 51200 Epernay	📞 +33 3 26 56 99 56
@ info@champagne-gosset.com	👤 Nathalie Dufour
🌐 www.champagne-gosset.com	[map p. 58]
📅 🏭 🏠 1 ha; 1,000,000 btl	Grande Reserve

The oldest house in Champagne, Gosset was established in Aÿ in 1584, when Pierre Gosset started producing red wine For much of the twentieth century, it produced champagne for sale by other brands. In 1994 it was sold to the owner of Cognac Frapin, and in 2009 they purchased Château Malakoff from Laurent Perrier for the new headquarters in Épernay. The underground caves are vast, with 2 km of galleries that can store 2.5 million bottles. Owning virtually no vineyards, Gosset purchases grapes from about 200 growers, cultivating 120 ha all over the region.

The house style emphasizes freshness. "We are one of the few houses that avoid MLF, we want to keep the freshness, the acidity, so the Gosset signature is to avoid malo. Until ten years ago we used oak, but never for the first fermentation. We were storing wines in oak to get more richness and roundness. But then the wines had sufficient richness, so we stopped using oak. Using oak doesn't really correspond to the Gosset style."

The style shows clearly on the Blanc de Blancs, and is softened by the broader flavors of the Grande Réserve. In addition to the Grande Millésime vintage, the prestige vintage cuvée, Celebris, has evident depth to nose and palate, cut by that trademark citric freshness. Rosé is unusually important at Gosset—it is at least 10% of production—but the style here is slightly different, a touch broader and more rustic without that characteristic freshness.

Champagne Gosset-Brabant ★

23 Boulevard Maréchal de Lattre de Tassigny, 51160 Aÿ	📞 +33 3 26 55 17 42
@ gosset-brabant@wanadoo.fr	👤 Christian Gosset
🌐 gosset-brabant.fr	[map p. 58]
😊 🏭 🍇 10 ha; 50,000 btl	Réserve Grand Cru

The Gossets have been in Aÿ since the sixteenth century. Christian Gosset's great grandfather founded Champagne Gosset, which became a Grand Marque. His grand

father Gabriel created Gosset-Brabant in the 1930 (Brabant was his wife's name.) Christian is the third generation and has been at the house for thirty years. "We have always been a Maison Familiale," he says. "We specialize in Pinot Noir, but unfortunately not all of our vineyards are in Aÿ." The premises are opposite Bollinger, with a group of buildings at the bottom of a long garden. About half the vineyards are in Aÿ, most of the rest in premier crus in the region, and a small plot in Chouilly on the Côte de Blancs.

"We've evolved somewhat, we look for more precision in expression now," Christian says. Winemaking is traditional, using vertical presses, fermentation in stainless steel, with all wines going through malolactic fermentation. The six cuvées distinguish between grand and premier crus. "We don't make cuvées from specific parcels, but we are close. Aÿ has a microclimate but there is much diversity among many parcels with differences in exposition and altitude."

There are six cuvées plus a Coteaux Champenoise red wine; about a third of the crop is sold off. All of the wines are dominated by Pinot, from a minimum of 70% in the Tradition cuvée, which is about half of production. The Réserve Grand Cru is definitely a step up; and the Nature Grand Cru, which has the same assemblage but no dosage, feels more like an Extra Brut, showing the intrinsic richness of the grapes. In the prestige cuvées, Gabriel is specifically from plots that face east, in order to focus on finesse and freshness, while Noirs d'Aÿ Grand Cru is an Extra Brut Blanc de Noirs from old vines (30-50-years old) on south-facing plots that makes a richer, more structured impression. The house style is firm, and the wines are a good representation of Aÿ.

Champagne Henri Goutorbe   *

9 bis rue Jeanson, 51160 Aÿ	📞 +33 3 26 55 21 70
@ *info@champagne-henri-goutorbe.com*	👤 *René Goutorbe*
🌐 *www.champagne-henri-goutorbe.com*	*[map p. 58]*
🗓️ 🏭 📷 🍇 🌿	*22 ha; 180,000 btl*

The family background was in the nursery business before they started making champagne. While Emile Goutorbe was Perrier-Jouët's vineyard manager in the 1920s, he established a nursery, and then bought some vineyards. His son Henri founded the champagne house at the end of the 1940s (while continuing the nursery business). Henri's son René took over in 1970; today he is helped by his son Étienne. In the 1960s, Henri bought the old cellars in which the house is now located from a negociant. The front is a discrete-looking building; underneath, the old cellars, probably dating from the nineteenth century, go down two stories underground and ramble much farther than you would expect. The House has moved into oenotourism by buying an old building farther along the street and turning it into a hotel.

Vineyards are in Aÿ and the neighboring villages, with 70% Pinot Noir, 25% Chardonnay, and just 5% Pinot Meunier. The approach to winemaking is quite traditional, using concrete and stainless steel: the demi-muids in the cellar are mostly for making the Coteaux Champenois still red wine. Dosage has come down from 12 g/l twenty years ago to around 9 g/l today for most cuvées, but remain high enough to give the wines a classic impression. The nonvintage Brut reflects the composition of the vineyards, and the dosage gives it quite a full impression on the palate. There is now an Extra Brut, but you get the impression that the Goutorbes regard this as going quite far enough.

Vintages are sourced only from grand cru Aÿ. The Cuvée Millésime is deeper and more textured than nonvintage Brut, with the same (traditional) flavor spectrum. In some vintages there is a Special Club Trésor as well as the Cuvée Millésime: it extends the sense of increasing depth and structure of the vintage. The rosé has 10% red wine from Ay, 70% Pinot Noir, and 20% Chardonnay, and actually has a fresher, less extracted impression than the other cuvées. Except for the Blanc de Blancs, all the cuvées have at least 75% Pinot Noir.

Champagne Alfred Gratien

30, rue Maurice Cerveaux, 51201 Épernay	📞 +33 3 26 54 38 20
@ contact@alfredgratien.com	👤 Mélissa Coquel
🌐 www.alfredgratien.com	[map p. 58]
🗓 €€ 🏭 🏠	2 ha; 300,000 btl

Alfred Gratien evidently had a love of sparkling wine as he founded two producers, more or less simultaneously, in Champagne and the Loire. Since 2000, both Champagne Alfred Gratien and Gratien & Meyer (in the Loire) have been owned by German sparkling wine producer Henkell & Söhnlein. However, tradition is emphasized, not least in chef de cave, Nicolas Jaeger, who is the fifth generation of his family to hold the position.

The change in ownership resulted in new investment, but the production method has not altered, with Gratien remaining one of the few Champagne houses that undertakes fermentation in oak barriques. House policy is to suppress malolactic fermentation to keep fresh acidity. Dosage is around 8 g/l, but feels less because of the higher acidity resulting from blocking MLF.

This is essentially a negociant house. Three quarters of production is the Brut Classique, which is a mainstream Champagne is the aperitif style: light and fresh, with a slight touch of sweetness at the end. The rosé is a little softer, the Blanc de Blancs is much in the same style as the nonvintage Brut, but the vintage Brut makes a more refined impression, and there's a little more character in the Cuvée Paradis vintage.

Champagne Charles Heidsieck   *

12 Allée du vignoble, 51100 Reims	📞 +33 3 26 84 43 50
@ charles@champagnes-ph-ch.com	👤 Véronique Lamotte
🌐 www.charlesheidsieck.com	[map p. 54]
🚫 🏭 🏠 85 ha; 1,000,000 btl	🍾 Brut Réserve
Owner: Groupe EPI	

Relationships between the various Heidsieck Champagne houses have changed over time. Charles Heidsieck was the last of the three to be established, in 1851: the houses that later became known as Piper-Heidsieck and Heidsieck Monopole had been founded at the end of the previous century. Founder Charles Camille Heidsieck broke away from his family to start Charles Heidsieck as a negociant business. Today Charles Heidsieck and Piper-Heidsieck are owned by EPI, the holding company of the Descours family (owners of various clothing brands), who purchased them from Rémy-Cointreau in 2011. (Heidsieck Monopole is part of the Vranken group.)

The same team is responsible for winemaking at Charles Heidsieck and Piper-Heidsieck, but Charles Heidsieck has the greater reputation, while Piper-Heidsieck has the greater volume. Charles Heidsieck has a flamboyant history, going back to when Charles Camille became known as "Champagne Charlie" during a stay in the United States, when he was imprisoned during the Civil War on suspicion of being a spy. The prestige cuvée was named for him until the name was changed after 1985 to Blanc de Millènaires. It was resurrected as a nonvintage cuvée in 2021, nonvintage becauase "Daniel Thibault (the winemaker who created it) understood that if you wanted to make great winew ith great consistency it had to be non-vintage," says current Chef de Cave, Cyril Brun. Production is up to 6,000- bottles, priced at about ten times the Brut Réserve. This has equal proportions of all three grape varieties, and is more than three quarters of production; it's a very solid Champagne, with dosage of 11 g/l making it soft and broad. There are also nonvintage rosé and both vintage Brut and rosé.

Champagne Piper-Heidsieck   *

12 Allée Du Vignoble, 51100 Reims	📞 *+33 3 26 84 43 00*
@ *contact.piperheidsieck@champagnes-ph-ch.com*	
🌐 *www.piper-heidsieck.com*	*[map p. 54]*
🚫 ▨ 🏠 ☙	*0 ha; 8,000,000 btl* *Owner: Groupe EPI*

Charles Heidsieck and Piper-Heidsieck are owned by EPI, the holding company of the Descours family (owners of various clothing brands), who purchased them from Rémy-Cointreau in 2011. The same team is responsible for winemaking at Charles Heidsieck and Piper-Heidsieck, but Charles Heidsieck has the greater reputation, while Piper-Heidsieck has the greater volume; as a negociant producing mainstream Champagne, its wines are perfectly sound but less interesting. The Brut and rosé are dominated by Pinot Noir and Pinot Meunier, and dosage seems just a little higher than it might be, generally around 9 g, giving the Champagne a fuller quality.

The style is quite flavorful, moving in a more savory direction going from Brut to the extended-aging cuvée to vintage. The Brut makes a smoky, mineral impression, and a sense of weight to the palate is emphasized by a nutty finish. Sold only to restaurants, the Essential Cuvée Reservée is the same blend of 55% Pinot Meunier, 25% Pinot Noir, and 20% Chardonnay but has extended aging, and has greater depth with more savory impressions. Some people will like the extra intensity, others will prefer the Brut. The vintage, which is 52% Pinot Noir and 48% Chardonnay, is flavorful and accentuates the savory elements. With 20% red wine, the rosé is relatively dark—"this has more red wine than most and is a gastronomic rosé"—but it's not really inclined towards red fruits, although showing more structure and depth. Occasionally, 11 times to date with the most recent release from vintage 2006, there is a Piper Rare cuvée, aged for at least seven years before release. This used to be the top cuvée of Piper-Heidsieck as such, but now has become a separate brand (following the example of luxury brands such as Dom Pérignon).

Champagne Henriot   *

81 rue Coquebert, 51100 Reims	📞 *+33 3 26 89 53 00*
@ *contact@champagne-henriot.com*	👤 *Laurent Fresnet*
🌐 *www.champagne-henriot.com*	*[map p. 54]*
📅 🏭 🏠 *35 ha; 1,500,000 btl*	🍾 *Blanc de Blancs*

The commercial history of this house is intricately linked with the ups and downs of Champagne. The family came to Champagne in 1640, and founded the house in 1808; it has remained in their hands, but with many changes of direction. The founder's grandson, Ernest, was involved in founding Charles Heidsieck (Charles was his brother-in-law). Under Joseph Henriot, who took over in 1962, Henriot actually purchased Charles Heidsieck in 1976 and sold it in 1985. At the same time, Joseph sold most of the 125 ha of Henriot estate vineyards to Veuve Clicquot, which he then ran until 1994, when he returned to rescue Henriot. Then Henriot expanded by purchasing Bouchard Père in Beaune, followed by William Fèvre in Chablis. Joseph's son, Stanislas, ran Henriot from 1999 until 2010, when he was replaced by his brother, Thomas.

Reduced to 35 ha of vineyards, without much in the way of grand crus, Henriot now buys 70% of its grapes. Vinification is exclusively in stainless steel, malolactic is usually performed, and a small proportion of reserve wines is kept as a perpetual reserve. Dosage is usually in the upper part of the Brut range, around 9-10 g/l. Until recently, Henriot did not use Pinot Meunier, but now includes some in its Brut Souverain and Rosé. Quality has revived in the present decade, and the style tends to be dense, with even Brut Souverain as suitable to accompany a meal as to enjoy as an aperitif. The prestige cuvée is the Cuvée des Enchanteleurs. François Pinault's Artemis Domaines (owner of Château Latour) bought a majority stake in 2022.

Champagne Jacquesson   **

68 rue du Colonel Fabien, Dizy, 51318 Épernay	📞 *+33 3 26 55 68 11*
@ *info@champagnejacquesson.com*	👤 *Jean-Hervé & Laurent Chiquet*
🌐 *www.champagnejacquesson.com*	*[map p. 58]*
📅 🥂 🏠 🍂 *28 ha; 250,000 btl*	🍾 *Cuvée #737*

Founded in 1798 in Châlons-sur-Marne, Jacquesson was a large producer by the mid nineteenth century, then collapsed and had a chequered history through several owners. Jean Chiquet was a grower in Dizy when he bought it in 1974. Production was transferred to the family property, where there's a charming house and courtyard on one side of the main road, and very large cellars on the other side. "I joined in 1977 and spent ten years negotiating with my father to change things," recollects Jean-Hervé Chiquet, who together with his brother, has transformed Jacquesson into a quality boutique. François Pinault (owner of Château Latour) bought a minority (one third) share in 2022. Providing three quarters of the grapes, the 28 ha of estate vineyards focus on premier and grand crus; grapes are purchased from another 8 ha. The Chiquet brothers reject conventional wisdom. "Our idea is the opposite of the non-vintage concept, we don't care about consistency, we want to make the best wine we can without hiding the base vintage," says Jean-Hervé. So a wine is made each year with the current vintage as base, and the previous two years as reserve; it's identified with a number (#738 has base year 2010). Dosage is always minimal—virtually everything is Extra Brut—and the style is crisp, mineral, and saline. "If we are making the best wine we can, we cannot also make a general vintage," explains Jean-Hervé, but there are small cuvées of vintage wines from single vineyards in Dizy, Ay, and Avize. There are late disgorgements of the numbered cuvées, which enhance the minerality of the house style. In addition there are single-vineyard wines released as conventional vintages. Flavorful would be a fair description of the style. I have the impression that is has become a little richer recently.

Champagne Krug ★★★★

5, rue Coquebert, BP 22, 51051 Reims	📞 +33 3 26 84 44 20
@ krug@krug.fr	👤 Margareth Henríquez
🌐 www.krug.com	[map p. 54]
📖 ✏️ 🏠 ☕ 20 ha; 500,000 btl	🍾 Grande Cuvée
Owner: LVMH	

The first time I visited Krug, a tour and tasting was followed by a leisurely lunch at a bistro in Reims with Henri Krug. The house was already owned by LVMH, but it still felt like a small family business. On more recent visits, it has felt like part of an international conglomerate. A professional guide conducted a tour and tasting, and a winemaker was full of corporate caution in discussing Krug's policies.

In spite of the change in atmosphere, however, the Champagne remains every bit as good, the only change perhaps being that the corporate environment has resulted in brand extension into more expensive special cuvées. The characteristic features of Krug's production have been maintained, in particular the unusual emphasis on Pinot Meunier, and the use of old oak casks to ferment the wine. (The barriques are moved into the courtyard and cleaned annually; it's quite a sight to see the whole courtyard filled with barriques, being watered by garden sprinklers.)

After fermentation, wine is transferred to stainless steel. MLF is neither encouraged nor discouraged. The Grande Cuvée goes into gyropalettes, but the other cuvées are still riddled by hand. There is no transvasage; sizes up to jeroboam are riddled in the bottle. All production is at Krug's premises in the center of Reims, where there are around 2 km of caves, running about 20 m underground. The focus on hospitality at Krug is being strengthened by the construction of a new visitor center from four houses along the street immediately adjacent to the winery.

Emphasis on blending is on identifying the character of individual lots: "You cannot say there is a specific proportion of a variety, we never speak of varieties, this is nonsense," says assistant winemaker Julie Cavil. Usually Krug is driven by Pinot Noir, but occasionally Chardonnay is more successful and predominates. The nonvintage Grande Cuvée is more than 80% of production. It is always has at least 50% of the base year; usually reserve wine is about 40%. It is aged for 7 years. The Grand Cuvée is tracked by a number for each release. Release #163 was based on 2007, and blended from 183 wines from twelve vintages going back to 1990. (If you go back 163 years, you get to 1844, which is when Joseph Krug first produced the nonvintage blend, Cuvée #1, which later became the Grand Cuvée.) Production level is secret but should be about 400,000 bottles annually. The Grande Cuvée ages unusually well in the bottle for nonvintage Champagne; a comparison of release #158 with #163 shows a slightly lighter impression for the current release, with a subtle evolution showing on #158, as an increase of stone fruits over citrus.

The vintage is aged for 10 years; on average it represents about 10% of produc tion. There are two single-vineyard wines. Clos de Mesnil is enclosed by a wall tha was built in 1698. Three hundred years later, it is an enclave completely surrounde by the village, which grew up in the nineteenth century. Krug purchased the vine yard of 1.85 ha in 1971, when it was all but abandoned, replanted it, and produce the first single vineyard wine in 1979. Clos d'Ambonnay is a Blanc de Noirs tha debuted in 1996. The Krug collection comes from re-releases, not necessarily from later disgorgement. Krug is always less than 6 g dosage, which means it is in the range of Extra Brut, but it is labeled as Brut, which anyway is a fairer description because the natural richness of the wine makes it seem relatively full in style.

Champagne Lallier *

4 place de La Libération, Bp 5, 51160 Aÿ	📞 *+33 3 26 55 43 40*
@ *contact@champagne-lallier.fr*	👤 *Francis Tribaut*
🌐 *www.champagne-lallier.fr*	*[map p. 58]*
📅 🏭 🏠 *15 ha; 400,000 btl*	🍾 *Blanc de Blancs*

The history of this house is relatively recent. Long estab lished in Aÿ, the Lalliers owned Deutz, but when they sol it in 1996, René James Lallier started the Lallier brand b constructing a winery on top of eighteenth century cellars i the center of Aÿ. When he retired in 2004, he sold Cham pagne Lallier to oenologist Francis Tribaut (himself fourth generation in Aÿ). The house has expanded greatly since then, and in 2012 constructed a new productio facility in Ogier; the wines are still aged in Aÿ. Francis Tribaut sold an 80% share i his holdings to the Campari group of Italy in 2020. A mid-sized house ("our aim i not to increase volume any further"), Lallier prides itself on using only Pinot Noi and Chardonnay from premier and grand cru vineyards. (In fact, it's mostly gran cru, premier cru being used only for the rosé.) The 43 parcels of estate vineyards ar on the slopes around Aÿ, and provide a quarter of the grapes; the rest come from th Côte des Blancs and Montagne de Reims. Fermentation takes place in stainless stee and malolactic is only partial in order to preserve freshness.

There are seven cuvées; except for the Blanc de Blancs, all are dominated by Pi not Noir. A new series, called R, for Récolte (harvest), was introduced in 2015 fo the nonvintage. "We decided to go back to our roots and make a wine that represent 80% of the recent vintage with less reserve wines," says Marie Malbois. Each year' release carries a number indicating the vintage of the base wine; R.012 is the firs release, and also has wines from 2002, 2004, and 2008. The blend is a little over on third Chardonnay. Using the same blend, R.012N is a zero dosage and R.012D i sweet. The house style is captured best in the very pure expression of the Blanc d Blancs, with precision of focus and clarity of fruits. The vintage has a denser style Ouvrage is an extra brut aged under cork. Francis Tribaut feels that natural cork al lows some breathing, and during aging the wine loses one bar of pressure. "We se this more like a wine than Champagne." It has a rich style.

Champagne Lanson *

66 rue de Courlancy, 51100 Reims	📞 *+33 3 26 78 50 50*
@ *info@lanson.com*	👤 *Hervé Dantan*

www.lanson.com   *[map p. 54]*

57 ha; 4,000,000 btl   *Black Label*

Owner: Lanson-BCC

One of the old grand marques, Lanson has had a chequered history. Founded in 1760 by François Delamotte, it was sold to Jean-Baptiste Lanson in 1837 and renamed. Lanson became well known in Britain. It was held by the Lanson family until the 1970s, then it was sold in succession to the Gardiner family, Danone yogurt, and LVMH, who stripped out its 200 ha of vineyards, and sold the brand on almost immediately. It was bought in 2006 by a group of three families, Baijot, Paillard, and Boizel, and became a key part of the Boizel Chanoine Champagne group to form the LANSON-BCC group, which is now the second largest group in Champagne.

Under Philippe Baijot and winemaker Hervé Dantan, who came in 2013, there has been a move to quality. Lanson has four pressing centers and a modern production facility in Reims, where they have been since 1924. The 7 km of tunnels underground date from 1870 and 1917. There are two vast vat rooms with stainless steel tanks, and a separate cellar with foudres, used for partial aging of the prestige cuvées since 2017. There used to be no malolactic fermentation, but Hervé Dantan introduced minimal MLF (10-30% depending on the year) for nonvintage.

Lanson now has some estate vineyards, but they provide only just over 10% of grapes. Its top vineyard is Clos Lanson, right by the winery in the city of Reims, surrounded by housing blocks. (It's described as facing the cathedral, which it is, sort of, from about a mile away.) It's now planted exclusively with Chardonnay (there used to be some Pinot Noir). Since 2006 there has been a vintage wine from the plot (barriques are used in aging with some new oak), producing about 8,000 bottles each year. There are bee boxes there and they also make a Clos Lanson honey.

The range has been reduced from 15 cuvées—"it was too much"—to 10. The Extra Age line was discontinued. Lanson distinguishes its wines by color labels. Black Label is the flagship—"we always talk about Lanson as being a good aperitif"—and it's quite crisp and lean. The rosé has the same dosage (8g) but the inclusion of red wine has made it softer and less lively. Hervé Dantan felt there was a gap between the nonvintage and vintage cuvées, and introduced two new cuvées: Black Label Reserve and the Blanc de Blancs. Black Label Reserve has a higher proportion of premier and grand cru (70% versus 50%) than Black Label, spends one year longer aging before disgorgement, has 1g less dosage, less MLF, and some lots aged in wood. It is rounder and deeper than Black Label, and more like the Blanc de Blancs in style, which is creamier. Green Label is a relatively new production from organic grapes grown in 16 ha of estate vineyards at Verneuil and Vandières in the Vallée de la Marne, and makes a more concentrated impression. The Gold Label vintage is broader and more obviously yeasty, with dosage of 3g into the Extra Brut range, and the finish can become quite savory.

Champagne Larmandier-Bernier   *

19 avenue du Général de Gaulle, 51130 Vertus	📞 +33 3 26 52 13 24
@ champagne@larmandier.fr	👤 Sophie, Pierre & Arthur Larmandier
🌐 www.larmandier.fr	*[map p. 59]*
18 ha; 150,000 btl	*Terre de Vertus*

The emphasis here is on terroir. The Maison has an unlikely location near a semi-industrial estate on the outskirts of Vertus, at the southern end of the Côte des Blancs, but inside the gates is a modern facility surrounded by a charming garden. Vineyards were expanded purchasing a plots of old vines in Avize and Oger in 2017. Their son Arthur joined Sophie and Pierre Larmandier in 2017.

Producing wine only from their own vineyards on the Côte des Blancs, the Larmandiers try to represent their vineyards by biodynamic viticulture, vinifying the wine in wood, and keeping it on the full lees in wood until bottling. Wood of various sizes is used, matched to the terroir. "The more powerful wines, like Cramant, go into barriques, and the more delicate, like Vertus, into foudres," Sophie Larmandier explains. Two concrete eggs are used for the rosé de saignée (mostly Pinot Noir), which has three days of maceration, and offers an unusual sense of precision for rosé. The biodynamic approach is all-inclusive. "Yeast is part of the terroir," Sophie explains, "We are trying to develop our own yeast for the second fermentation."

All the cuvées are extra brut or zero dosage in order to focus on terroir. Latitude is an extra brut, and Longitude is a premier cru extra brut, showing a savory palate with a mineral finish; in vintage, Terre de Vertus is a zero dosage premier cru exhibiting saline delicacy when young, softening with age. Les Chemins d'Avize offers a more creamy expression that relieves the usual tightness of style, and the Vieille Vigne du Levant (from Cramant) stands out as the richest wine in the range. There's a distinctive character here, with an authenticity far from the manipulated quality of many Champagnes.

Groupe Laurent-Perrier   *

Avenue de Champagne, Bp 3, 51150 Tours-sur-Marne	📞 +33 3 26 58 91 22
@ *direction.communication@laurent-perrier.fr*	👤
🌐 *www.laurent-perrier.fr*	*[map p. 53]*
🚫 🏭 🏠 🕊 *150 ha; 7,000,000 btl*	*Ultra Brut*

"Brut dosage, reliance on Chardonnay, vinification in stainless steel to maintain freshness—we were the first to abandon barriques—it is the root of our style of lightness and elegance that made Laurent Perrier an ambassador for contemporary champagne, that is, for an aperitif wine," says Anne-Laure Domenichini.

Laurent-Perrier was founded in 1812, and was in dire straits by 1939, when it was sold to the de Nonancourts. After the war, Bernard de Nonancourt established the principles on which the Maison is still run today by the third generation. One of the five largest houses, it is a public company, however, and expanded significantly by taking over Château Malakoff in 2004: it also owns Salon-Delamotte and de Castellane. The winery is located in an extensive estate on the main road through Tours-sur-Marne (east of Aÿ, away from the other major houses).

Estate vineyards provide 11% of the grapes, the rest coming from 1,200 growers. With 50% Chardonnay and 11 g/l dosage, the Brut was a very mainstream aperitif. The style was fragrant and elegant and lightly aromatic, very much an aperitif Champagne. It was the fifth best-selling Champagne in the world when it was replaced in 2017 with La Cuvée. This marks a significant change in style. Grape soruces remain similar (more than 50% Chardonnay, 30-35% Pinot Noir, and 10-

15% Pinot Meunier, with 15-30% of reserve wines), but the style is weightier and fresher, moving towards Blanc de Blancs in balance and towards lower dosage wines in austerity. It tastes much drier than the reduction to 9g dosage would predict, more of a wine to match with food.

I find the Ultra Brut, an equal blend of the ripest Chardonnay and Pinot Noir, re-launched in 1981, to be a step up in refinement: more precise rather than particularly drier in its impression, even though it has zero dosage. The rosé ("launched in 1968 when rosé was considered a froufrou") is famous as a saignée, conveying an unusual sense of structure. Grand Siècle (created in 1959) is a prestige cuvée blended from three vintages that were declared by Laurent Perrier. The vintage releases are more intense versions of the original delicate style of the nonvintage.

Champagne A. R. Lenoble   *

35, rue Paul Douce, BP 6, 51480 Damery	📞 *+33 3 26 58 42 60*
@ *antoine.malassagne@champagne-arlenoble.com*	👤 *Antoine Malassagne*
🌐 *www.champagne-lenoble.com*	*[map p. 56]*
📅 🏭 🍇 🕰 *18 ha; 300,000 btl*	*Blanc de Blancs Chouilly*

This house has been producing Champagne since 1920, and since 1993 has been run by the great-grandchildren of the founder, sister and brother Anne and Antoine Malassagne. (The founder, d'Armand-Raphaël Graser, came from Alsace, but named the house with his initials followed by Lenoble to reflect his view of Champagne as a noble wine.) The Maison is located in Damery, in the Vallée de la Marne, but also has vineyards in Bisseuil (to the east of Aÿ) and Chouilly (the northernmost village of the Côte de Blancs), with plantings of Chardonnay predominant.

The wines fall into three series. The Classique collection are distinguished by dosage or variety: Zero Dosage, Brut, Sweet, and a Blanc de Blancs. The Terroir collection showcases wines from specific villages, including rosé and vintage Blanc de Blancs and Blanc de Noirs. There are also two further Blanc de Blancs from vineyards in Chouilly, described as the Prestige Collection. More than half of the vineyards are in Chouilly, and several cuvées focus on expressing this terroir. There is a certain focus on wood: wines are variously fermented in barriques, foudres, or stainless steel, reserve wines are all stored in either barriques or foudres, and malolactic fermentation depends on the lot and the year.

The style is quite soft, emphasized by the use of wood, and dosage is moderate, always below 6 g/l. "Chouilly has a creamy character," Antoine says. The Intense cuvée, which is Extra Brut with under 5 g dosage, is soft in style but quite assertive, while the Brut Nature is just a little more linear. The Malassagnes are proud of being among the first to produce Zero Dosage, and the wine is rich and flavorful; it might easily pass for an Extra Brut. The Chouilly Blanc de Blancs comes from a single parcel of 0.5 ha, and with the lowest dosage of all at 2 g, is the softest and roundest. The Blanc de Blancs vintage, with only 3 g dosage, is quite intense. The rosé is soft and a little nutty.

Champagne Lombard   *

1, rue des Côtelles Bp 118, 51204 Épernay	📞 *+33 3 26 59 57 40*

84

@ info@champagne-lombard.com   👤 *Thierry Lombard*

🌐 *www.champagne-lombard.com*   *[map p. 58]*

📅 🍾 🏠 🥂 *6 ha; 600,000 btl*   *Premier Cru*

"We focus on terroir, we have a blend from premier crus, a blend from grand crus, and then we have several village wines and single-vineyard wines. This is a new approach to Champagne, we moved from blends to the single village and single plot wines when my son Thomas joined," says Thierry Lombard, who is the third generation at this medium-sized house in Epernay. The house was founded in 1925, moved to cellars in Épernay in 1936, and expanded its winery in Épernay in 1987. Thierry has been in charge since then. A separate line is produced under the name of Maison Lombard, from grapes bought from 55 ha. Dosage is less for the cuvées of Champagne Lombard. Under the marque Médot, there are cuvées from organic grapes made without added sulfur.

"We don't want to add sugar, we want to show the taste of the terroir. All cuvées are Extra Brut for premier cru, and zero dosage for grand cru. All the Pinot Noir comes from the Montagne de Reims and all the Chardonnay from the Côte des Blancs," Thierry says. The estate vineyards are in the Montagne de Reims; grapes from the Côte des Blancs are purchased.

The style is very finely textured and elegant. The premier crus have some vinification in old oak barriques, and grand crus are entirely in old barriques. Premier crus age for 2-3 years, and grand crus age for 5 years before disgorgement. The Extra Brut premier cru has a nice sense of roundness, the premier cru Blanc des Noirs is a little fuller and rounder, but maintains a great sense of precision, and the grand cru Brut Nature is just a touch more linear, reflecting its 50% Chardonnay.

The village wines from Verzenay and Le Mesnil sur Oger are a great illustration of the difference between Montagne de Reims and Côte des Blancs. The Brut Nature from Verzenay has 80% Pinot Noir and 20% Chardonnay, and the Pinot Noir conveys enough sense of fullness that the zero dosage is reflected in a very fine texture of the palate rather than in any austerity. The Blancs de Blancs from Verzenay has an even finer texture, with an increased sense of precision, and a faint mineral tang.

Champagne Moët et Chandon

20 *Avenue de Champagne, 51333 Épernay*	📞 *+33 3 26 51 20 00*
@ *contact@moet.fr*	
🌐 *www.moet.com*	*[map p. 58]*
📅 €€ 🍾 🏠 🥂 *1190 ha; 30,000,000 btl*	*Owner: LVMH*

With its imposing headquarters at the start of the Avenue de Champagne in Épernay, Moët and Chandon is one of the major Champagne houses. Owned by LVMH, it's by far the largest owner of vineyards in Champagne (partly because LVMH has gobbled up smaller houses that owned vineyards). A quarter of the estate vineyards are premier crus, and half are grand crus (including the top sites that are used for Dom Pérignon). Moët's total production amounts to 10% of all Champagne. Dom Pérignon (see pro-ile), which started as Moët's prestige cuvée, is now regarded as a separate brand within Moët.

Moët's quality has been variable. Until 2012, dosage was on the high side, generally around 12 g/l, making the style a bit muddy. The White Star brand sold in the United States had 20 g/l, making it distinctly sweet. White Star was discontinued in 2012, and the dosage in the general cuvée (Impérial) was reduced to 9 g/l, which improved the situation. There is no Extra Brut or Brut Natur in nonvintage, but there is an Ice Impérial with 45 g/l making it very sweet. The vintage has lower dosage, typically about 5 g/l. A new multi-vintage prestige cuvée, MCIII, was introduced in 2015 (just 15,000 bottles at €450 per bottle), but it may be a one-off as it was based on the unusually powerful 2003 vintage.

Given the huge volume of production, and the need to appeal as widely as possible, it would be surprising if Moët met the highest standards for flavor interest, but it's a distinct notch below Veuve Clicquot, which is also owned by LVMH.

Champagne Pierre Moncuit   *

1, rue Persault-Maheu, 51190 Le Mesnil-sur-Oger	📞 +33 3 26 57 52 65
contact@pierre-moncuit.fr	👤 Nicole Moncuit
www.pierre-moncuit.fr	[map p. 59]
😊 🏭 🍷 ☺ 20 ha; 180,000 btl	Cuvée Pierre Moncuit-Delos

The third generation runs this family domain, divided between 15 ha on the Côte des Blancs and 5 ha at Sézanne. All wines are Blanc de Blancs, except for a rosé. There are three nonvintage cuvées, a Brut (Hughes à Coulmet), the prestige Brut (Pierre Moncuit-Delos), and a rosé grand cru. For vintage wines, there is a Brut and an Extra Brut (or sometimes a non dosé); and a Vieilles Vignes is made occasionally. Except for the Extra Brut, dosage is always around 7-8 g/l. Vinification is in stainless steel, and malolactic fermentation always occurs.

The style here makes few concessions, even to vintage: nonvintage cuvées actually come from a single recent vintage (in 2013 the cuvées I tasted at the Maison all came from 2010). This unusual policy started when Pierre Moncuit decided he wanted to capture the spirit of each year. Vintage-dated wines are reserved for exceptional years.

Although there is more variation in the nonvintage cuvées than usual in Champagne, the style generally tends towards the austere, highlighting purity of fruits, which can be aggressive in some vintages. The moderate dosage only just cuts the acidity, and even the Brut gives somewhat of the drier impression of an Extra Brut. Fruits are pure and clean but not overly generous. These are wines that may need extra time in bottle to show at their best. When the Moncuits are asked to define house style, the answer is rather bland: "To maintain continuity of style, without any change from the past."

Maison G. H. Mumm

34 rue du Champ de Mars, 51100 Reims	📞 +33 3 26 49 59 69
guides@mumm.com	👤
www.mumm.com	[map p. 54]
🏭 🏠 ☺ 216 ha; 9,000,000 btl	Owner: Pernod Ricard

Mumm's has certainly had a chequered past. Founded in 1827 by the Mumm brothers from Germany, the house became successful in the late nineteenth century with its Cordon Rouge cuvée. However, the house was confiscated during the first world war as the Mumms had remained German citizens. It was sold in 1920, passed on to Seagrams in 1955, then sold to a venture capitalist group, and finally wound up in Pernod-Ricard in 2005.

Although Mumm has important vineyard holdings, for much of the twentieth century the focus was clearly not on quality. The flagship Cordon Rouge always seemed to me to have a soapy quality with too much dosage making for a clumsy impression. Although there has been significant improvement in the past decade, Cordon Rouge still seems somewhat rustic and too soft. The rosé is a bit muddy, but the vintage shows a nicely textured impression, and the Blanc de Blancs comes closest to overcoming Mumm's slightly muddy style.

Visits are designed for tourists, starting with a movie, then a tour of the old caves (complete with waxworks!) but also an interesting exhibition of old winemaking implements, before winding up with a tasting. Mumm's also has a winery for producing sparkling wine in Napa Valley, California.

Champagne Nicolas Feuillatte *

Route de Pierry, 51200 Chouilly	📞 +33 3 26 59 64 61
@ *contact@atelierxy.com*	
🌐 *www.nicolas-feuillatte.com*	*[map p. 58]*
🗓 € 🏭 ▬ *0 ha; 10,000,000 btl*	Blanc de Blancs

Reflecting the unusual importance of cooperatives in Champagne, Nicolas Feuillatte is probably the most prestigious of France's cooperatives. (There really was a Nicolas Feuillatte, and he sold his brand to the Centre Viticole in 1987.) Feuillatte's annual production of almost 10 million bottles places it as one of the largest Champagne houses, third in worldwide sales, behind Moët & Chandon and Veuve Clicquot. It represents 82 of the 140 cooperatives in the Champagne region, with its growers covering 2,250 ha (about 7% of the vineyards), including holdings in grand and premier crus. It became even larger when it announced a merger with Champagne Castelnau, another major cooperative, in 2021. Altogether, that brings the combined operation to represent 6,000 growers. Production facilities are on an industrial scale (the plant occupies 11 ha, with 15 individual tank halls), employing a highly automated vinification process. Malolactic fermentation occurs for all cuvées, and the nonvintage wines are aged for three years before disgorgement.

The range includes almost 20 cuvées. The regular Brut cuvées are not especially interesting (but the same might be said about most of the major brands). However, Nicolas Feuillatte goes head to head with the major brands in developing prestige cuvées (the Palme d'Or Brut and rosé cuvées come from grand crus), and a series of single vineyard vintage wines (from Mesnil, Cramant, Verzy, and Chouilly). For a cooperative, this is a dynamic venture, and there isn't a whole lot to distinguish its quality from standard major brands, except perhaps slightly more reasonable prices. The style tends to freshness.

Champagne Bruno Paillard ★★

Avenue de Champagne, 51100 Reims	📞 +33 3 26 36 20 22
@ *info@brunopaillard.com*	👤 *Bruno Paillard*
🌐 *www.champagnebrunopaillard.com*	*[map p. 54]*
🚫 🏭 🏠 ⌖ *32 ha; 450,000 btl*	*Première Cuvée, rosé*

Bruno Paillard had worked with his father as a grape broker for six years when he decided to found his own house in 1981. "I tried to persuade my father, but he thought I was crazy," he recollects. "The idea was to take the north face road, to make the best quality wines for restaurants." The winery is a striking modern building of glass and steel on the outskirts of Reims. "It was difficult—and expensive—to acquire vineyards," Bruno says, but estate vineyards now provide more than half the grapes; the rest comes from 60 growers.

The style here is airy and delicate. "I like tension and vibrancy, and that's why people sometimes find the wines a little austere at first; perhaps I should not say austere, but they are discrete and open slowly, they need a little more time." Vinification uses a mix of stainless steel and barriques. Aging on the lees more than doubles the legally required period, and there is a delay before release as Bruno feels strongly that disgorgement is a trauma to the wine. The Brut is a classic blend with almost half Pinot Noir; the rosé uses a mix of short and long maceration (and has a little Chardonnay for freshness); and the Blanc de Blancs has a slightly lower atmospheric pressure to enhance its finesse. Dosage has been lowered steadily and now is typically 6 g/l for nonvintage; vintage wines are slightly lower at 5 g/l. Both vintage and nonvintage show great fruit purity with a silky finish.

Bruno not only takes close charge of his Champagne house, but also is the CEO of the Lanson-BCC group, which owns several Champagne houses.

Champagne Joseph Perrier ★

69 Avenue de Paris, BP 31, 51016 Châlons-en-Champagne	📞 +33 3 26 68 29 51
@ *visite@josephperrier.fr*	👤 *Benjamin Fourmon & Nathalie Laplaige*
🌐 *www.joseph-perrier.com*	*[map p. 53]*
📅 🏭 🏠 *23 ha; 700,000 btl*	*Blanc de Blancs*

Joseph Perrier is proud of its origins. It was founded in 1825 in Châlons-en-Champagne when this was the most important town in the region, surrounded by 1,000 ha of vineyards. "But phylloxera finished all that," says Svetlana Bodineau. Now the only Champagne house left in Châlons, where there are no longer any vineyards, Joseph Perrier is still located in the same premises, where several slightly dilapidated-looking large buildings are grouped around a courtyard behind an imposing entrance. The tasting room is in the first building, which hasn't changed. "We believe in conservation." Tradition runs deep: just beside the winery is a small house for the cellarmaster, who is the fourth generation of the same family.

The extensive cellars run for 3 km under the city in what is now black chalk—black because mold has formed on the walls over the decades. The caves are about 20m underground, with air shafts running up to the surface, with old metal reflectors that were used to direct light into the cellars before electricity was introduced. The winery is filled with modern equipment, however, including stainless steel vats for fermentation, and gyropalettes for riddling. Some prestige cuvées are still riddled by hand, as are large formats (there is no transvasage). All wines go through MLF.

The house is run today by the fourth generation of the Pithois family, who took over in 1888, in the form of Jean-Claude Fourmon. (The house is part of the group Thiénot Bordeaux-Champagnes; Jean-Claude Fourmon and Alain Thiénot are cousins.) Estate vineyards provide a third of the grapes; purchased grapes come from agreements with growers who have supplied Joseph Perrier for a long time. "We are a family business and expansion is not a word in the vocabulary of the company." Vineyards are mostly in the Montagne de Reims, with some at Hautvillers, and some Chardonnay farther south around Vitry-le-François. There are nine cuvées. "We are known for our Blanc de Blancs, but I wouldn't call it our specialty because there are also rosé and Brut Nature."

The style is lively. "Our aim is that it should make you want to eat." The Brut has a bright aperitif style. The Blanc de Blancs shows a stronger style, moving from citrus more towards stone fruits; character is enhanced in the vintage, with greater density and more sense of evolution (and it will be Extra Brut from 2010). Cuvée Josephine, which comes from grand and premier crus, continues that smooth, dense impression. Coming from a single vineyard parcel at Hautvillers, which always ripens first, the Blanc de Noirs Brut Nature follows with a dark impression of smooth supple fruits. After the Brut, indeed these seem wines to go with food.

Champagne Perrier-Jouët   *

26 Avenue de Champagne, BP 31, 51201 Épernay	📞 +33 3 26 55 40 04
📠 +33 3 26 54 54 55	👤 Frédérique Baveret
🌐 www.perrier-jouet.com	[map p. 58]
📅 ⛏ 🏠 65 ha; 2,500,000 btl	🍾 Grand Brut
Owner: Pernod Ricard	

Founded in 1811, Perrier-Jouët has rather grand quarters on the Avenue de Champagne in Epernay, just across the street from Château Perrier, built by the family in 1854. In 2005 Perrier-Jouët became part of Pernod Ricard (who also own Mumms). Perrier-Jouët (or P-J as it's known in the trade) has around 10 km of galleries in its extensive underground caves, which can store 10 million bottles.

About a third of the grapes are supplied by estate vineyards, with half on the Côte des Blancs, giving strong emphasis to Chardonnay; this contributes to a more feminine style, says cellarmaster Hervé Deschamps. Perrier-Jouët makes only Brut Champagne. Dosage is usually 8-10 g/l, depending on the year. "We don't change the dosage, low dosage is a fashion," cellarmaster Hervé Deschamps explained a few years back. Vinification is in stainless steel, and all wines go through malolactic fermentation. "Malo opens the wine, when fermentation was in oak we did not use MLF, but kept the wine longer before shipping," Hervé said. Nonvintage spends three years before disgorgement, and vintage spends six years.

The house style is clear and elegant; you might say Perrier-Jouët is the archetypal aperitif champagne. A characteristic cleanness of line, a very fine floral impression, runs from the Grand Brut nonvintage through cuvées such as the nonvintage Blanc de Blancs (a little weightier) to the Belle Époque prestige vintage wines, showing elegance and delicacy rather than power. Belle Epoque comes in Brut, Rose, and

Blanc de Blancs, made in only occasional vintages. It's rare for all three to be produced in the same year, which has happened only in 1999, 2006, and 2012. Blanc de Blancs adds silkiness, while the rosé is softened, but that characteristic clarity runs throughout.

The Belle Epoque Blanc de Blancs is the smallest cuvée Perrier-Jouët produces, from two small vineyards in Cramant, bought in 1848 by the son of the founders. Cellarmaster Séverine Frerson, who took over in 2020, says "it's a picture of place and terroir." It ages at least 8 years before disgorgement. The seven releases between 1993 and 2012 (the next is 2014) show remarkable consistency of style. For the Brut and rosé, Séverine says, "I also select plots for the style," so the composition may change with each vintage release.

Champagne Pierre Péters   *

9 rue de l'Eglise, 51190 Le Mesnil-sur-Oger	📞 +33 3 26 57 50 32
@ info@champagne-peters.com	👤 Rodolphe Péters
🌐 www.champagne-peters.com	[map p. 59]
🗓 🏛 🌾 🍇 ⌚ 20 ha; 160,000 btl	Cuvée de Réserve

This family domain is now into the sixth generation. Production started with still wine; the first Champagne was a demi-sec, called Veuve Peters, in 1919. The Pierre Peters label was introduced in 1944. The premises in Mesnil-sur-Oger look like a private residence, but behind and underneath is a modern cellar. Vineyards are almost exclusively Chardonnay on the Côte des Blancs, three quarters in Grand Cru villages.

The objective is to bring out fruit: grapes are harvested for freshness, the wine goes through malolactic fermentation, and dosage for the nonvintage Brut is only 6-7 g/l. There is an Extra Brut with dosage of 2 g/l. Vintage wines have 4-5 g/l dosage. "I use stainless steel to safeguard the pure character of the wine. Dosage for me is a means of compensating between cool and warm years to maintain consistency in the nonvintage. The vintage is different, it shows the style of the year," says Rodolphe Peters. Kept in tulip-shaped cement cuves designed to maximize contact with the lees, the reserve goes back a long way. "I assemble all my wines into one reserve, it's a reserve perpetuelle that has almost 15 years."

The style extends from the relatively straightforward Brut to the precision of the Extra Brut (in fact an undeclared vintage); the same variation is reprised in the vintage wines, with breadth to L'Esprit, the general vintage wine, but a wonderful tight precision to Les Chétillons, a single-vineyard wine from Mesnil-sur-Oger.

Champagne Philipponnat   **

13 rue du Pont, Mareuil-sur-Aÿ, 51160 Aÿ-Champagne	📞 +33 3 26 56 93 00
@ info@philipponnat.com	👤 Thierry Garnier
🌐 www.champagnephilipponnat.com	[map p. 58]
🗓 🏛 🏭 🏠 ⌚ 17 ha; 600,000 btl	Royale Réserve Brut
Owner: Lanson-BCC	

The Philipponnats were growers and merchants at Aÿ in the sixteenth century, but the house was officially founded in 1910 in Mareuil-sur-Aÿ. The family sold the house in the seventies, its reputation declined during the nineties, and in 1997 it be-

came part of the Lanson-BCC group. Charles Philipponnat, grandson of one of the founders, came from Moët to run it in 2000. "We haven't really changed the style, we've made it more precise," Charles says, but that's understating the effect of the first change he made, to drop dosage for non-vintage (Royale Réserve) from 12 g/l to 8 g/l. For vintage, "We use 4.5 g/l dosage in every vintage (called cuvée 1522), so if there are differences in perception they reflect vintage character."

All of the cuvées except the Grand Blanc (a Blanc de Blancs) have a majority of Pinot Noir. Fermentation and maturation use a mix of stainless steel and barriques. The top wine is the Clos des Goisses, which comes from a narrow strip of land rising up steeply from the river Aÿ just along the road from the Maison. This achieves an unusual degree of ripeness, and (perhaps uniquely in Champagne) is made in virtually every vintage; it has the same blend as 1522, two thirds Pinot Noir and one third Chardonnay. The style of the house is full and powerful, showing the dominance of Pinot Noir, but there's a refreshing catch of citrus at the end, reflecting the use of only partial malolactic fermentation.

Champagne Pol Roger **

1, rue Winston Churchill, 51200 Épernay	📞 +33 3 26 59 58 00
@ polroger@polroger.fr	👤 Laurent d'Harcourt
🌐 www.polroger.com	[map p. 58]
🚫 🏭 🏠 🕰 92 ha; 1,800,000 btl	🍾 Blanc de Blancs

The most famous consumer of Pol Roger was Winston Churchill, for whom the prestige cuvée was named in 1975. (He once described Pol Roger's Maison as "the world's most drinkable address.") One of the Grand Marques, founded in 1849, this is still a family-run company, with an impressively massive headquarters on the Avenue de Champagne in Epernay. A buying spree has increased estate vineyards to provide just over half of needs. Pol Roger has always been a popular Champagne in the U.K., which remains its major export market.

The cellars are completely modernized, with vinification exclusively in stainless steel—"there is no oak in any of our Champagnes—and the wine goes through malolactic fermentation." All riddling is still done by hand. The house attributes its extra-tiny bubbles and finesse to the fact that the caves at Pol Roger are unusually deep and cold, so everything takes longer. The White Foil cuvée was introduced in 1955 with a back label "Reserved for Great Britain." Dosage on the White Foil (now officially called the Extra Cuvée de Reserve) was reduced in 2010 to 9-10 g/l, and the wine now lives up better to the house's aspiration for freshness, but I would still be inclined to describe it as firm rather than airy. The Pure cuvée has zero dosage (although labeled Extra Brut), and the Rich cuvée is a 35 g/l demi-sec. All of these are blended from equal proportions of each of the three grape varieties.

Vintages wines include Brut, Brut Rosé, and Blanc de Blancs. The vintage cuvées come exclusively from estate grapes. Vintage is more important at Pol Roger than most producers, and comprises as much as 20% of production. The vintage Brut is a deeper version of the nonvintage, but the Blanc de Blancs tends to a distinctive, more savory, character. Cuvée Sir Winston Churchill is dominated by Pinot Noir to achieve a rich, full-bodied style in keeping with its name; definitely a Champagne to accompany a meal rather than to have as an aperitif. Pol Roger Champagnes always nake a mainstream impression, and progressing from nonvintage to vintage to Sir Winston Churchill, the main effect is increasing refinement together with more grip on the palate.

Champagne Pommery

Villa Demoiselle, 56 boulevard Henry Vasnier, 51100 Reims	📞 +33 3 26 61 62 63
@ domaine@vrankenpommery.fr	
⊕ www.champagnepommery.com	[map p. 54]
☺ €€ ⋔ 🏠	54 ha; 6,000,000 btl
	Owner: Vranken-Pommery Monopole

One of the grand marques of Champagne, Pommery has its headquarters in the city of Reims. The best thing about Pommery may be their caves, among the most spectacular in Champagne, extensively tunneled under Reims,. Visitors are transported along them in a little train. Pommery is now part of the Vranken group of Champagne houses. The style is on the lighter side: in fact, the style used to be distinctly thin and a little acid, but improvements in recent years have seen some deepening. Pommery is probably best known for wines at both ends of the spectrum: Cuvée Louise (named for the founder of the house) is a prestige Champagne from grand cru vineyards; and Pommery POP is a range intended to appeal to the younger consumer, sold in small, colorful bottles.

Champagne Éric Rodez   **

4 rue de Isse, 51150 Ambonnay	📞 +33 3 26 57 04 93
@ contact@champagne-rodez.fr	👤 Éric & Mickael Rodez
⊕ www.champagne-rodez.fr	[map p. 57]
🗒 ⋔ 🍇 🥂 6 ha; 45,000 btl	Cuvée des Crayères

The Rodez family has been making wine in Ambonnay since 1757. Éric is the eighth generation, and after a stint in Burgundy followed by experience as an oenologist at a large Champagne house, he came back to run the family domain. "My first vintage was an exceptionally bad year, 1984, and this created a tsunami in me. I felt no emotion in my new wine," he recollects. Éric bubbles over with comparisons between wine and music, all the while drawing parallels between the emotions they create. "When you go to a concert, every concert is a new emotion, it's not just a repeat. For me this is the logic for terroir wine. Every year I am writing a melody with a new interpretation."

This is a small family domain—Éric was recently joined by his son Mickael—run from Éric's house in a back street of Ambonnay. There are separate cellars close by in the town, but they have run out of space, so a new winery is being constructed around the house. Éric is committed to biodynamic viticulture, but that is not enough, and now he is using aromatherapy to reduce the need for copper and sulfate. Out in the vineyards, he explains the fragmented character of his holdings, which consist of 35 separate parcels. "These 13 rows of Pinot Noir come from my father, these 39 rows of Chardonnay come from my mother." Fervent about the advantages of biodynamics, he points out that the berries and bunches are smaller than those of conventionally cultivated vines.

Winemaking is traditional in some respects and unconventional or modern in others. "Traditionally Champagne is 80% the new year and 20% reserves, but I use 70% reserve wines and only 30% of current vintage." Pressing uses old manual presses constructed in 1936. "I don't want to use a modern press. It's very important to press slowly." But there are a couple of gyropalettes, so Eric is not stuck thoughtlessly in tradition. The cellar contains stainless steel vats and barriques; 20% of the wine is fermented in old oak, and most élevage is in oak.

Dosage is always low here. "All my wines are Extra Brut, but I put Brut on the label because I never know for the next vintage." The style really showcases cépage, and you see the differences between the character of each cépage in a way that is unusually clear for Champagne. The Blanc de Blancs says, "I am Chardonnay," and the Blanc de Noirs says, "I am Pinot Noir." Coming from the Ambonnay grand cru, the blends have only Chardonnay and Pinot Noir. "I'm not interested in Pinot Meunier because it doesn't age well," Éric explains. All the wines have a great sense of balance and integration between density and vivacity.

"Cuvée des Crayères blends the structure of Pinot Noir with the sensuality of Chardonnay," says Éric, and it shows that characteristic balance of the house. The Blanc de Blancs comes from Ambonnay and has a typically elegant uplift. The Blanc de Noirs has that characteristic sense of Pinot Noir's density. "For the Blanc de Noirs I did not do MLF in order to have more sensuality." The Zero Dosage is perfectly balanced, with no sense of anything missing, as sometimes happens in the category. It comes from a plot in the middle of the slope which gives good ripeness. The Cuvée des Grands Vintages is "a blend of the best vintages, it is very complex. "Les Beurys is "one plot, one vintage, one cépage," from a plot of Pinot Noir with east exposure and 35 cms of soil. "It's almost an anti-Champagne because there's no assemblage." The vintage Blanc de Blancs, Empreinte De Terroir Chardonnay, "is my view of the terroir of Ambonnay."

Champagne Louis Roederer   ★★

21 Blvd Lundy, BP 66, 51053 Reims	📞 +33 3 26 40 42 11
@ *com@champagne-roederer.com*	👤 *Frédéric Rouzaud*
⊕ *www.louis-roederer.com*	*[map p. 54]*
📅 ⚒ 🏠 ▨ Ⓒ *242 ha; 3,500,000 btl*	Rosé

Roederer describes itself as one of the last independent family-run Champagne houses, but this is a little deceptive as it is now quite a wine conglomerate: it created Roederer Estate in California, purchased Champagne Deutz (which continues to be run independently), and also owns Château Pichon Lalande in Pauillac, Domaines Ott in Provence Delas Frères in the Rhône, Ramos Pinto Port in Portugal, and wineries in Napa Valley and Sonoma. Louis Roederer, who inherited the company from his uncle in 1833 focused on purchasing vineyards, and today the estate vineyards supply two thirds of the grapes, an unusually high proportion in Champagne. All estate vineyards are planted by selection massale using Roederer's own nursery and selections. Half of the estate vineyards are certified organic.

The house is famous for its prestige cuvée, Cristal, which was created (as a sweet blend) for Tsar Alexander II in 1876; the name reflects the fact that it was bottled in clear crystal. It became Roederer's commercial prestige cuvée after the first world war, and remains one of the best known ultra-prestige cuvées. It comes from 45 dedicated plots of the oldest vines, the oldest being 70 years and the youngest 25 years.

A proportion of the wine is fermented in large oak vats (about 5% for nonvintage, 30% for vintage, 100% for Cristal). Malolactic is partial for nonvintage and vintage, but blocked for Brut Nature and Cristal.

There was a significant change in the style of nonvintage in 2021. Until then, the major nonvintage cuvée was Brut Premier, showing an elegant and precise style, almost tight when young, and very consistent. Brut Premier was a blend of 40% Pinot Noir, 40% Chardonnay, and 20% Pinot Meunier; with dosage has been reduced to 9 g/l from 12 g/l a decade ago. Brut Premier has now been replaced by Collection, with a composition that changes each year. The number of the release is indicated very discreetly on the label. Dosage is slightly lower than Brut Premier, at 8g. One change in production is that 34% comes from a Réserve Perpetuelle (effectively a solera) kept in stainless steel, and 10% from reserve wines of individual vintages stored in oak. Consistent with a view that consumers now want wines that are readier to drink, this feels more mature on release, showing greater weight to the palate and something of a move from citrus fruits towards stone fruits.

The nonvintage rosé still shows the classic Roederer style: only a touch darker than Collection (it is made by a method Roederer call infusion, which is close to direct pressing), it is very elegant, slightly citric, slightly spicy, and might be hard to identify as rosé in a blind tasting. If you are devoted to the old Roederer style, this is the cuvée to have.

The vintage Brut and Rosé both have 70% Pinot Noir to 30% Chardonnay. The vintage Blanc de Blancs has a great sense of tension: some people might call the style delicate. The Brut Nature comes from 10 ha in Cumières where all three varieties are planted (on soils with more clay). They are all picked together when Pinot Noir is ready and then pressed together. Recently a small production of still wines (Coteaux Champenoise) has been started for all three colors.

Maison Ruinart ★★

Crayères, 51100 Reims	📞 +33 3 26 77 51 51
@ *contact@ruinart.com*	👤 *Frédéric Panaïotis*
🌐 *www.ruinart.com*	*[map p. 54]*
📅 🍷 🏭 🏠 ☺ *17 ha; 1,700,000 btl Owner: LVMH*	🍾 *Blanc de Blancs*

In 1735, Nicolas Ruinart moved from the textile trade to selling "wine with bubbles." One of the Grand Marques, the house remained independent until after the seventh generation the family lost interest, and it was taken over by Moët in 1962;. today it is part of LVMH. It is one of the oldest Champagne houses, and claims to be the first devoted exclusively to sparkling wine. It's located in very grand headquarters in the Les Crayères area of Reims, with extensive underground caves cut into the chalk. Ruinart's historic vineyard is at Sillery, in the Montagne de Reims, and this is still the heart of its top cuvées, but grapes are also sourced from LVMH's other holdings. The winemaking team of four is led by chef de cave Frédéric Panaïotis, who plays some cards close to his chest. No one else knows when the next vintage declaration will be.

Ruinart calls itself a Chardonnay house. "The style of Ruinart is about revealing Chardonnay and keeping aromatic freshness," says winemaker Louise Bryden. "We struggle against oxidation." The entire winemaking process is designed around maintaining freshness. Nonvintage cuvées use only young reserve wines; typically a nonvintage includes 25% of wines from the previous two years to supplement the 75% from the current. Crushing uses a pneumatic press, not the traditional basket press, and fermentation is at low temperature to maintain aromatics. There's even a special shaped bottle, with a narrow neck to admit less oxygen. In 2010, aging for the vintage cuvées switched from using the usual crown caps to using corks, because this reduces exposure to oxygen over a longer period. The latest adjustment is the use of jetting to reduce oxygen ingress at disgorgement.

The style of the Ruinart Blanc de Blancs is quite deep. Indeed, I find more of the crisp brightness of Chardonnay in the "R" de Ruinart Brut (which has the atypical blend for the house of 45% Chardonnay, 50-55% Pinot Noir, and 5-10% Pinot Meunier) than in the nonvintage Blanc de Blancs, which is deeper and nuttier. The prestige vintage cuvées are called Dom Ruinart (after Nicolas Ruinart's uncle). The Blanc de Blancs is intensely savory; indeed I call it an umami wine, as for me the character is savory rather than mineral. With age it can develop a complex creaminess that deepens to caramel and toffee. Dom Ruinart is about 2% of production. The vintage rosé is 80% Chardonnay, and made in the same vintages as Dom Ruinart Blanc de Blancs so long as the red wine has sufficient quality.

Champagne Salon   ★★★★

5-7 rue Brèche d'Oger, 51190 Le Mesnil-sur-Oger	📞 +33 3 26 57 51 65
@ *champagne@salondelamotte.com*	👤 *Didier Depond*
🌐 *www.champagne-salon.fr*	*[map p. 59]*
🚫 🗡 🏠 ☕	*10 ha; 60,000 btl* *Owner: Champagne Delamotte*

The most unusual house in Champagne, Salon has only one wine, a vintage Blanc de Blancs coming exclusively from Le Mesnil, made in 43 vintages since the house was founded in 1911. Eugène Aimé Salon came from Champagne, but he made a fortune in furs before establishing Champagne Salon. "Even the locals didn't understand what he was doing: using a single cépage to make only a vintage," says Audrey Campos of Salon. After M. Salon died in 1943, the house remained in family hands for twenty years until it was sold to Pernod-Ricard, who sold it on to Laurent-Perrier in 1989. Today it is run in association with Delamotte, which is next door: "You cannot speak of one without the other." When Salon is not made, the grapes are used by Delamotte.

Salon did not buy vineyards; a 1 ha vineyard behind the house, known as the garden, is the only one owned by the house. Grapes come from 10 ha of 19 parcels, all in mid-slope, owned by various proprietors, but mostly worked by Laurent-Perrier. (The only change has been that Clos de Mesnil was part of Salon until it was purchased by Krug in 1979.) Vinification switched from large oak vats to stainless steel in 1995, and malolactic is always blocked. With dosage of only 5 g/l, and around ten years before disgorgement, the style shows restrained minerality when young, but with an infinitely refined sense of tension. Needing twenty years to reach its peak, this is surely the most precise Champagne of all.

Champagne Jacques Selosse   ***

59 rue Ernest Vallée, 51190 Avize	📞 *+33 3 26 57 53 56*
@ *champagne@selosse-lesavises.com*	👤 *Guillaume Selosse*
🌐 *www.selosse-lesavises.com*	*[map p. 59]*
⊘ 🍇 🔪 🍎 ◻ 🍇 *9 ha; 57,000 btl*	*Version Originale*

CHAMPAGNE

INITIALE
Brut
JACQUES SELOSSE

This house has a reputation for marching to the beat of a different drum. Jacques Selosse was a baker who bought land in Avize in 1949, and sold the fruit to Lanson. In the 1960s he started bottling his own Champagne, and his son Anselme went to Burgundy to learn oenology. When Anselme started making the wine—"1974 was my first vintage, not one to make a millésime"—he began following a Burgundian model, focusing on parcels (or groups of parcels given that the vineyards are divided into 47 different plots). Most of the vineyards are grand cru, with 4 ha in Avize; there is some premier cru in Mareuil.

Anselme divides his vineyards into those with less than 15% incline and those with more, as this determines types of soils, especially how much clay accumulates at the bottom of the slope. This leads to four "topographic" nonvintage cuvées (two Blanc de Blancs and two rosé). The emphasis here is on differences: differences between vintages and differences between places. For vintage wines, "I prefer that each wine should be different. I do not want the wine to be the same every year... And there is a false idea that the vintage ends when the vigneron decides to harvest, but conditions after are different too—which is why malo is left to happen or not happen," he says. Bottlings from individual lieu-dits are nonvintage: "The objective is to display terroir rather than vintage." They are made as a blend of several recent vintages, which may develop into something equivalent to a Perpetual Reserve. Bottling from lieu-dits started in 2003; today there are six nonvintage lieu-dit cuvées, three Blanc de Blancs and three Blanc de Noirs, as well as vintage wines.

The lieu-dits make the point forcefully that even after the involved process of making Champagne, terroir can show: Les Carelles from Mesnil has a very fine impression of the minerality of the village, whereas Sous le Mont from Mareuil has a more powerful linear impression. Anselme sees the differences as resulting from the minerals in the soil: more magnesium at Mareuil makes the limestone harder, and the wine sterner.

Burgundian methods extend to fermenting and aging the base wine in fûts (with 15% new oak) using barriques of 228 liter and larger casks of 400 liter. The Selosse wines have sometimes been criticized for showing too much oak, but for me it seems that the oak is not so much obvious directly as indirectly, in the increased richness and more oxidative style. The wines tend to seem more mature, reflecting the generally oxidative style of winemaking, but are not oaky in any conventional sense, allowing the lieu-dits to show their differences. Anselme can pull this off successfully because of the sheer quality of his wines, but it might be problematic at another producer.

Certainly these are powerful wines, more suited for a meal than an aperitif. The style shows wide breadth of flavor and a strong body, sometimes with a trademark touch of minerality or salinity on the finish. These are wines that make a statement. Expanding into oenotourism, Anselme also has a hotel and restaurant at the Maison.

96

Champagne De Sousa ★★

12 place Léon Bourgeois, 51190 Avize	📞 *+33 3 26 57 53 29*
@ *contact@champagnedesousa.com*	👤 *Erick De Sousa*
🌐 *www.champagnedesousa.com*	*[map p. 59]*
🗓 🏭 🏠 ⌚ *10 ha; 100,000 btl*	*Brut Reserve*

This small house has a distinctive style. The family arrived when Erik de Sousa's great grandfather came from Portugal during the first world war. Erik's parents created the marque, and Erik took over in 1986, making wine in two cuveries on either side of the main square in Avize. Estate vineyards have increased from the original 3 ha, and now include two vineyards in Aÿ and Ambonnay, bringing Pinot Noir to complement the Chardonnay of the Côte des Blancs.

There are 7-8 nonvintage cuvées as well as vintage wines: "We take care that each cuvée has a specific character whether it's cépage, terroir, or use of wood," Erik explains. Brut Tradition comes from vines that aren't grand cru, while Brut Reserve is Chardonnay from grand crus. Both are vinified in cuve. Cuvée 3A is a blend from Avize, Aÿ, and Ambonnay, poised between Chardonnay and Pinot Noir. Cuvée des Caudalies nonvintage is a Blanc de Blancs from old vines, vinified in wood. Cuvée des Caudalies vintage is vinified in wood with 15% new oak, and the Le Mesnil cuvée comes from the oldest vines. Umami is a vintage made once so far, in 2009, when conditions fulfilled Erik's aim, conceived after a visit to Japan, of representing umami in a wine. Two rosés come in a presentation box, one from assemblage, one from saignée. The style develops from fruity for the Brut, mineral for Blanc de Blancs, powerful for Caudalies, and quite savory for Umami and vintage Caudalies. These are wines of character.

Champagne Taittinger ★★

9 Place Saint Nicaise, BP 2741, 51100 Reims	📞 *+33 3 26 85 45 35*
@ *contactez-nous@taittinger.fr*	👤 *Axel Gillery*
🌐 *www.taittinger.com*	*[map p. 54]*
😊 €€ 🏭 🏠 *290 ha; 3,000,000 btl*	*Cuvée Prelude*

The largest family-owned house in Champagne, Taittinger has headquarters in Reims, with a stylish reception area, a cinema for showing movies about the house, and all the other accoutrements of a Grand Maison. It stands on the site of the Abbey of St. Nicaise, which was destroyed in the Revolution. The caves underneath go back to the monks, dating from the thirteenth century (with a lower level of even older caves dating from the fourth century). There are 4 km of cellars at this site—which is used for producing prestige cuvées—and in the center of Reims is another even larger site, more mechanized, with another 10 km of cellars.

It's difficult to define house style here, given a wide range of cuvées, every one apparently designed to fit a different niche. The Brut Réserve and Rosé are mainstream. The premium cuvée Prélude has a level of refinement and tension, while the vintage is broader and more opulent, although both have equal proportions of Pinot Noir and Chardonnay coming from grand and premier cru sites. "With the vintage we are looking for the specificity of the harvest, but also something with more roundness and aromatics, more of a match for food," says Director Dominique Gareta. The flagship Comtes de Champagne is fine and precise, the quintessence of the Blanc de Blancs style. And then there is Nocturne, a Sec champagne designed for nightclubs, in purple packaging that might glow in the dark. The various cuvées are interestingly different.

Champagne Tarlant   **

21, rue Principale, 51480 Oeuilly/Épernay	📞 +33 3 26 58 30 60
@ champagne@tarlant.com	👤 Benoit Tarlant
🌐 www.tarlant.com	[map p. 56]
🗓 ⚒ 🍇 🏭 14 ha; 100,000 btl	🍷 Blanc de Noirs

Dating from 1687, this is an old family domain, presently run by Benoît Tarlant and his sister Mélanie, with its own vineyard holdings in 55 separate parcels in the Vallée de la Marne, mostly on the south side of the river. It was necessary to replant after the second world war, so the vines date from 1946 to the 1970s. There's an emphasis on single vineyards, with wine from each plot vinified separately. "Terroir is more determinative than cépage," Benoît says. "The final tasting for assemblage is blind, with little attention paid to variety." About 60% is fermented in barriques, and reserve wines are aged in wood. There is no malolactic fermentation. As well as the usual varieties, Benoît has planted some of the old varieties: Pinot Blanc, Petit Meslier, and Arbanne.

In addition to the range of nonvintage and vintage wines, there are some special cuvées. La Vigne d'Or comes from Pinot Meunier in a single plot. "When I made the first Blanc de Meunier, in 1999," Benoît says, "it was considered to be pushing the limits, but now there are several others." There's also a plot of ungrafted Chardonnay on (relatively) sandy soil, which makes the special cuvée Vigne d'Antan (a Blanc de Blancs whose name means, vines of yesterday).

There is little or no dosage; most cuvées are Extra Brut, so the house style is crisp and precise. In the past decade, Benoît has moved steadily towards zero dosage. The Zero Brut Nature is a little austere, but the Zero Rosé takes the edge off the style and gives a flavorful impression. Ripeness of the grapes shows through the Argilite vintage zero dosage, which is tight, precise, and elegant. The vintage wines age well, with the Vigne d'Antan 2000 showing at its peak in 2013, and Cuvée Louis 2000 quite splendid in 2016.

"Recently disgorged" (not to mention zero dosage) got a whole new meaning on a visit to the house when we compared the Blanc de Meunier with the Blanc de Noirs made exclusively from Pinot Noir. The vintage had not yet been released, so Benoît Tarlant knocked off the crown caps, a gush of disgorgement, and the freshly disgorged wine was ready to taste.

Champagne Vazart-Coquart   *

5 rue-des-Partelaines, 51530 Chouilly	📞 +33 3 26 55 40 04
@ contact@vazart-coquart.com	👤 Jean-Pierre Vazart
🌐 www.champagnevazartcoquart.com	[map p. 58]
🗓 ⚒ 🍇 🏭 11 ha; 70,000 btl	🍷 Brut Réserve, Blanc de Blancs

98

The involvement of the Vazart and Coquart families with winemaking dates from 1785, and the house was created in 1953 by Louis Vazart and his son Jacques. The brick Maison in the main street of Chouilly was constructed in 1865, but a modern winery was constructed recently. Jean-Pierre Vazart, Jacques's son, has been in charge since 1995. All the vineyards are in the grand cru of Chouilly at the northern edge of the Côte des Blancs. In fact, Vazart-Coquart is the third-largest landholder in Chouilly (albeit dwarfed by Moët and Roederer). Vineyards are almost entirely (95%) planted with Chardonnay.

Wines are matured exclusively in stainless steel "for purity." Reserve wines are kept in a "solera," started by Jacques in 1982, which provides a quarter of the wine for the Brut Réserve and the Extra Brut Réserve, both Blanc de Blancs. The Réserve spends 30 months before disgorgement; the Extra Brut spends 42 months. Dosage for the Brut has decreased from 7 g to 5g; for the Extra Brut it is 2.5 g/l. Cuvée Camille, a blend of 70% Chardonnay with 30% Pinot Noir, is where the Pinot goes. The top wine is the vintage Special Club, which spends more than seven years aging on the lees, and is broader and deeper. House style seems to have become richer in recent years, with the cuvées that are all 100% Chardonnay (except Camille) showing more the weight and texture of Blancs de Noirs than Blanc de Blancs. Stone fruits dominate a firm palate.

Champagne Veuve Clicquot   *

Albert Thomas, 51100 Reims 51100 Reims	📞 +33 3 26 89 54 40
@ *communication@veuve-clicquot.fr*	
🌐 *www.veuve-clicquot.com*	*[map p. 54]*
🛅 €€ 🏭 🏠	*393 ha; 14,000,000 btl* *Owner: LVMH*

Introduced in 1873, Veuve Clicquot's vivid yellow label is one of the most effective marketing images in Champagne, immediately identifying one of the largest and most successful Champagne houses. (The yellow label was introduced in 1877 to distinguish the new drier style from the original demi-sec white label). Founded in 1772, Veuve Clicquot's history is bound up with the history of Champagne, since, after taking over in 1805, it was the eponymous Veuve Clicquot who invented the pupître for riddling in 1816. Veuve Clicquot is the second largest house in Champagne (behind Moët), with estate vineyards providing about 25% of the grape supply, and since 1987 has been part of LVMH. The criticism, of course, is that volume prevents it from scaling the heights, but it's an achievement in itself to keep consistency at this level. The production site occupies 19 ha on the east side of Reims; massive Crayères, cut into the chalk since the 13th century, extend for 15 miles underneath. "Every bottle of Clicquot around the world comes through here," they say. There is a dedicated visitor center at the site, with a charming garden where you can taste outside in good weather.

The number of cuvées is relatively restricted for such a large house. With a majority of Pinot Noir in all, the style of the Brut is relatively full, the vintage is definitely more refined and inclined towards minerality, and the prestige vintage cuvée (La Grande Dame) has real weight (and seems more in keeping with the style of Yellow Label than the regular vintage). Cellarmaster Dominique Demarville was increasing the proportion of Pinot Noir before he retired in 2020. The nonvintage yellow label is by far the most important cuvée (it can be as much as 90% of production), and Dominique said that Clicquot will be "declaring fewer vintages than we did in the past and ageing the reserve wines a bit further to add complexity," with the intention of improving quality.

Veuve Clicquot are not believers in zero dosage—the wine needs to be protected with some sugar, they say—and dosage is usually moderate, 10g for Yellow Label, 7-8g for vintage, and 7g for Grande Dame. However, there has been a move towards the fashion for lower dosage with the introduction of the Extra Old extra brut cuvée, which has 3g dosage. This comes 100% from reserve wines (there is no base vintage), with releases planned for every 2-3 years: for the first edition. the reserves started with 1988; for the second edition the reserves came from 1990 up to 2012. The back label lists all the vintages that are included. It spends 3 years in stainless steel before disgorgement and then 3 years in bottle. (Disgorgement date is put on the back label only for this wine and the vintage cuvée.) The style is closer to vintage than to Yellow Label.

Champagne Veuve Fourny et Fils ★★

5, rue du Mesnil, B.P. 12, 51130 Vertus	📞 +33 3 26 52 16 30
@ info@champagne-veuve-fourny.com	👤 Charles-Henry & Emmanuel Fourny
🌐 www.champagne-veuve-fourny.com	[map p. 59]
📅 🏭 🏠 ⌚ 29 ha; 250,000 btl	🍾 Cuvée R, Blanc de Blancs, Extra Brut

A small family domain since 1856, Veuve Fourny has been run by the fifth generation of brothers Charles-Henry and Emmanuel Fourny since 1993. "My brother and I started making wine together for two years as an experiment," says Charles-Henry. They are very hands-on: when I arrived at the winery, Charles-Henry was supervising the loading of a tractor-trailer with wine for Australia. The winery runs back along the road from the gracious family house on the corner, and has expanded on to the other side of the street.

All in the premier cru of Vertus, vineyards comprise around 30 individual parcels. Clos Faubourg Notre Dame, one of the few remaining walled vineyards in Champagne, is adjacent to the tasting room. All vineyards are premier or grand cru; most of the 50 parcels are in the chalky northern part of Vertus. Estate grapes supply about half of production, supplemented by purchased grapes, but all sources remain local. Many of the estate vineyards are old, because after Roger Fourny died when the brothers were young teenagers, their mother took over the domain, but did not have time for the replanting that was popular in the era.

Dosage is minimal for all cuvées. "Dosage for us is not to make the wine sweet, it's to balance acidity, texture, and minerality," says Charles-Henry. "It's always below 6 g, so it has to be very precise. We do not use cane sugar, but the syrup of grapes." Emphasized by the low dosage, the style is fresh. "We believe in RD (recent disgorgement) for everything, and we disgorge when there's demand."

Production is Blanc de Blancs except for some Pinot Noir in the Grand Réserve Brut (80% Chardonnay and 20% Pinot Noir) and the rosé. Tasting starts with the Vertus Brut Nature. "We've been making this a long time, it's not a fashion, it's just a few south-facing plots that deserve to be Brut Nature." Its silky sheen would make it hard to identify as zero dosage in a blind tasting; it feels more like Extra Brut in its sense of depth and roundness. The impression of purity continues with the Brut premier cru, where the dosage smoothes out the texture, but style remains crisp and linear. The Grande Reserve Brut (80% Chardonnay, 20% Pinot Noir), has 50% reserve wines, and makes a weightier impression, with a creamy palate pushing salinity more into the background.

Nonvintage wines use some vinification in oak, but vintage is all in stainless steel. Monts de Vertus Extra Brut (2-3g dosage) is fuller than nonvintage, but with typical salinity on the palate. Cuvée "R" is a blend of two recent vintages from older (60-year) vines; aged exclusively in barrique, it has more intensity all round, with a more textured impression from oak aging. Malolactic fermentation is usually partial for nonvintage cuvées, and varies with the cuvée for vintage.

The rosés are all top of the line. The premier cru rosé is an assemblage of Chardonnay and Pinot Noir that maintains the linearity of Vertus. The MV13 rosé cuvée (MV stands for multivintage, 13 means the base is 2013) is softer, but still shows that savory impression of the Côte des Blancs. Monts de Vertus rosé is a saignée of Pinot Noir and has a great sense of completeness.

Running through the cuvées is great purity of style, always with a catch of salinity at the end. "When you open one of our wines, it will be rich and full, but after 30 minutes you will see the linearity as the backbone comes back," says Charles-Henry. "Since we're in Vertus, there is always citrus," says Emmanuel. This is a fair description of the house style, which shows through the range, with citrus sometimes turning to minerality or even salinity, but always with an overlay of intensity and even richness.

Champagne Vilmart et Cie   *

5 rue des Gravières, BP 4, 51500 Rilly-La-Montagne	📞 +33 3 26 03 40 01
@ patricia@champagnevilmart.fr	👤 Laurent Champs
🌐 www.champagnevilmart.fr	[map p. 57]
🚗 🍇 ⚏ 🥂	Grand Cellier

Known for its extensive use of wood and full-bodied style, Vilmart is a boutique house located in the northern part of the Montagne de Reims. Vineyards are relatively compact, with 12 separate plots, almost all in the village of Rilly-La-Montagne (and therefore premier cru). Vilmart was established in 1872, but really came to fame (or to notoriety at the time) about forty years ago when it began to ferment and mature the base wines in wood. (This seems to have started by accident when there was a shortage of vats.) Today foudres are used for the nonvintage, and barriques or demi-muids for the vintage wines, comprising a mix of new wood with one-year and two-year. The wine stays in the wood for ten months. Since 1989, Vilmart has been run by René Champs, the fifth generation of the family.

The basic nonvintage cuvée (not exported to the U.S.) is called the Grande Réserve and is 70% Pinot Noir to 30% Chardonnay; the rosé, Cuvée Rubis, is 90% Pinot Noir. All the other cuvées are dominated by Chardonnay. There is no Pinot Meunier. The Grand Cellier nonvintage has 70% Chardonnay to 30% Pinot Noir. The vintage wines, Grand Cellier d'Or and Coeur de Cuvée, have about 80% Chardonnay. Coeur de Cuvée comes from the oldest vines (about 60 years) and is made almost every year; it's a little more intense than Grand Cellier d'Or, which moves in a savory direction as it ages. Malolactic fermentation is blocked for all cuvées, but the impression on the palate shows stone fruits more than citrus. Dosage is well into the brut range, usually 7-11 g/l. The style is consistent across the range, and the major transition is increased intensity and flavor variety going from nonvintage to vintage.

Profiles of Important Estates

Champagne Allouchery-Perseval

11, rue de l'Église, 51500 Écueil	📞 +33 3 26 49 74 61
@ *contact@alloucheryperseval.com*	👤 *Émilien Allouchery*
🌐 *www.alloucheryperseval.com*	*[map p. 55]*
🗓 🏭 🍇 🍂	*8 ha; 60,000 btl*

Émilien Allouchery qualified in oenology and then worked in the New World before taking over the family estate just south of Reims in 2006. He is the fourth generation. Vineyards are in Écueil, and are classified as premier cru. Plantings are mostly Pinot Noir with some Chardonnay. The Tradition Brut (7 g/l dosage) and Extra Brut (3 g/l dosage) are Blanc de Noirs; there is also a demi-sec (32 g/l dosage). They age for 2-3 years before disgorgement. The rosé has 12% dry red wine, 78% Pinot Noir, and 10% Chardonnay, with a dosage of 8g/l. The Réserve nonvintage is 60% Pinot Noir and 40% Chardonnay, and ages for five years on the lees. It has 6-7 g/l dosage. The vintage is an Extra Brut (4 g/l dosage) assemblage of equal Pinot Noir and Chardonnay, and ages for 8 years. There is also a Blanc de Blancs vintage, Eclipse, with 40% vinified in barriques, which spends 3-4 years on the lees before disgorgement.

Champagne André Chemin

3 Rue Châtillon, 51500 Sacy	📞 +33 3 26 49 22 42
@ *champagneandrechemin@wanadoo.fr*	👤 *Eva Chemin*
🌐 *www.champagneandrechemin.fr*	*[map p. 55]*
🗓 🏭 ▬ ☕	*7 ha; 55,000 btl*

"We are in the Montagne de Reims, and what we do best is Pinot Noir," says Eva Chemin. Her husband Sébastian is the grandson of André Chemin, who established this small grower house just outside Reims in 1948. The general policy here is to use low dosage, combined with malolactic fermentation for almost all cuvées. Celstynka is a Blanc de Noirs from 100% Pinot Noir with zero dosage; Tradition is the same wine with 6 g dosage. It's more accessible, in fact, it's an unusual example in which the fruits are brought out more clearly by the dosage. "The first one doesn't please everyone," Eva says. Cuvée Selectionée is three quarters Pinot Noir and one quarter Chardonnay, and spends an extra three years aging. It's a little fuller on the palate, and is a Champagne for food. The rosé d'assemblage has the same basis as Cuvée Selectionée, but the addition of the red wine rounds up the palate, and together with higher dosage (7 g), makes this one of the most accessible wines in the range. Low dosage of 3 g reinforces the crisp, linear impression of the Blanc de Blancs, Excellence, which is the only cuvée not to go through malolactic fermentation.

Champagne André Jacquart

63, avenue de Bammental, 51130 Vertus	📞 +33 3 26 57 52 29
@ *marie.doyard@andrejacquart.com*	👤 *Marie Doyard*
🌐 *www.andrejacquart.com*	*[map p. 59]*
🗓 €€ 🏭 🍇 ☕ *24 ha; 100,000 btl*	*Le Mesnil, Blanc de Blancs*

André Jacquart created the house that bears his name in 1958. (It should not be confused with Champagne Jacquart—see profile—which is a cooperative based in Reims.) André's grand-daughter, Marie Doyard, and her brother Benoît, took over in 2004, when their parents decided to combine the family estates from the Jacquart and Doyard sides. The cave was originally in Mesnil-sur-Oger, but then moved to Vertus (where the Doyards come from). The style changed with the new generation. "I made three big decisions," Marie says. "Long aging for four to five years before being released, and eight to nine years for vintage Champagne. A really low dosage of zero to four grams of sugar. And the biggest decision was to work in old barrels from Burgundy." Vineyards include 16 ha in Mesnil-sur-Oger and in Vertus. The other vineyards are divided between the Aube and the Aisne. The Doyard family also own Château Cantegrive in Puisseguin St. Emilion. Base wines age 80% in oak, and malolactic fermentation is always blocked. The wines with dosage are labeled Brut, although dosage is typically 4 g/l. All the wines are Blanc de Blancs except for the rosé. Brut Expérience comes 60% from Vertus and 40% from Mesnil, Pur Chardonnay Mesnil Expérience comes from the Doyard vines in Mesnil-sur-Oger, and there is also a Brut Nature from Mesnil-sur-Oger. The rosé, made by saignée, is 80% Pinot Noir from Vertus blended with 20% Chardonnay from Mesnil-sur-Oger. The style is quite firm; the difference between the Brut Nature from Le Mesnil and the Extra Brut is quite slight, with such good ripeness it would be hard to identify the Brut Nature as having zero dosage in a blind tasting.

Champagne Apollonis

13 rue de Bel Air, 51700 Festigny	📞 +33 3 26 58 34 01
@ contact@champagneapollonis.com	👤 Michel Loriot
🌐 www.champagne-michelloriot.com	[map p. 56]
🛈 € 🏭 🍇 🍷	7 ha; 55,000 btl

The name Apollonis suggests a new house, but the Loriot family have been involved in Champagne since the nineteenth century. They started estate-bottling in 1931 because conditions were bad they could not sell the grapes. Michel Loriot took over in 1977, and changed the name of the house to Apollonis in 2016. Michel's daughter Marie has taken over viticulture. Michel is known for taking his interest in music to the point of playing music in the cellars (this is called protéodie in France), starting with Beethoven during fermentation, and moving on to Mozart, Brahms, Vivaldi, or Elgar. "The notes arising from these melodies bring vibrations that reach the wine, the yields and the proteins of which it is composed." Located in the Vallée de la Marne, the focus is on Pinot Meunier. The cuvée Authentic Meunier is a Blanc de Noirs from 100% Pinot Meunier. The nonvintage Brut Patrimony is a blend of 70% Pinot Meunier and 30% Chardonnay. The rosé is 50% Chardonnay, 15% each of Pinot Noir and Pinot Meunier, and another 15% of Pinot Noir as red wine. Dosage is a touch on the high side, at 9g/l for the Brut cuvées. In Extra Brut, the vintage Inspiration de Saison is unusual in having a high proportion (65%) of Pinot Meunier, the rest being Chardonnay, Monodie is a Blanc de Noirs from Pinot Meunier old vines planted in 1942, the Blanc de Blancs has 6 g/l dosage, and Palmyre is Brut Nature.

Champagne Michel Arnould et Fils

28 rue de Mailly, 51360 Verzenay	📞 +33 3 26 49 40 06
@ info@champagne-michel-arnould.com	👤 Patrick Arnould
🌐 www.champagne-michel-arnould.com	[map p. 57]
🐓 🏭 🍇 🍷	12 ha; 95,000 btl

The family has been at Verzenay in the Montagne de Reims since the end of the nineteenth century. Like many others, the decline in grape prices pushed them into producing their own wine in 1929, under the name of Henri Lefevre; the marque Michel Arnould dates from 1961 when Michel Arnould married Henri's granddaughter Françoise. Michel's son Patrick and son-in-law Thierry run the estate today. The range starts with the Réserve Grand Cru (Pinot Noir and Chardonnay), Blanc de Noirs (from Verzenay), and Rosé (100% Pinot Noir), all with dosage of 9.5 g/l. Grande Cuvée grand cru has Pinot Noir from Verzenay and Chardonnay from the Côte des Blancs, with dosage dialed down just a fraction to 8.5 g/l. Fleur de Rosé is 100% Pinot Noir from old vines from a single year. with dosage at 9 g/l. In vintage, Carte d'Or has equal Pinot Noir and Chardonnay (all grand cru), and Mémoire de Vignes is the Blanc de Noirs, both from the oldest vines, with dosage at 8 g/l. B50 is a vintage from equal Pinot Noir and Chardonnay, with base wines vinified in barriques, and dosage at 7.5 g/l. There is one extra brut, a Blanc de Noirs.

Champagne Aspasie

4-8 Grande Rue, 51170 Brouillet	📞 *+33 3 26 97 43 46*
@ *contact@champagneaspasie.com*	👤 *Paul-Vincent Ariston*
🌐 *champagneaspasie.com*	*[map p. 53]*
🔲 € 🏭 🍾 🍇 🍶 🔵	*12 ha; 65,000 btl*

About twenty miles to the west of Reims, the Ariston family traces its involvement in growing grapes to 1714 with Aspasie Ancien, for whom the house is named. Paul-Vincent took over from his father Rémi in 2011. In addition to the three major varieties, the house specializes in growing the old varieties, Petit Meslier, Arbanne, Pinot Blanc, and Fromenteau (Pinot Gris). The range starts with the usual styles in nonvintage, then there is a Brut Prestige from old vines (50% Chardonnay, 25% each of Pinot Noir and Pinot Meunier), Brut de Fût (same blend from the oldest vines, but with base wines vinified in oak), and Cépages d'Antan (40% Arbanne, 40% Petit Meslier, and 20% Pinot Blanc).

Champagne Aubry Fils

4-6 Grande Rue, 51390 Jouy lès Reims	📞 *+33 3 26 49 20 27*
@ *contact@champagne-aubry.com*	👤 *Pierre & Philippe Aubry*
🌐 *www.champagne-aubry.com*	*[map p. 55]*
🔲 🏭 🍇	*12 ha; 120,000 btl*

The Aubrey twins, Pierre and Philippe, are the current generation in this family house dating from 1790. They are known for their focus on the old varieties, Arbanne, Petit Meslier, Fromenteau (Pinot Gris), and even Enfumé (a variant of Pinot Meunier), which started when they made a special cuvée to celebrate 200 years of the house. Now even the regular Brut cuvée has 5% of the old varieties. It is based on 50% current vintages and 50% from a perpetual reserve. Le Nombre d'Or has all 7 varieties that are allowed in Champagne. Sablé Blanc des Blancs has all the white varieties, and there is also a Sablé rosé. Vinification is in stainless steel, and because acidity is usually high, there is complete malolactic fermentation.

Jean Baillette-Prudhomme

4 Rue de La Gare, 51500 Trois Puits	📞 *+33 3 26 82 37 14*
@ *l.baillette@yahoo.fr*	👤 *Marie-France Baillette*
🌐 *champagnejbp.com*	*[map p. 57]*
🔲 🏭 🍇	*5 ha*

Just southeast of Reims, this small family domain has been run since Jean Baillette died in 2005 by his wife Marie-France and her daughters Laureen and Justine. Winemaking is traditional, from using an old Champagne press to riddling by hand for the top cuvées. The Brut Réserve has the classic blend of a third of each variety, Rosé de Saignée is 100% Pinot Noir, Brut Nature is 80% Pinot Noir and 20% Chardonnay and ages for 7-8 years before disgorgement, sometimes even longer than the vintage which ages for 70 years and has 60% Pinot

Noir, 30% Chardonnay, and 10% Pinot Meunier, Memoris is an assemblage from the years of 80% Pinot Noir and 20% Chardonnay, aged for 6-8 years, and Héritage is a Blanc de Blanc with the base wines aged in barrique.

Champagne Barfontarc

18 Route de Bar-sur-Aube, 10200 Baroville	📞 +33 3 25 27 07 09
@ *champagne@barfontarc.com*	🏭 *Olivier Martin*
⊕ *www.champagne-barfontarc.com*	*[map p. 60]*
🏃 € ⛏ ▬	*127 ha; 1,500,000 btl*

The cooperative of Barfontarc was founded in 1962—the name is an amalgam from the names of the villages Baroville, Fontaine, and Arconville on the Côte des Bar—by 50 growers, all of whom are still members. (A handful have started to produce their own wines, but they distribute them through the coop.) Vineyards are in 7 villages within a 10 mile range of the coop. Cuvées range from entry-level to specialized, and there is also a separate high-end label called Eugène III (mostly distributed in the United States). The two brands together account for about a quarter of all production. The Barfontarc nonvintage Brut is 80% Pinot Noir with 20% Chardonnay and is not overly fruity. The Eugène III Blanc de Noirs makes a classic impression, more full-bodied than the Brut. The Eugène III rosé is made by assemblage and makes quite a savory impression.

Champagne Edmond Barnaut

1 place André Collard, 51150 Bouzy	📞 +33 3 26 57 01 54
@ *contact@champagne-barnaut.fr*	🏭 *Philippe Secondé*
⊕ *www.champagne-barnaut-bouzy.com*	*[map p. 57]*
🏃 € ⛏ 🍇 ☺	*12 ha; 80,000 btl*

Founded in 1874, the house takes its name from its founder; it is now in the fifth generation under Philippe Secondé, who took over in 1985. Located in Bouzy, Pinots are three quarters of plantings, and the focus is on Pinot Noir (90%). Most of the vineyards are in Bouzy, and most of the cuvées are marked Grand Cru. The house is known for producing still red Bouzy as well as a complete range of champagnes. A perpetual reserve is used for the champagnes, and malolactic fermentation usually occurs. Dosage is low, 6 g/l for the Brut cuvées, and actually zero for the Extra Brut. In the center of Bouzy, there is a shop and tasting room in an old house above the cellars, managed by Laurette Secondé.

Champagne Barrat-Masson

20 rue Jaillard, 10370 Villenauxe La Grande	📞 +33 6 76 68 87 35
@ *champagnebarrat-masson@orange.fr*	🏭 *Aurélie & Loïc Barrat*
⊕ *champagne-barrat-masson.com*	
📅 ⛏ 🍇 ▨	*4 ha; 18,000 btl*

Loïc Barrat took over his family vineyards on the Côte de Sézanne in 2005, together with Aurélie, who is an oenologue. They converted to organic viticulture in 2009 and started to produce their own Champagne from plantings of 90% Pinot Noir and 10% Chardonnay. Although the domain is small, there is a range of 6 nonvintage cuvées as well as a vintage. Dosage is very low or zero. To increase flavor diversity, base wines for nonvintage cuvées age in a mix of (15-70%) barriques or demi-muids and vat for 9 months on the lees. Fleur de Craie is a Blanc de Blancs, and Grain d'Argile is 70% Chardonnay and 30% Pinot Noir, both labeled as Extra Brut, but actually they may have no dosage. Labeled as Brut Nature, Les Margannes is Blanc de Blancs, La Grande Homée is Blanc de Noirs, Les Volies has equal Pinot Noir and Chardonnay, and Nuances de Cornoie has 60% Chardonnay and 40% Pinot Noir. The vintage is a Blanc de Blancs from the best plots of Chardonnay. (The vintage base wine ages entirely under oak.) Disgorgement for all cuvées is done in the old style, à la volé. This is a very artisanal domain.

Champagne Phal B de Beaufort

25 rue de Tours sur Marne, 51150 Bouzy	📞 +33 3 26 52 12 49
@ contact@phalb-de-beaufort.fr	👤 Brigitte Beaufort
🌐 www.champagne-phalb-de-beaufort.fr	[map p. 57]
📅 €€ ⛏ 🍇 🍷	4 ha; 6,000 btl

The family has long owned vineyards but did not produce Champagne until Brigitte Beaufort gave up her career in computing and founded the house in 2008. Her children Pierre-Herbert and Anne-Louise are now involved. This is a small house, but even so, its vineyards are divided into 14 separate parcels, in the grand cru villages of Bouzy, Ambonnay, and Tours sur Marne. Vines have an average age of 35 years. The house has an unusual policy of producing only vintage Champagne. There are three cuvées, Expression is 75% Pinot Noir and 25% Chardonnay, with dosage of 6-8 g/l, depending on vintage. Privilège is Extra Brut (with 4 g/l dosage), exclusively from three parcels in Bouzy, with 80% Pinot Noir and 20% Chardonnay. The rosé, Harmonie, also comes only from Bouzy, and has 12% Bouzy red wine plus a mix that varies from 44-86% Chardonnay, with the rest Pinot Noir. None of the cuvées have malolactic fermentation.

Champagne Beaumont des Crayères

64 Rue de La Liberté, 51530 Mardeuil	📞 +33 3 26 55 29 40
@ contact@champagne-beaumont.com	👤 Olivier Piazza
🌐 www.champagne-beaumont.com	[map p. 56]
🧍 ⛏ 🍇	86 ha; 600,000 btl

This cooperative was founded in 1955 by a group of growers around Mardeuil, and takes its name from the famous hill in the vicinity. Today it has 245 members. A new cuverie was built in 2012. 70% of production is sold under its own label or other marques, with another 10% labeled directly with the names of its members, and 20% sold to negociants. Pinot Meunier represents 60% of plantings, 15% is Pinot Noir, and 25% is Chardonnay. The objective is to produce "a very fruity style of Champagne." The style here shows a break from the obvious fruits and dosage of the Grande Réserve Brut (which exactly represents the proportion of plantings) and the Rosé Brut nonvintage (with more Pinot Noir) to the better integrated impressions of the vintage Blanc de Blancs or Blanc de Noirs. The Blanc de Noirs is 70% Pinot Noir and 30% Pinot Meunier and is quite full-bodied. The exception to the usual dosage of 9-10 g is Fleur de Meunier, a 100% Pinot Meunier Blanc de Noirs that is Brut Nature, and surprisingly full on the palate. Another exception is the Fleur de Prestige vintage—"this goes against the grain for the house and is 50% Chardonnay"—which is deep with something of the tang of Blanc de Blancs. The wines are generally best enjoyed fairly soon after release.

Champagne Françoise Bedel

71 Grand Rue, 02310 Crouttes-sur-Marne	📞 +33 3 23 82 15 80
@ contact@champagne-bedel.fr	👤 Françoise Bedel
🌐 www.champagne-bedel.fr	
🧍 €€ ⛏ 🍇 🍷	9 ha; 45,000 btl

Almost off the map of Champagne, located at the far western border, this domain was created when Fernand and Marie-Louise Bedel turned from polyculture to making wine in 1957. Their daughter Françoise took over in 1976, and has worked with her son Vincent since 2003. A new cellar was built in 2015. With a classic mix for the Vallée de la Marne, most of the plantings are black, almost all Pinot Meunier. In nonvintage, Origin'elle is 90% Pinot Meunier and 10% Pinot Noir; Dis "Vin Secret" comes from limestone, whereas Entre Ciel and Terre comes from calcareous clay. In vintage. l'Ame de Terre is a selection of lots to bring out vintage character, and Comme Autrefois is the sole cuvée to be aged solely in oak. All except Comme Autrefois are Extra Brut.

Champagne H.Billiot & Fils

1 Place de la Fontaine, 51150 Ambonnay	📞 +33 6 11 31 51 51
@ contact@champagnebilliot.fr	👤 Laetitia Billiot
🌐 www.champagnebilliot.fr	[map p. 57]
📅 € 🏭 🍇 🍷	5 ha; 32,000 btl

Eugène Billiot purchased vineyards in 1896 and sold the grapes, Louis Billiot started producing wine in 1937, and the eponymous Henri Billiot took over in 1960. Laetitia Billiot, the fifth generation, took over in 1910. All the vineyards are in Ambonnay, planted with 75% Pinot Noir and 25% Chardonnay. Tradition is the principal cuvée, with the same blend as the vineyards. Reserve has the same assemblage but spends a year longer on the lees. The rosé is made by saignée. Julie is a prestige cuvée, with equal Pinot Noir and Chardonnay, aged in oak. Laetitia is a "perpetual cuvée," which is to say that the blend goes back to the 1980s and is refreshed in the best years.

Champagne Maxime Blin

11 rue du Point du Jour, 51140 Trigny	📞 +33 3 26 03 10 97
@ contact@champagne-blin-et-fils.fr	👤 Maxime Blin
🌐 maxime.blin@champagne-blin-et-fils.fr	[map p. 54]
🏃 🏭 🍇 🍷	12 ha; 100,000 btl

Founded by Robert Blin in 1960, this was originally known as Champagne R. Blin et fils, producing its own Champagne since 1988. Robert's son Gilles took over, was joined by his son Maxime in 2004, and then handed over in 2014. Wines are now produced under the label of Maxime Blin. Vineyards are in the Massif de St Thierry, northwest of Reims. Vineyards are around Trigny. Blends include Grande Tradition (90% Chardonnay, 10% Pinot Noir) and Maxime Blin (a third of each variety). The rosés come from Pinot Noir, including L'Authentique (rosé de saignée). Carte Blanche is (Blanc de Noirs from 80% Pinot Meunier and 20% Pinot Noir), Carte Douce has the same blend but is demi-sec. In vintage, there is a Blanc de Noirs Brut and a Blanc de Noirs Brut Nature. La Clé d'Éole is a tiny production of Blanc de Blancs, vinified in barrique.

Champagne Boizel

46 Avenue de Champagne, 51205 Épernay	📞 +33 3 26 55 21 51
@ boizelinfo@boizel.fr	👤 Florent Roques-Boizel
🌐 www.boizel.com	[map p. 58]
🏃 € 🏭 🏠 🍷	7 ha; 500,000 btl Owner: Lanson-BCC

Founded in 1834 as a negociant house, and since 1994 part of the Lanson-BCC group, Boizel is in the fifth generation under Evelyne and Christophe. Estate grapes provide 10% of sources. The wines are divided into three ranges. There are four Essential cuvées. In nonvintage, Brut Réserve is 55% Pinot Noir with 30% Chardonnay and 15% Pinot Meunier; with a nice weight to the palate, it is flavorful. The rosé is made by assemblage, and is softer, with more amorphous fruits. The Blanc de Blancs comes from the Côte des Blancs. All have dosage of 8 g/l. The Exceptional range has a Blanc de Noirs, the Ultime cuvée, a demi-sec, and the Cuvée Sous-Bois vintage matured in oak. The Ultime Extra Brut is in fact a zero dosage; the same blend as the Brut Réserve, longer aging compensates for the lack of sugar, and the wine is only a touch drier, and a little more linear. With only 4 g dosage, the vintage has an increased sense of precision. Joyau de France is a vintage using only premier and grand cru grapes; with equal proportions of Pinot Noir and Chardonnay, and its longer aging shows in greater depth.

Champagne Bonnet-Gilmert

10 Bis, rue de La Côte, 51190 Oger	📞 +33 3 26 53 86 08
@ contact@champagne-bonnet-gilmert.com	👤 Aude Vauban-Menuel
🌐 www.champagne-bonnet-gilmert.com	[map p. 59]
📅 ⛏ 🍇 ☖ 7 ha	🍾 Extra Brut Réserve

"My grandparents established the domain," says Aude Vauban-Menuel. It was created when Colette Gilmert, whose grandfather had started producing Champagne in 1910, married Robert Bonnet in the 1950s. The estate vineyards have only Chardonnay, and the focus is on three cuvées of Blanc de Blancs: the Réserve, the Extra Brut, and the vintage. Spending a year longer before release, the Extra Brut shows the character of Blanc de Blancs more clearly, and there is another step up to the greater density of the vintage. There are two rosés: the Rosé d'Assemblage is based on Chardonnay with a little Pinot Noir; the Rosé de Saignée is Pinot Noir and Pinot Meunier (for which grapes are purchased). Dosage is moderate, around 6g/l for most cuvées (the Brut Réserve is a little higher).

Champagne Franck Bonville

9 rue Pasteur, 51190 Avize	📞 +33 3 26 57 52 30
@ contact@champagnebonville.fr	👤 Olivier Bonville
🌐 www.champagne-franck-bonville.com	[map p. 59]
📅 ⛏ 🍇 ☖	15 ha; 150,000 btl

Alfred Bonville started buying vineyards at the start of the twentieth century, just after phylloxera struck. With his son Franck, he started to make wine in 1937. The estate grew to its present size after the second world war, and is now run by the fourth generation. Vineyards are in Cramant, Oger et Avize (all grand cru), planted exclusively with Chardonnay. Except for the rosé (which uses some red wine from Ambonnay) all the cuvées are Blanc de Blancs. Dosage is moderate, 5 g/l for the Brut, 2.5 g/l for the Extra Brut. and 8 g/l for the vintage. The Brut Prestige (7 g/l) is a selection of the best lots, and Les Belles Voyes (2.5 g/l) comes from a single vineyard in Oger.

Champagne Francis Boulard & Fille

13 Rue de la Censé Flancourt, 51170 Faverolles et Coëmy	📞 +33 3 26 61 52 77
@ contact@francis-boulard.com	👤 Delphine Boulard
🌐 www.francis-boulard.com	[map p. 53]
📅 €€ ⛏ 🗄 🍇 ◐ 🍇	4 ha; 25,000 btl

This is both a new and an old producer. The three siblings who inherited Champagne Raymond Boulard split up in 2009, and Francis Boulard, together with his daughter Delphine, formed his own house with his share of the vineyards. Francis retired in 2018. The estate is one of the few located to the north of Reims; most of the vineyards are in the Massif de Saint Thierry, with 30% each of Chardonnay and Pinot Noir, and 40% of Pinot Meunier. Vinification is casks of old oak of varying sizes. The flagship wine is Les Murgiers, a Blanc de Noirs that comes exclusively from Pinot Meunier. The Vieilles Vignes is a Blanc de Blancs. Vintage cuvées include a Grand Cru Blanc de Blancs from Mailly, Les Rachais from Saint Thierry, and Les Rachais rosé. Dosage is always very low, either at the lower end of Extra Brut (2-3 g/l) or zero.

Champagne Bourgeois-Diaz

43 Grande Rue, 02310 Crouttes-sur-Marne	📞 *+33 3 23 82 18 35*
@ *bourgeois-diaz@wanadoo.fr*	👤 *Charlotte & Jérôme Bourgeois*
⊕ *www.bourgeois-diaz.com*	
🗓 🏭 🍇 🍷	*7 ha; 40,000 btl*

In the far west of the Champagne area, half way between Reims and Paris, close to the Marne, Jérôme Bourgeois-Diaz took over his family estate in 2001, after previously working in industrial sales. Plantings are 40% Pinot Meunier and 30% each of Pinot Noir and Chardonnay. The style is lean, with really low dosage for all cuvées. BD'3C represents the domain as a whole, with a blend of all varieties, and dosage of 3 g/l, aged for 24 months. BD'3CC ages for longer, up to 60 months, with only 2 g/l dosage. BD'N is a Blanc de Noirs from 70% Pinot Noir and 30% Pinot Meunier. BD'M is 100% Pinot Meunier from 60-year-old vines with no dosage. BD'N and BD'M are vinified in a mix of stainless steel and used barriques. The BD'B is Blanc de Blancs from a single parcel of old vines, fermented and partially aged in barriques including some new wood, with only 1 g/l dosage. BD'RS is a rosé de saignée from 100% Pinot Meunier with zero dosage.

Champagne Château de Boursault

2 Rue Maurice Gilbert, 51480 Boursault	📞 *+33 3 26 58 42 21*
@ *info@champagnechateau.com*	👤 *Alex Fringhian*
⊕ *champagne-chateau-de-boursault.fr*	*[map p. 56]*
🗓 € 🏭 🍇 🕯	*13 ha*

This is an unusual property for the Champagne area, a real château, constructed in 1843-1850 in neo-Renaissance style by the Veuve Clicquot on the left bank of the river Marne, and given to her granddaughter as a marriage present. The domain is in a single holding, with the vineyard surrounded by a stone wall. The château was sold and became a military hospital in the first world war. Achod Fringham bought the property in 1927, and it was run by his grandson Harald Fringham since 1975, joined in 2015 by his son Alex, who has now taken over. Reflecting the location in the Marne, Pinot Meunier is strong here. The Tradition cuvée is in aperitif style, with 40% each Pinot Noir and Pinot Meunier, and 20% Chardonnay. The Brut Nature is 50% Pinot Meunier and 25% each Pinot Noir and Chardonnay. The rosé is made by saignée, and has 47% Pinot Meunier, 27% Pinot Noir, and 26% Chardonnay. The Blanc de Noirs is 60% Pinot Meunier and 40% Pinot Noir. Only two cuvées exclude Pinot Meunier. Prestige has equal Pinot Noir and Chardonnay, and spends four years on the lees before disgorgement. Vintage has three quarters Pinot Noir and a quarter Chardonnay, and spends 14 years on the lees before disgorgement. The house is into oenotourism and offers a range of tours and tastings. Tours of the vineyards are available as well as tastings and visits to the cellars.

Champagne Breton Fils

12 Rue Courte Pilate, 51270 Congy	📞 +33 3 26 59 31 03
@ *contact@champagne-breton-fils.fr*	👤 Reynald Breton
🌐 *www.champagne-breton-fils.com*	*[map p. 53]*
🧍 🏭 🍇	*16 ha*

The domain was founded in 1945 when Olivette and Ange Breton started to produce Champagne from a few rows of vines: the first year was 3,000 bottles. Ange expanded the vineyards with plots in 11 communes and built cellars at Congy, between the Côte de Sézanne and the Côte des Blancs; he handed over to his son Reynaud in 2009. The Classic range has Brut (a third of each variety), Rosé, and Blanc de Blancs, and the Brut de Brut zero dosage (equal Pinot Noir and Chardonnay). There is also a Prestige range with all styles. The Caviste range has the Symphonie Brut (equal Pinot Noir and Chardonnay), the Sarabande rosé, and the Impromptu Blanc de Blancs from Sézanne. Vintage is Blanc de Blancs. All the brut cuvées have dosage of 9 g/l. The classic range ages for 3 years before disgorgement, Caviste and Prestige for 5-6 years, and Vintage for 10 years.

Champagne Louis Brochet

12 Rue Villers au Noeuds, 51500 Écueil	📞 +33 3 26 49 77 44
@ *contact@champagne-brochet.com*	👤 Hélène Brochet
🌐 *www.champagne-brochet.com*	*[map p. 55]*
🗓 🍷 🏭 🍇 🍃	*13 ha; 90,000 btl*

The Brochet family has been growing grapes at Ecueil, a premier cru village in the Petite Montagne de Reims, since 1674. They've been producing their own Champagne since 1943. Alain Brochet ran the domain for 45 years until 2011, when Louis and his sister Hélène took over. Vineyards are in 50 separate plots around Ecueil. Cuvées are dominated by Pinot Noir, typically with around 80% Pinot Noir, 15% Chardonnay, and 5% Pinot Meunier, including brut, extra brut. and rosé. La Réserve Perpetuelle is a Blanc de Noirs from a solera system established in 2010. L'Extra Noir and L'Extra Blanc come from parcels in premier cru vineyards and are extra brut. The vintage is typically about two third Pinot Noir and a third Chardonnay, with a prestige vintage, HBH, in some years from equal Pinot Noir and Chardonnay. There are several possibilities for tours and tastings, including yoga and other workshops.

Brun Servenay

Place Léon Bourgeois, 51190 Avize	📞 +33 3 26 57 52 75
@ *contact@champagnelebrun.com*	👤 Gauthier Brun
🌐 *www.champagnelebrun.com*	*[map p. 59]*
🗓 🏭 🍇 🍃	*7 ha; 40,000 btl*

The house was created in 1955 after a marriage between the Le Brun family, who have had Chardonnay in Avize for four generations, and the Servenays, who had Pinot Noir and Pinot Meunier in Mancy to the west of Avize. The domain started with 4 ha, in the next generation Patrick took over in 1992 and expanded the domain, and then after a divorce it was reduced to today's size, more or less with half in Avize, Cramant, and Oger, and half in Mancy. Patrick's son Gauthier took over in 2017. Plantings include many old vines, with an average age for the nonvintage cuvées of 35 years, rising to 65 years for the vintage. Vinification is in stainless steel, and malolactic fermentation is usually blocked. The nonvintage Réserve is 50% Chardonnay and 25% each of Pinot Noir and Pinot Meunier, and comes as Brut (with 7 g/l dosage) and Extra Brut (with 3 g/l dosage). Rosé is 90% Chardonnay and also comes as Brut or Extra

Brut. There's some wood aging for the rosé. In vintage there is the Exhilarante blend of 80% Chardonnay with 10% each of Pinot Noir and Pinot Meunier, with dosage of 4 g/l. The vintage Blanc de Blancs comes from the oldest (80-year) vines, and is also Extra Brut. The style is pushed further with the X.B. (Extra Brut) cuvées, which have 2.5 g/l dosage for the Blanc de Blancs, and 3.2 g/l for the rosé.

Champagne Canard-Duchêne

1 rue Edmond Canard, 51500 Ludes	☎ +33 3 26 61 11 60
@ info@canard-duchene.fr	
⊕ www.canard-duchene.fr	[map p. 57]
🉑 € ⛏ 🏠	55 ha; 4,000,000 btl
	Owner: Champagne Joseph Perrier

This well-known house has a curious history. It started in 1959 as a Maison in the Montagne de Reims when Victor Canard married Léone Duchêne. Canard-Duchêne was purchased by Veuve Clicquot in 1978 and became part of LVMH, but was sold in 2003 to the Alain Thiénot group when LVMH decided to concentrate on its best-known brands. Laurent Fédou, who was the cellarmaster at Champagne Alain Thiénot (see profile) became cellarmaster at Canard Duchêne also. The style is middle-of-the-road: well made, but rarely exciting, easy to drink with dosage a little on the high side, around 10 g/l for the Brut.

Champagne Cattier

6-11 rue Dom Pérignon, BP 15, 51500 Chigny Les Roses	☎ +33 3 26 03 42 11
@ champagne@cattier.com	👤 Alexandre Cattier
⊕ www.cattier.com	[map p. 57]
🉑 ⛏ 🏠	20 ha

This old family domain started with grape-growing at Chigny Les Roses, in the Montagne de Reims, in the seventeenth century. Bottling Champagne from estate grapes started in 1918, and was extended by purchasing grapes after 1978. Alexandre Cattier took over in 2011, representing the 11th generation. "We use more Pinot Meunier than average," he says. The Brut premier cru is 40% Pinot Meunier, 35% Pinot Noir, and 25% Chardonnay. Style is quite mainstream. The Blanc de Blancs is more linear. The rosé has 40% Pinot Meunier and 50% Pinot Noir, and is soft and perfumed—"this is a wine for summer." Even the vintage has a third Pinot Meunier, together with a third each of Pinot Noir and Chardonnay; it shows greater depth than the non-vintage. The style reflects the focus on Pinot Meunier, tending towards breadth on the palate.

Champagne Claude Cazals

28 rue du Grand Mont, 51190 Le Mesnil-sur-Oger	☎ +33 3 26 57 52 26
@ contact@champagne-cazals.fr	👤 Delphine Cazals
⊕ www.champagne-cazals.fr	[map p. 59]
🉑 ⛏ 🍃 🥂	9 ha; 80,000 btl

Ernest Cazals founded the house in 1897; now it is in the fourth generation under Delphine Cazals. Vineyards are in four communes of the Côte des Blancs: grand crus Oger and Le Mesnil-sur-Oger, and premier crus Vertus and Villeneuve. The top cuvée, Clos Cazals, comes from a 3.7 ha vineyard in Oger (purchased in 1950 by Delphine's grandfather). It is a vintage Extra Brut Blanc de Blancs made from the oldest (60-year) vines, and spends 10 years on the lees. La Chapelle du Clos is a vintage Brut from younger vines in the Clos, and spends 8 years on the lees. There is also a vintage Brut Blanc de Blancs from the other vineyards. The three non-vintage cuvées include Brut, Extra Brut, and Grand Cru. Delphine's father, Claude Cazals, also had the distinction of inventing the gyropalette.

Champagne Roland Champion

19 Grande Rue, 51530 Chouilly	📞 +33 3 26 55 40 30
@ contact@champagne-roland-champion.com	👤 Carole Champion
🌐 www.champagne-roland-champion.com	[map p. 58]
🗓 🏭 🍇	18 ha; 85,000 btl

The Champions were well established as grape growers when André Champion started to produce champagne in 1929. His son Roland subsequently took over, expanded the vineyards, and founded the house in 1951. Roland's son François is in charge today, together has daughter Carole. Vineyards consist of 40 parcels in Chouilly (on the Côte des Blancs) and Verneuil and Vandière (in the Vallée de la Marne). About half the production is bottled under the Roland Champion label; the rest is sold to negociants. The nonvintage Carte Blanche and vintage Carte Noir are grand cru Blanc de Blancs from Chouilly; Cuvée d'Aramis comes from the Vallée de la Marne. The domain is a member of the Special Club organization and makes a Blanc de Blancs vintage under that label.

Champagne Georges de la Chapelle

Champagne Prat, 9 rue des Ruiselots, 51130 Vert Toulon	📞 +33 3 26 52 12 16
@ info@champagneprat.com	👤 Aurèlia Prat
🌐 www.georgesdelachapelle.com	[map p. 53]
🧑 🏭 🍇 14 ha; 100,000 btl	🍾 Blanc de Blancs

There are effectively two brands under one roof. Yveline and Alain Prat created their Champagne house in 1975. They describe the style of Champagne Prat as "light and fruity." In 2002 they created a higher-end brand, which they called Champagne Georges de la Chapelle after Uncle Georges, who helped them start up. The house is located on the edge of the Côte des Blancs, but there 41 different vineyard plots in 9 villages. Lower dosage gives the Extra Brut more definition than the Brut, but the Blanc de Blancs is distinctly a notch further up. Nostalgie is a selection of the best lots and has greater density and weight. All the wines are vinified in steel, except Fûts de Chêne, aged in 4-year-old barriques, with a more savory style.

Champagne Denis Chaput

8 Rue de la Souche, 10200 Arrentières	📞 +33 6 38 48 71 67
@ contact@champagne-denischaput.com	👤 Nicolas & Xavier Chaput
🌐 www.champagne-denischaput.com	[map p. 60]
🧑 € 🏭 🍇 ⟳ 12 ha; 35,000 btl	🍾 Blanc de Noirs

This family domain dates from 1862. The house is located on the Aube, in the Côte des Bar, with 26 different plots. Plantings are only Pinot Noir and Chardonnay: there is no Pinot Meunier. The cuvées have all been nonvintage, but in 2019 the first vintage (2012) is being released. Sometimes the Blanc de Blancs comes from a single year, and so is effectively an undeclared vintage, but this is not always the case. Cuvées Tradition and Réserve have 70-75% Pinot Noir: Tradition represents the Côte des Bar in the house style of elegance and minerality, Réserve has a slightly drier and more savory impression. The Blanc de Blancs has that crisp dryness of Chardonnay, and the Blanc de Noirs shows the richness of Pinot Noir and the Côte des Bar.

Champagne Guy Charlemagne

4 rue de la Brèche d'Oger, 51190 Le Mesnil-sur-Oger	📞 +33 3 26 57 52 98
@ champagneguycharlemagne@orange.fr	👤 Elodie Caraskakis
🌐 www.champagne-guy-charlemagne.com	[map p. 59]
📅 🏭 🏠 🌿	14 ha; 90,000 btl

Founded in 1892, this house is now in its fifth generation under Philippe Charlemagne, who took over in 1988. Most of the vineyards are on the Côte des Blancs, in Le Mesnil and Oger, but there are also some farther south on the Côte de Sézanne. Brut Classic and Brute Nature come from the Côte de Sézanne, while Réserve Blanc de Blancs comes from the Côte des Blancs. Cuvée Charlemagne is a Blanc de Blancs selected from the best lots in Le Mesnil and Oger. The top wine is Mesnillésime, a vintage Blanc de Blancs from the oldest vines in Le Mesnil. The rosé comes exclusively from Pinot Noir.

Champagne Vincent Charlot

23, rue des Semons, 51530 Mardeuil	📞 +33 3 26 51 93 92
@ champcharlottanneux@free.fr	👤 Vincent Charlot
🌐 champagne-charlot-tanneux.fr	[map p. 58]
📅 € 🏭 🍇 🍶	4 ha; 30,000 btl

Vincent Charlot is committed to biodynamics and beyond, meaning that he not only makes the standard preparations, but also adds some experimental recipes of his own. Grapes from his family domain were sold to the negociants until he took over in 2001. Just to the west of Épernay, most of his 39 plots are planted with Pinot Meunier. Wines blended from several parcels are labeled as Champagne Charlot-Tanneux, while single-vineyard wines, produced only in top vintages, are labeled as Champagne Vincent Charlot. All the latter are Extra Brut.

Champagne Chassenay d'Arce

11 rue du Pressoir, 10110 Ville-sur-Arce	📞 +33 3 25 38 30 70
@ champagne@chassenay.com	👤 Florie Landry
🌐 chassenay.com	[map p. 60]
📅 €€ 🏭 ▬	315 ha

This cooperative was founded by five growers in 1956 and now has 130 members, who cultivate more than 300 ha in 12 villages across the Arce valley (near Bar-sur-Seine). As usual for a cooperative, there is a wide range, biased towards use of Pinot Noir that's common on the Côte des Bar. All wines ferment and are held in stainless steel. There is usually partial malolactic fermentation. Wines age longer than regulations require, typically about 4 years for nonvintage, and up to 10 years for vintage. Dosage tends to be a touch on the sweet side, at 8-10 g/l for brut. The top cuvée is the vintage Confidences, which comes from the oldest vines, has 8% aged in barriques, and dosage at 7 g/l for both brut and rosé. One unusual feature here is the use of Pinot Blanc, in small proportions in Confidence and some other cuvées including the vintage Blanc de Blancs, and making the monovarietal Pinot Blanc vintage release, an extra brut with 3 g/l dosage.

Champagne La Closerie

65 rue des Dames de France, 51390 Gueux	📞 +33 3 26 03 48 60
@ champagnelacloserie@orange.fr	👤 Jérôme Prévost

www.champagnelacloserie.fr	*[map p. 55]*
	*2 ha; 14,000 btl*

Jérôme Prévost created this tiny estate just outside Reims in 1987 with vineyards he inherited from his grandmother, who had been renting out the vineyards. He started selling the grapes, but started to make wine in 1998 under the advice of Anselme Selosse, initially borrowing some space in the Selosse cellars until his own cellar was constructed at his house in Gueux. His vineyard is planted with Pinot Meunier (94%) and a tiny amount of Chardonnay and Pinot Gris, and it makes a single cuvée, produced as an Extra Brut with only 2.5 g/l dosage each year (effectively as an undeclared vintage). It carries the name of the vineyard, Les Béguines, and has become something of a cult. Occasionally he also makes a rosé, called Fac Similé, also based on Les Béguines. Wines are aged in a range of oak casks from barriques to tonneaux.

Champagne André Clouet

8 rue Gambetta, 51150 Bouzy	📞 *+33 3 26 57 00 82*
@ *secretariatandreclouet@yahoo.fr*	👤 *Jean-François Clouet*
🌐 *www.andreclouet.com*	*[map p. 57]*
	9 ha

"Everything is 100% Pinot Noir and 100% Grand Cru," says Jean-François Clouet. Vineyards are mostly around Bouzy with some in Ambonnay. I'm inclined to say that flavor is the hallmark of the house, as all the cuvées have a certain intensity, ripe on the palate with a mineral tang at the end. The Grand Réserve Blanc de Noirs is relatively crisp. Rosé No. 3 uses Clouet's own Bouzy red, is barely softer than the other cuvées, and inclined in a savory direction. The best known cuvée is the 1911, a selection from the best plots of Pinot Noir. The story goes that it's a homage to the 1911 vintage, after a case was found in 1991, and turned out still to be in top condition. (1911 was the year of the riots in Champagne). It's a multivintage blend from recent vintages, and only 1,911 numbered bottles are made each year. It spends 7 years on the lees and has 6 g/l dosage.

Champagne Paul Clouet

place André Tritant, 51150 Bouzy	📞 *+33 3 26 53 97 58*
@ *contact@champagne-paul-clouet.com*	👤 *Jean-Emmanuel Bonnaire*
🌐 *www.champagne-paul-clouet.com*	*[map p. 57]*
	6 ha; 60,000 btl

Paul Clouet founded the domain in 1907, it was subsequently taken over by his daughter, and when she died in 1970, her two daughters continued. After some difficulties, Marie-Thérèse Clouet-Bonnaire relaunched the brand in 1992, based on the family vineyards in Bouzy, effectively all planted with Pinot Noir. Her husband, Jean-Louis Bonnaire, had his own domain in Cramant (see profile), and made the wines until his death in 2015. Their son, Jean-Emmanuel Bonnaire, now makes the wines in Cramant for both houses. Brut and rosé are the same for both houses, but the rest of the range is distinct. Grand Cru Brut is quite tight. Cuvée Prestige comes from the oldest vines, and is weightier and broader, but still in a relatively austere style. The wines have the richness of Bouzy in a restrained style.

Champagne Coessens

Chemin Les Farces, 10110 Ville-sur-Arce	📞 *+33 3 51 63 70 48*
@ *contact@champagne-coessens.com*	👤 *Jérome Coessens*

www.champagne-coessens.com

[map p. 60]

7 ha; 20,000 btl

This small family estate has a single vineyard holding on the Côte des Bar. Although it's one block, and planted exclusively with Pinot Noir, Jérôme Coessens has been producing eight micro-cuvées to focus on different aspects since he took over in 2008. The parcel is called L'Argillier, referring to its terroir of clay and Kimmeridgian limestone, and Jérôme divides it into four parts which he calls, Minéral, Fruit, Fleur (flower), and Matière (extract). The best parts, with the oldest vines, are used for production: grapes from some other parts are sold off. Except for a solera, all the cuvées come from single vintages, so here is the extreme expression of terroir and climate. "I compose eight different wines by playing the game of blending or not from the four sub-parcels, with the effect of the vintage as well as vinification," Jérôme says. There are six Champagne cuvées and two dry red wines. With one exception the Champagnes all see only stainless steel. Malolactic fermentation is done for all cuvées. Blanc de Noirs is a blend from Fruit and Fleur, Brut Nature comes from Minéral, Rosé de Saignée comes from Matière, Les Sens Boisé also comes from Matière but ages in barriques, Millésime is a declared vintage Extra Brut, and at the other extreme, Caresse d'Automne comes from a solera containing lots from all four sub-parcels. Jérôme took advice from Yves Confuron of Domaine Confuron-Cotetidot in Burgundy on making still red wine (labeled Coteaux Champenois), and even here cannot resist the opportunity to play with the variables. Vendange Egrappé has all the berries destemmed, while Vendange Entière is made from whole clusters.

Champagne Colin

101 avenue du Général de Gaulle, 51130 Vertus	📞 +33 3 26 58 86 32
@ *info@champagne-colin.com*	👤 *Delphine Colin*
⊕ *www.champagne-colin.com*	[map p. 59]
	11 ha; 90,000 btl

This small family domain in the Côte des Blancs has a typical focus on Chardonnay. The heart is the 6 ha in the premier cru village of Vertus, and there are smaller plots totaling 1 ha in the grand cru villages of Cramant and Oiry. Pinot Noir and Pinot Meunier come from 3 ha in Sézanne. The house is now effectively in its third generation of producing Champagne, but has been growing grapes for two centuries. The nonvintage Alliance cuvée (7 g/l dosage) is a blend of various holdings, but the house really expresses its style with the Blanc de Blancs Blanche de Castille, which comes from the premier cru villages. "This is typical of the house," Delphine Colin says. The Extra Brut Blanc de Blancs (3 g/ dosage), Parallèle, spends a year longer on the lees, and moves in a more savory direction. The vintage Blanc de Blancs comes from the Grand Cru holdings and conveys a sense of greater depth and extraction. Breaking the mold, the Rosé de Saignée (only 1,500 bottles) comes from 100% Pinot Noir; "this is rare on the Côte des Blancs," Delphine says. Fresh, with a sense of red berry fruits, it retains the elegance and savory character of the Côte des Blancs. The wines have character and are good value.

Champagne Collard-Picard

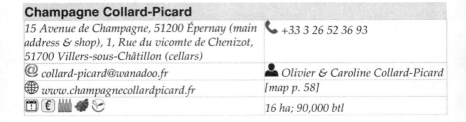

15 Avenue de Champagne, 51200 Épernay (main address & shop), 1, Rue du vicomte de Chenizot, 51700 Villers-sous-Châtillon (cellars)	📞 +33 3 26 52 36 93
@ *collard-picard@wanadoo.fr*	👤 *Olivier & Caroline Collard-Picard*
⊕ *www.champagnecollardpicard.fr*	[map p. 58]
	16 ha; 90,000 btl

The house was founded relatively recently, resulting from the marriage of Olivier Collard and Caroline Picard in 1996, which brought together vineyards in the Vallée de la Marne from the Collard side, and in Côte des Blancs from the Picard side. The winery is a modern building in the Vallée de la Marne, where most of the crop is Pinot Meunier, but Chardonnay comes from the vineyards in Le-Mesnil-sur-Oger. Malolactic fermentation is usually blocked; dosage varies from 12g to 8g (except for zero dosage). Vinified in stainless steel, the Blanc de Noirs and rosé are both half Pinot Noir and half Pinot Meunier. Cuvée Prestige is half Pinot Noir and Meunier from Vallée de la Marne, and half Chardonnay from the Côte des Blancs, vinified in tonneau, with 12g dosage at the limit for Brut. The same blend is used for the vintage Cuvée Prestige Millésimée. Cuvée des Merveilles Rosé is a single-vineyard wine from Vertus with 80% Pinot Noir, 20% Chardonnay, made by saignée. Dom Picard is a Blanc de Blancs from Côte des Blancs, Essential is the zero dosage equivalent of the Prestige Millésimée. The top cuvée is the Cuvée des Archives, 80% Chardonnay from the Côte des Blancs and 20% Pinot Noir from 100-year old vines in the Vallée de la Marne. The main address and shop are in Epernay; visits to the cellars in Villers-sous-Châtillon are available only as a (very expensive) VIP tour.

Champagne Ulysse Collin

19-21 rue des vignerons, 51270 Congy	📞 *+33 3 26 59 35 48*
@ *champagne-ulysse.collin@orange.fr*	👤 *Olivier Collin*
🗓 ⚗ 🍷 🕸 *9 ha; 50,000 btl*	*[map p. 53]*

His experience working with Anselme Selosse in 2001 drove Ulysse Collin to take back the family vineyards, at Congy between the Côte de Sézanne and the Côte des Blancs, that had been rented out to Pommery. "At the time I wasn't sure if I'd ever be a vigneron; you don't regain an estate from a négociant that easily," he recollects. He started with 4.5 ha and rented equipment in 2003; his first cuvée was a Blanc de Blancs from the 1.2 ha plot of Les Perrières the following year. The Blanc de Noirs Les Maillons followed in 2006. The estate expanded when he took back a further 4.2 ha in 2005, together with cellars. Les Roises is the third cuvée, a Blanc de Blancs from 60-year-old vines. Wines are aged in old oak, dosage is minimal (1-2 g/l), because grapes are harvested late to be riper than normal.

Champagne Marie Copinet

chemin Plessis, Z.a. Bassin, 10370 Villenauxe Grande	📞 *+33 6 71 62 43 63*
@ *champagne@marie-copinet.com*	👤 *Marie-Laure Copinet*
🌐 *www.champagne-marie-copinet.com*	
🗓 🏭 ⚗ ▨ ◈	*9 ha; 66,000 btl*

Jacques Copinet founded the domain in 1975 when he was working for Taittinger, stopped selling the fruit, and started to bottle his own cuvées. His daughter Marie-Laure and her husband Alexandre Kowal took over in 2008, and started producing wine under their own label in 2016. Most of the vineyard parcels are on the Côte de Sézanne, near the tiny home village of Montgenost (the official address; but tastings take place at the cellars in Villenauxe La Grande); there are also some plots in the Vallée de la Marne and on the Côte des Bar. Wines are vinified in stainless steel, but the reserve is kept in 50 hl foudres and 300-liter barrels. The standard range has all styles of Brut (with dosage at 5-6 g/l) and a Blanc de Blancs Brut Nature. The Prestige range comes from more restricted sources: Monsieur Léonard and Alexandrine are Blanc de Blancs from the Coteaux Crayeux de Montgenost, with Alexandrine containing grapes only from vintage years. La Ruelle des Loups is a Blanc de Noirs from 60% Pinot Meunier and 40% Pinot Noir at Montigny in the Vallée de la Marne, and has the distinction of aging in a custom-built stainless steel egg. Dosage is 3 g/l. Argilla Villonissa is a Blanc de Blanc vinified in eggs. Two further ranges don't even mention Marie Copinet on the front

116

label. The Jardin range is the same wine at three different dosages: Jardin Sauvage has zero dosage, Jardin d'Été (extra brut) has 5g/l, and Jardin d'Automne (brut) has 11 g/l. Epreuve d'Artiste (with a large EA on the front label and Champagne Copinet shown discreetly only on the capsule) is a series of undeclared vintage Blanc de Blancs from different terroirs.

Champagne Vincent Couche

29 Grande Rue, 10110 Buxeuil	📞 +33 3 25 38 53 96
@ contact@champagne-couche.fr	👤 Vincent Couche
🌐 www.champagne-couche.fr	[map p. 60]
🗓 ⚒ 🍇 🍷 🍂 ∅	14 ha; 100,000 btl

Located on the Côte des Bar, Vincent Couche has Chardonnay at Montague, on 3 ha of south facing chalk terroir, with his main holding at Buxeuil, mostly planted with Pinot Noir, on soil varying from Kimmeridgian to limestone-clay. Planting density is high, around 10,000 vines/ha. Harvest is late to achieve sufficient ripeness to avoid the need for chaptalization. The focus here is on purity of expression, and the wines are generally Extra Brut except for two zero dosage cuvées. Elégance (80% Pinot Noir and 20% Chardonnay) lives up to its name, light on the palate, its elegant balance makes this an excellent aperitif. Brut Nature Chloé is based on a solera and is more reserved, less open, and is a halfway house in style to the Brut Nature Selection Parcellaire, which gives an impression of power. The vintage cuvée is a more intense version of Chloé. Chardonnay de Montague has the most textured impression and grip on the palate, and is more a wine to match food. The Rosé Desiré is softer and richer.

Champagne R.h. Coutier

7 rue Henri Iii,10 Boulevard des Fosses de Ronde, 51150 Ambonnay	📞 +33 3 26 57 02 55
@ info@champagnerhcoutier.fr	👤 Antoine Coutier
🗓 ⚒ 🍇 ▦ 9 ha; 60,000 btl	[map p. 57]

The organization of this house is a bit unusual. It is registered as RC, meaning that it can supply grapes to a cooperative, and receive wine in return to sell under its own label. However since 2015 it has left the cooperative, and Antoine Coutier functions as a grower, producing all four cuvées from estate grapes (although some grapes are still sold off). The style is not quite typical for Ambonnay, because Antoine's father, René, planted Chardonnay; he was the first grower to do so in Ambonnay. The nonvintage Brut Tradition and the vintage Brut both have 60% Pinot Noir and 40% Chardonnay, and there is also a nonvintage Blanc de Blancs. The top cuvée is Henri III, a Blanc de Noirs, and the only one to age in wood. Partial malolactic fermentation is used to preserve acidity.

Champagne Dehours & Fils

2 Rue de la Chapelle, 51700 Mareuil Le Port	📞 +33 3 26 52 71 75
@ contact@champagne-dehours.fr	👤 Jérôme Dehours
🌐 www.champagne-dehours.fr	[map p. 56]
🗓 ⚒ 🏠 🌿	14 ha; 85,000 btl

Located in the Vallée de la Marne, about 10 miles west of Épernay, the house was founded in 1930 by Ludovic Dehours. His son, Robert, died young, and the estate was managed by a financial group. Robert's son Jérôme took the estate back in 1996. Vineyards are dispersed into 42 parcels on the south side of the river, with the focus typical for the area on Pinot Meunier which amounts to about 60% of plantings, together with 30% Chardonnay and 10% Pinot

Noir. Jérôme introduced the "solera" or perpetual reserve system in 1998, in which some wine is added to the reserve each year. The Grande Réserve Brut includes about a quarter of reserve wine and has low dosage at 7 g/l. There is also a zero dosage version with an extra year's aging. Trio (S) is a Brut that comes entirely from a separate solera, from which 30% is withdrawn each year. Aside from the Brut blends, the wines are extra brut or zero dosage "to give the greatest purity of expression." Wines are aged in a mix of oak and steel, and malolactic fermentation is taken to completion. There are several single vineyard vintage wines, coming from the best locations on the middle of the slopes overlooking the river. Made in small amounts, there are usually around 200 cases per vintage. Les Genevraux and La Croix Joly come from plots of 50-year-old Pinot Meunier, La Côte en Bosses is a blend from all three varieties fermented together, and Brisefer is Blanc de Blancs.

Champagne Benoît Déhu

3 Rue Saint Georges, 02650 Fossoy	📞 +33 3 23 71 90 47
@ contact@champagne-dehu.com	👤 Benoît Déhu
🌐 www.champagne-dehu.com	
🚶 🏭 🍇 ▦	4 ha; 16,000 btl

Not quite off the map, but certainly at the far west of the Vallée de la Marne in AOP Champagne, the Déhu family has grown grapes for eight generations since 1787. They produced Champagne under their own name at the cooperative from the 1980s, until Benoît Déhu started his own production. Benoît worked previously for four years at Bollinger, and follows the same regime of vinifying in barriques. In fact, he makes his own barrels with wood from the estate. He started making wine from just a hectare of Pinot Meunier, from the plot La Rue des Noyers, producing one champagne and two still Coteaux Champenois, one white and one red. Then in 2013, he added two more plots, one Pinot Meunier and one Pinot Noir. From these came Initiation (a blend of Pinot Meunier from Rue des Noyers and Pinot Noir from another plot), and L'Orme (100% Pinot Noir from a plot at the bottom of the hill of Rue des Noyers). In addition to the initial focus on micro-cuvées from specific plots and varieties, which are labeled as Champagne Benoît Déhu, Benoît also produces more conventional blends under the name Champagne Déhu Père and Fils in both brut (usually with dosage of 9.5 g/l) and extra brut.

Champagne Maurice Delabaye et Fils

6 Rue Anatole France, 51480 Damery	📞 +33 3 26 51 94 91
@ champagne-delabaye@outlook.com	👤 Germain Delabaye
🌐 scev-delabaye@wanadoo.fr	[map p. 56]
▣ 🏭 🍇	10 ha

The estate started when Victor Delabaye began to grow grapes in 1921 at Damery. His son Maurice started to produce Champagne and founded the house in 1959. His son Germain took over in 2001, and was joined by his son Victor in 2014. Vineyards are around Epernay, with holdings in the premier crus of Cumières, Hautvillers, Dizy, and in grand cru Aÿ, and include 4 ha each of Pinot Noir and Pinot Meunier with 2 ha of Chardonnay. The blend of the Brut Original reflects plantings in the vineyards, aged for 24 months. The Brut Prestige comes only from premier cru plots, has more Chardonnay and less Pinot Meunier, and ages for 36 months. The Brut Grand Cru is mostly Pinot Noir with a little Chardonnay. Rosé Brut de Saignée comes from Pinot Noir and Pinot Meunier at Cumières. The prestige cuvée Victor Delabaye, the vintage Brut, and vintage rosé, all are exclusively Pinot Noir and Chardonnay, with the base wines aged partly in barriques. All the Brut cuvées have 8-9 g/l dosage. The demi-sec Gourmand has 32 g/l dosage, and is also found as a rosé.

Champagne Delamotte

5-7 rue de la Brèche d'Oger, 51190 Le Mesnil-sur-Oger	📞 +33 3 26 57 51 65
@ *champagne@salondelamotte.com*	👤 *Didier Depond*
🌐 *www.champagne-delamotte.com*	*[map p. 59]*
🚫 ⛏ 🏠 ☺	*5 ha; 850,000 btl*

Owned by Laurent-Perrier since 1988, Delamotte functions in conjunction with the mythic Champagne Salon (see profile). The sister houses share facilities, and the wines are made by Michel Fauconnet, Laurent-Perrier's chef de cave. As Salon is made only in top vintages, its grapes go into Delamotte in other vintages. Otherwise, Delamotte is a classic Maison, with estate vineyards providing just over 10% of the grapes. There are four cuvées: Brut, Blanc de Blancs, the vintage Blanc de Blancs, and a rosé. The style is on the full-bodied side for the Côte des Blancs, tending more towards stone fruits than citrus.

Champagne Maurice Delot

3, place de l'Église, 10110 Celles-sur-Ource	📞 +33 3 25 38 50 12
@ *contact@champagne-delot.fr*	👤 *Jean Baptiste Dangin*
🌐 *www.champagne-delot.com*	*[map p. 60]*
🚶 ⛏ 🍇	*8 ha; 75,000 btl*
	Owner: Champagne Dangin Paul et Fils

Maurice Delot founded the house in 1933, his son Vincent took over in due course, but when Vincent had no heirs to take over, he sold the house in 2006 to Champagne Paul Dangin, a somewhat larger neighbor a couple of streets away in Celles sur Ouce on the Côte des Bar. The purpose was to keep the house going independently, rather than to merge into one of the large houses, and Jean-Baptiste Dangin, who had been working at Champagne Dangin, came to take over, aged only 22. The range is fairly typical for the area, including extra brut and brut, with a focus on Blanc de Noirs, and some cuvées from late disgorgement.

Champagne A. & J. Demière

2 Rue Dom Pérignon, 51480 Fleury La Rivière	📞 +33 3 26 58 43 36
@ *a-j-demiere@wanadoo.fr*	👤 *Audrey Demière*
🌐 *champagnedemiere.com*	*[map p. 56]*
📅 ⛏ 🍇 *8 ha; 70,000 btl*	🍾 *Blanc de Noirs, Prestige Rochelle*

This family domain is now its third generation. Located in the Vallée de la Marne, vineyards are in one village, and the cuvées are driven by Pinot Meunier. "These are *wines* of Champagne," says Audrey Demière. The aim is to preserve citrus fruits and show minerality; there is no malolactic fermentation in order to preserve the wines for longer aging. The wines have long aging before release, six years for the nonvintage Brut. There are 12 Champagne cuvées, including the classic range and smaller-production runs called Confidential. The Blanc de Noirs is a blend of 60% Pinot Meunier and 40% Pinot Noir. The Lysandre vintage Extra Brut is 100% Pinot Meunier. All wines age in cuve, except for Solera23, another 100% Meunier, which spends twenty years on the lees before release. "This gives the lie to the idea that Pinot Meunier can't age," says Audrey. The wines move in a savory direction as they age.

Champagne Paul Déthune

2 rue du Moulin, 51150 Ambonnay	📞 +33 3 26 57 01 88
@ *info@champagne-dethune.com*	👤 *Pierre Déthune*

⊕ *www.champagne-dethune.com*	*[map p. 57]*
🚪 📛 🦋 ▨	*7 ha; 55,000 btl*

The Déthunes have been growing vines in Ambonnay since the seventeenth century. Today the this small house is run by Pierre and Sophie Déthune. All the vineyards are in Ambonnay, and from the 7 ha there are 9 cuvées. all blends across various parcels. The nonvintage range includes all categories: Brut Nature, Extra Brut, Brut, rosé, and demi-sec. The vintage blend ages in large oak casks, while the vintage Blanc de Blancs, Blanc de Noirs, and Cuvée à l'Ancienne age in barriques. The flagship wine is the Princesse des Thunes, aged in oak.

Champagne Devaux

Domaine de Villeneuve, 10110 Bar-sur-Seine	📞 *+33 3 25 38 63 85*
@ *manoir@champagne-devaux.fr*	👤 *Pascal Dubois*
⊕ *www.champagne-devaux.com*	*[map p. 60]*
🧍 📛 ▬	*100 ha; 750,000 btl*

Devaux was a family house on the Côte des Bars, founded in 1846, but was sold in 1987 to the cooperative Union Auboise, the largest on the Côte des Bars. The official name is now the Groupe Vinicole Champagne Devaux. The Devaux line uses about 100 ha of the 1,400 ha controlled in total by the Union. The top line is the collection D, where the focus is on maintaining freshness because everything is aged for at least 5 years. There is no MLF and there is some oak aging. The style of the nonvintage cuvée D is quite fragrant, and relatively round with 6-8 g dosage; with only 2 g dosage the Ultra D is crisper and tighter with more obvious citrus fruits. Impressions of soft red fruits cut the acidity on the rosé, and the vintage follows in a rounder, deeper style than nonvintage.

Champagne Diebolt-Vallois

72 Rue Neuve, 51530 Cramant	📞 *+33 3 26 57 54 92*
@ *contact@diebolt-vallois.com*	👤 *Famille Diebolt-Vallois*
⊕ *www.diebolt-vallois.com*	*[map p. 59]*
🚪 📛 🏠	*15 ha; 150,000 btl*

The Diebolt family has been in Cramant since the nineteenth century, and the Vallois family in Cuis for even longer, so when Jacques Diebolt married Nadia Vallois and established the Maison in 1959, they had vineyards from both communes. The house was originally registered as RM, but changed to NM to enable them to purchase grapes from 3 ha of vineyards held by another branch of the family. Jacques is in the process of handing over to his children, Arnaud and Isabelle. The cuvées are Blanc de Blancs except for Tradition and the rosé. The nonvintage and vintage Blanc de Blancs are blends from all their holdings; Cuvée Prestige comes only from the Côte des Blancs and is aged in large oak casks. The flagship Fleur de Passion comes from the parcels of oldest vines in Cramant and ages in barriques. Dosage is 6-8 g/l for all cuvées.

Champagne Pascal Doquet

44 Chemin du Moulin de la Censé Bizet, 51130 Vertus	📞 *+33 3 26 52 16 50*
@ *contact@champagne-doquet.com*	👤 *Pascal Doquet*
⊕ *www.champagne-doquet.com*	*[map p. 59]*
🚪 📛 🏠 ▨	*9 ha; 65,000 btl*

Pascal Doquet joined the family Maison, Doquet Jeanmaire, in 1982, and made the wine from 1995 to 2003; then he bought out his sisters' share and created his own house in 2004. Most of the vineyards are at the southern end of the Côte des Blancs, with the rest about 40 miles to the east in the Vitryat. Plantings are 95% Chardonnay, and except for the rosé, all the cuvées are Blanc de Blancs. The Horizon cuvée comes from Vitryat, the Premier Crus is an assemblage from the Côte des Blancs, and there is also a Vertus cuvée. The top wines come from Le Mesnil-sur-Oger, with both vintage and nonvintage cuvées; these are aged in oak, and some oak is also used in the other cuvées.

Champagne Dosnon

4bis rue du Bas de Lingey, 10340 Avirey Lingey	📞 +33 3 25 29 19 24
@ *nicolas@champagne-dosnon.com*	👤 *Davy Dosnon*
⊕ *www.champagne-dosnon.com*	*[map p. 60]*
◗ ▨ 🏠	*2 ha; 50,000 btl*

This boutique negociant house started out as Dosnon and Lepage in 2004, and then became known simply as Dosnon from 2014. Grapes from 2 ha that Davy inherited, and he buys grapes from another 5 ha, also on the Côte des Bar. Wines are fermented in old barriques. The nonvintage wines are simply labeled as Récolte Brute (Extra Brut), Récolte Blanche (Blanc de Blancs), Récolte Noir (Blanc de Noirs), and Récolte Rosé. The top wine is l'Alliance, an equal blend of Pinot Noir and Chardonnay; with only 40 cases each year it is effectively an undeclared vintage.

Champagne Didier Doué

Chemin des Vignes, 10300 Montgueux	📞 +33 3 25 79 44 33
@ *doue.didier@wanadoo.fr*	👤 *Didier Doué*
⊕ *champagne-didier-doue.fr*	
🗓 ▥ 🍇 ▨	*5 ha; 40,000 btl*

Located well off the beaten track, even for the Côte des Bar, the house is a few miles to the west of Troyes. Didier is the fifth generation at this family estate, having taken over from his grandfather in 1975 when he was 18. The terroir at Montgueux is chalk, so the emphasis is on Chardonnay, which is 90% of plantings in the 7 parcels. Didier is often described as Burgundian because of a focus on single parcels. The Brut, La Chanose, is 80% Chardonnay and 20% Pinot Noir. The Brut Nature, La Corres, is 70% Chardonnay and 30% Pinot Noir, and comes from a single parcel in Corre. Le Truchat comes from a single plot of Chardonnay. The vintage also is solely Chardonnay, and comes as Brut or Brut Nature. The cuvée with the most Pinot Noir is the Cuvée Prestige, 40% Pinot Noir and 60% Chardonnay, a special selection that is intended to age. Vinification is in stainless steel, and everything goes through malolactic fermentation.

Champagne Doyard

39, avenue du Général Leclerc, 51130 Vertus	📞 +33 3 26 52 14 74
@ *contact@champagnedoyard.fr*	👤 *Yannick & Guillaume Doyard.*
⊕ *www.champagnedoyard.fr*	*[map p. 59]*
◗ ▨ 🍇 ☍	*11 ha; 50,000 btl*

The Doyards have been growing grapes in Vertus, at the southern end of the Côte des Blancs for a long time, and started producing Champagne four generations ago. Yannick Doyard took over in 1979. He was handing over to his older son Charles when Charles died unexpectedly young in 2017; his younger son Guillaume then took over. The 54 separate plots are mostly Chardonnay on the Côte des Blancs, but there is 1 ha of Pinot Noir at Vertus and Aÿ. The practice here is to replace individual vines if they die, rather than to replant entire plots, which has kept the average age of vines around 40 years. Together with a policy of keeping yields low, this increases concentration in the wines. Wines are aged for a minimum of 48 months on the lees before disgorgement. There is partial malolactic fermentation only for the nonvintage, none for the vintage cuvées. Blanc de Blancs cuvées are divided into premier and grand cru for both nonvintage and vintage. In nonvintage, Vendémiaire is the premier cru Blanc de Blancs, with 40% fermented in barriques, and 4 g/l dosage. Révolution is the grand cru, with 50% fermented in barriques, and zero dosage. Vintage cuvées ferment entirely in 5-year barriques. Premier cru Clos de l'Abbaye comes from an 0.5 ha plot planted in 1956 and has dosage of 3 g/l. The grand cru has minimal dosage (less than 1 g/l). Moving on from Blanc de Blancs, Oeil de Perdrix is an extra brut rosé, made by direct pressing, from 25% Chardonnay and 75% Pinot Noir. La Libertine is an unusual cuvée attempting to represent the style of the first Champagnes from the eighteenth century; it ages for more than 12 years before disgorgement, has lower pressure than usual, and dosage of 65 g/l.

Champagne Duménil

38 rue du Puits, 51500 Sacy	📞 +33 3 26 03 44 48
@ contact@champagne-dumenil.com	👤 Hugues & Frédérique Poret
🌐 www.champagne-dumenil.com	[map p. 55]
🆔 €€ 🏠	8 ha; 80,000 btl

Emile-Paul Duménil founded the Maison in 1874, and his great granddaughter Frédérique Poret is the winemaker today, together with her husband Hughes who manages the vineyards. Vineyards are in three premier cru villages of the Montagne de Reims. Cuvée Jany Poret is dominated by Pinot Meunier (60%), Grand Réserve is a blend with a third of each variety, and Nature has no dosage. In addition to the vintage wine, there are late releases of vintages in the Oenothèque series. Les Pêcherines comes from a single plot of old vines in Chigny-les-Roses, and Amour de Cuvée is a prestige cuvée based on selection. Duménil is a member of the Trésors de Champagne and makes a Special Club cuvée in some vintages.

Champagne R. Dumont et Fils

3, rue de Champagne, 10200 Champignol Lez Mondeville	📞 +33 3 25 27 45 95
@ rdumontetfils@wanadoo.fr	👤 Bernard Dumont
🌐 www.champagnedumont.fr	[map p. 60]
🚶 👑	23 ha; 110,000 btl

The Dumonts are a long-established family on the Côte des Bar. Today the house is run by three brothers. Vineyards on Kimmeridgian terroir are planted with 90% Pinot Noir and 10% Chardonnay. The nonvintage Brut is a representative blend from the vineyards with 9 g/l dosage, aged for two years. The rosé is 100% Pinot Noir, produced by saignée, with slightly higher dosage at 10 g/l. The Brut Nature is 100% Pinot Noir from three recent vintages, matured longer, for 4 years before disgorgement. The Solera Reserve is a Blanc de Blancs based on a single tank of Chardonnay, first filled in 1991, and added to every year, with the first release in 2010; it has dosage of 6 g/l. Cuvée Intense comes from three specific parcels, with two thirds Pinot Noir and a third Chardonnay, with base wines aged for six months in barriques, before three years' aging on the lees and disgorgement with 5 g/l dosage. Vintage wines are 65% Pinot Noir and 35% Chardonnay, labeled Brut, but actually in the Extra Brut range with 5 g/l dosage.

Champagne Charles Ellner

1-6 Rue Côte Legris, 51200 Épernay	📞 +33 3 26 55 60 25
@ *info@champagne-ellner.com*	👤 *Stéphane Dubois*
🌐 *www.champagne-ellner.com*	*[map p. 58]*
🗓 € ⛏ 🏠	*50 ha; 500,000 btl*

This mid-sized house started when Charles Ellner, who was a riddler, started buying vineyards at the end of the nineteenth century. The first Champagne under the name of the house was released in 1905. Vineyards expanded under his son Pierre and grandsons. Grandson Jean-Pierre is in charge today, together with his nephews and daughters. In 1972, the house took on NM status, allowing it to purchase grapes, and today production comes about half from estate grapes and half from purchased grapes. Everything is fermented in stainless steel, and malolactic fermentation is blocked.

Champagne Fallet Dart

2 Rue Clos du Mont Drachy, 02310 Charly	📞 +33 3 23 82 01 73
@ *contact@champagne-fallet-dart.fr*	👤 *Adrien & Paul Fallet*
🌐 *www.champagne-fallet-dart.fr*	
🧍 ⛏ 🍇 🍃	*20 ha; 160,000 btl*

Somewhat off the beaten track in the far west of the Vallée de la Marne, the house traces its origins back to the Fallets in 1610. Louis Fallet was producing wine from 1903. A marriage in 1953 hyphenated the name of the house. Daniel and Gérard Fallet ran the domain from 1985 to 2016, when Adrien and Paul took over. Vineyards are in 5 villages around Charly-sur-Marne, 25 miles west of the Côte des Blancs and a little south of Château-Thierry. Most wines are vinified in stainless steel and go through malolactic fermentation. The nonvintage Cuvée de Réserve Brut is effectively a Blanc de Noirs from 70% Pinot Meunier and 30% Pinot Noir, with 9 g/l dosage, and 36 months before disgorgement. Grand Sélection is 70% Pinot Noir and 15% each of Pinot Meunier and Chardonnay, with 9 g/l dosage and 48 months before disgorgement. The rosé is 60% Pinot Meunier and 40% Pinot Noir. Le Clos du Mont is Chardonnay and Pinot Noir from a single parcel, vinified in barriques, and aged for 13 years before disgorgement. The vintage is 70% Chardonnay and 30% Pinot Noir, with base wines partly aged in barriques.

Champagne Nathalie Falmet

1, rue Saint-Maurice, 10200 Rouvres-les-vignes	📞 +33 6 07 02 74 27
@ *nathalie.falmet@orange.fr*	👤 *Nathalie Falmet*
🌐 *www.champagne-falmet.com*	*[map p. 60]*
🗓 🌾 🍇 🍃 *3 ha; 28,000 btl*	🍾 *Brut*

Nathalie Falmet qualified in oenology in 1993. She started by running an oenology laboratory in Bar-sur-Aube, and then took over her tiny family domain, with her first vintage in 2009. This focus here is towards individual years and parcels with very low or zero dosage. Plantings are 2.4 ha of Pinot Noir and less than 0.5 ha each of Chardonnay and Pinot Meunier. Most wines are vinified in stainless steel. Only one cuvée follows the conventional route of using a blend of the current vintage with reserve wines; this is the Brut, two thirds Pinot Noir and one third Chardonnay, using 20-30% reserve wine from a solera. Dosage is 4-5g, but this barely perceptible by comparison with the Brut Nature, which is a Blanc de Noirs. There is a Solera cuvée, half Pinot Noir and half Chardonnay, effectively a more or less equal blend of several recent vintages. It comes from Val Cornet, and has zero dosage. The other cuvées come from single years, although not described as vintage on the label. Val Cornet comes from a single parcel planted equally with Pinot Noir and Pinot Meunier. The base wine for this cuvée is vinified half in stainless steel and half in 350 liter oak barrels. Dosage is 4g. Tentation Rosé is a rosé de saignée from the same blend, also from a single parcel and single year, with 5g dosage. Terra is 100% Chardonnay from a single parcel and single year, with the distinction that the base wine is vinified in amphorae. Dosage is very low at 1g. Overall the style is light and elegant, lively and fresh, with ripe grapes that carry the low dosage well. Brut and Brut Nature are lovely aperitif Champagnes, Val Cornet has a steelier character, and Solera Extra Brut shows its zero dosage more clearly. The wines develop slowly and typically are still fresh five years or so after disgorgement.

Champagne Faÿ Michel

21, rue Pasteur, 02850 Barzy-sur-Marne	📞 +33 3 23 70 21 44
@ contact@champagne-fay.fr	👤 Murielle Faÿ
🌐 www.champagne-fay.fr	
📅 €€ ⛏ 🍇	9 ha; 150,000 btl

The Faÿ family traces their involvement with wine to 1695, and the estate has been handed from father to son ever since. Michel Faÿ started to produce his own Champagne in 1975. His son Stéphane took over in 1997, and was joined by his sister Murielle in 2007. The range of 10 cuvées starts with Tradition, which has a classic assemblage of 40% each of Pinot Noir and Pinot Meunier and 20% Chardonnay; Grande Réserve has 50% Pinot Meunier, 35% Chardonnay, and 15% Pinot Noir. The rosé Grand Réserve is made by assemblage, while Coeur de Rosé comes from saignée. The regular vintage has a third of each variety, while the special vintage Cuvée Alexander has 50% each of Pinot Noir and Chardonnay.

Champagne Émilien Feneuil

32 rue du Franc Mousset, 51500 Sermiers	📞 +33 6 87 93 68 33
@ lafeuille@hotmail.fr	👤 Émilien Feneuil
🌐 emilienfeneuil.com	[map p. 55]
🍇 ▦ 🍇 ⊘	3 ha

Émilien Feneuil took over his family property in 2006. His father had sold grapes (and other fruits or vegetables) and Émilien continued to sell his grapes until 2014 when he started to produce wine. Plantings are 40% Pinot Meunier, 28% Chardonnay, 22% Pinot Noir, and 7% Petit Meslier. Vineyards are dispersed into 17 plots, in the Montagne de Reims just southwest of Reims. There are plots in Chamery, on slopes of clay on top of limestone facing northeast, and in Sermier and Eucueil, where the soils are denser. The first vintages were pressed at friends' wineries; in 2020 Émilien obtained his own press. The wines are vinified in old barriques and 400-liter barrels. He produces three Coteaux Champenois: Les Goulats is a red from Chamery, Les Basses Croix & Les Gillis is a white from Sermiers, and Les Puits is a 100% Petit Meslier from Sermiers. There are four Champagnes. Totum is a blend from all the plots. Les Goulat is a rosé (by maceration) from Chamery. Les Puits (Blanc des Noirs) comes from Chamery, and Les Basses Croix & Les Gillis (Blanc des Blancs) comes from Sermiers. The first vintage was disgorged in 2019, all as zero dosage.

Champagne Feneuil Pointillart

21 rue du Jard, 51500 Chamery	📞 +33 3 26 97 62 35
@ champagne.fp@wanadoo.fr	👤 Astrid Feneuil
🌐 www.champagne-fp.com	[map p. 55]
📅 ⛏ 🍇 ☺	8 ha

This relatively new domain (in the context of the history of Champagne) was launched in Chamery in the Montagne de Reims by a marriage in 1972 between the Feneuil and Pointillart families, both occupants of the village since the seventeenth century. Astrid and Benjamin Feneuil took over in 2011. The Tradition range includes brut (8.5 g/l dosage), rosé (9 g/l dosage), and demi-sec (20 g/l dosage), all about 30-35% Pinot Noir, 25% Chardonnay, and 40-45% Pinot Meunier. Cuvée Réserve is 50% Chardonnay, 40% Pinot Noir, and 10% Pinot Meunier, with dosage 6 g/l, aged for 6 years before release. The Blanc de Blancs Marquis de Luth ages for 4 years and has 5 g/l dosage. The vintage cuvée has slightly unusual composition for a vintage release, 70% Chardonnay and 30% Pinot Meunier, with 6 g/l dosage, aged for 6 years before release.

Champagne Alexandre Filaine

17 rue Raymond Poincaré, 51480 Damery	📞 +33 3 26 58 88 39
	👤 Fabrice Gass
🍇 🍂 2 ha; 5,000 btl	[map p. 56]

This is a tiny operation, but the winemaker has an impressive pedigree. Fabrice Gass started producing his own Champagne while he was a winemaker at Bollinger, and now it has become a full-time project. The wines are made in his garage. The vineyard consists of 10 dispersed plots, with all three varieties planted. Production resembles the process at Bollinger, with base wines fermented and aged in old barriques from Bollinger, and then kept after the second fermentation in bottles under cork until disgorgement. Even from this tiny plot, there are three cuvées. Speciale and Confidence are 45% Pinot Noir, 35% Chardonnay, and 20% Pinot Meunier; Speciale has 6 g/l dosage and Confidence has 4 g/l. Cuvée Sensuum Vertigo is a Blanc de Noirs. There is no malolactic fermentation, not because it is specially blocked, but because it is prevented by natural high acidity. Production is so small that the wines are very hard to find.

Champagne Forget Chemin

15 rue Victor Hugo, 51500 Ludes-le-Coquet	📞 +33 3 26 61 12 17
@ champagne.forget.chemin@gmail.com	👤 Thierry Forget
🌐 www.champagne-forget-chemin.fr	[map p. 57]
🧍 🏭 🍇 🍷	12 ha; 100,000 btl

Thierry Forget is the fourth generation at this family domain, and has been the principal winemaker since 1991. The domain took its present name in the late 1960s when Thierry's father, Edmond, married Denise Chemin. Vineyards are in 60 parcels spread over eleven villages. The majority of plantings (70%) are Pinot Meunier. The Carte Blanche nonvintage range includes Extra Brut, Brut, and Demi-Sec, Marie-Forget (Extra Brut) and Carte Noire (Brut) are special selections, and Heritage Paul Forget is intended to be made in a more traditional style; there is also a Special Club cuvée. Dosage is moderate, around 8 g/l.

Champagne Philippe Fourrier

39 Rue de Bar sur Aube, 10200 Baroville	📞 +33 3 25 27 13 44
@ contact@champagne-fourrier.fr	👤
🌐 www.champagne-fourrier.com	[map p. 60]
📅 € 🏭 🏠 🍷	23 ha

In its fifth generation since the domain was founded in 1847, this family estate on the Côte des Bar is located in Baroville, the largest town in the area. It's been producing its own Champagne since the beginning of the twentieth century. Julien is the winemaker, working with his siblings Stéphanie and Mathilde. Vineyards are around Baroville, with 70% Pinot Noir, 29% Chardonnay, and 1% Pinot Meunier. Vinification is in stainless steel. Aside from the Cuvée Réserve (60% Pinot Noir, 40% Chardonnay), most of the cuvées are single varietals: there are nonvintage Blanc de Blancs from Chardonnay and also one from Pinot Blanc, and both vintage and nonvintage Blanc de Noirs. Dosage is on the high side for Brut, usually 8 - 12g.

Frèrejean Frères

66, rue Pasteur, 51190 Avize	📞 *+33 1 80 50 20 03*
@ *visit@frerejeanfreres.com*	👤 *Didier Pierson*
🌐 *frerejeanfreres.com*	*[map p. 59]*
🏠 🏢 🏭 🏠	*8 ha; 120,000 btl*

The objective of the three brothers, Guillaume, Rodolphe and Richard Frèrejean-Taittinger, was to create a high-end Maison when they created their company in 2005. The winery is in Avize, but there are also offices in Paris. Didier Pierson, from a local winemaking family, is the winemaker. Grapes come only from premier and grand cru villages. Wines are vinified in stainless steel, malolactic fermentation is performed, riddling is by hand, and dosage is kept low. The range starts with the nonvintage premier cru Brut and Extra Brut, each with 50% each of Pinot Noir and Chardonnay. More or less doubling in price, there are Blanc de Blancs and rosé Brut. After that, there is a big jump in price to the rest of the range. The vintage Extra Brut comes from 40-year-old vines Grand cru Blanc de Blancs VV26 comes from 90-year-old vines (the name refers to the date of the oldest planting in 1926); the base wines for this cuvée are vinified in barriques. Solaire is the grand cru vintage Blanc de Blancs.

Gallimard Père Et Fils

18 Rue Gaston Cheq Le Magny Haut, 10340 Les Riceys	📞 *+33 3 25 29 32 44*
@ *champ.gallimard@wanadoo.fr*	👤 *Didier Gallimard*
🌐 *www.champagne-gallimard.com*	*[map p. 60]*
🏠 🏭 🍇	*12 ha*

This family domain has been passed from father to son for six generations, having started to produce its own Champagne in 1930. Didier Gallimard runs the House today with his son Arnaud. About two thirds of production, the major nonvintage cuvée is the Cuvée de Reserve Blanc de Noirs, which uses 30% reserve wines and 10% from a solera. A Grande Réserve Blanc de Blancs is produced in much smaller amounts. Two rosés are produced by saignée: the Brut is 80% Pinot Noir and 20% Chardonnay, while Les Riceys is a vintage from 100% Pinot Noir. Reducing the dosage, Quintessence is an extra brut Blanc de Blancs, with base wines aged in oak, Les Murgers is extra brut Blanc de Noirs, and Amphoressence is a zero dosage blend of equal Chardonnay and Pinot Noir with base wines aged in amphorae. Prestige is a vintage blend of two thirds Pinot Noir with one third Chardonnay.

Champagne Gaston Chiquet

912, Avenue du Général Leclerc, 51530 Dizy	📞 *+33 3 26 55 22 02*
@ *info@gastonchiquet.com*	👤 *Nicolas Chiquet*
🌐 *www.gastonchiquet.com*	*[map p. 58]*
🧑 💶 🏭 🍇 ☕	*23 ha; 180,000 btl*

The family has been growing grapes here since 1746; the Chiquet brothers established an estate in 1919, and then Gaston Chiquet created his own marque and started bottling wine in

1935. This relatively large grower estate is now in the hands of Antoine and Nicolas Chiquet, the grandsons of the founder. Vineyards are spread between Aÿ, Dizy, and Hautvillers. There is more Chardonnay than usual for the area, 40% of plantings, with the rest split equally between the two Pinots. Brut Tradition is almost half Pinot Meunier, and Cuvée de Réserve is essentially a later disgorgement of the same wine. There is an unusual Blanc de Blancs from Aÿ, reflecting its terroir in unusual richness for Blanc de Blancs; there is also a vintage version.

Champagne Gatinois

7 rue Marcel Mailly, 51160 Aÿ	📞 +33 3 26 55 14 26
@ contact@champagnegatinois.com	👤 Pierre Cheval
🌐 www.champagnegatinois.com	[map p. 58]
🎫 €€ 🏭 🍇	7 ha; 50,000 btl

With 27 parcels of vines on the slopes around Aÿ, almost all planted with Pinot Noir, Gatinois makes a full-bodied style of champagne. Louis Cheval, formerly a geologist. took over from his father Pierre, who died in 2016 after running the house for thirty years. Some of the crop is sold to neighboring Bollinger, but an increasing proportion is being used for estate production. Brut Tradition is a blend from all parcels, and the Réserve is held a year longer on the lees. The vintage includes most of the grapes from the Petit Pinot d'Aÿ clone, which is considered to be the best Pinot Noir clone used in Champagne. The red wine used for the rosé comes from the same Pinot Noir source used for the blend.

Champagne Pierre Gerbais

10110 Celles-sur-Ource	📞 +33 3 25 38 51 29
@ contact@gerbais.com	👤 Aurélien Gerbais
🌐 www.gerbais.com	[map p. 60]
🎫 🏭 🍇 🍷	15 ha; 140,000 btl

Pierre Gerbais bought the vineyards at Celles sur Ource in the Aube that are the basis for this small grower-producer, including 10 ha of Pinot Noir, 4 ha of Chardonnay, and (unusually) 4 ha of Pinot Blanc. His grandson Aurélien now runs the house. Aurélien describes the extra brut cuvée, Grains de Celles (50% Pinot Noir, 25% each of Pinot Blanc and Chardonnay) as "anti-parcellaire." There's also a rosé with the same base. Other cuvées are based on single varieties. L'Osmose is 100% Chardonnay, l'Audace is 100% Pinot Noir, l'Originale is 100% Pinot Blanc, and Rosé de Saignée is 100% Pinot Noir. Except for l'Audace and Rosé de Saignée, which are zero dosage, all cuvées are extra brut, with 3-4 g dosage. There's a good deal of experimentation here, trying alcoholic and malolactic fermentations in oak, comparing natural yeast with inoculated fermentations, and a focus on terroir. "I consider myself more Burgundian than Champenois," Aurélien says.

Champagne Gimonnet-Gonet

Lotissement bas-des-Auges, 51190 Le Mesnil-sur-Oger	📞 +33 9 82 29 93 15
@ contact@champagne-gimonnet-gonet.com	👤 Charles Gimonnet
🌐 www.champagne-gimonnet-gonet.com	[map p. 59]
🎫 🏭 🍇	15 ha

Gimmonet and Gonet are both well-known names on the Côte des Blancs, and the house was formed after the marriage of Philippe Gimmonet and Anne Gonet in 1986. Their son Charles took over in 2012. Half of the vineyard holdings are Chardonnay in grand cru villages on the

Côte des Blancs; the other half consists of Pinot Noir and Pinot Meunier in the Vallée de la Marne. Wines are vinified in stainless steel, and pass through malolactic fermentation. Brut Tradition (dosage 8 g/l) is half Chardonnay and half Pinot Noir; this is the only cuvée not based exclusively on Chardonnay. Brut d'Or (dosage 6 g/l) is in fact a Blanc de Blancs from grand cru villages, as is Extra Brut (dosage 2 g/l). The rosé is Chardonnay except for the 10% of red wine. Cuvée Prestige comes from Chardonnay only in Cramant and Le Mesnil-sur-Oger, and Carat du Mesnil (extra brut with 3 g/l dosage) comes only from the oldest vines (60 years' age) in Le Mesnil-sur-Oger.

Champagne Philippe Glavier

82 rue Nestor Gaunel, 51530 Cramant	📞 +33 6 67 61 86 73
@ *info@champagne-philippe-glavier.com*	👤 *Philippe Glavier*
🌐 *www.champagne-philippe-glavier.com*	*[map p. 59]*
	5 ha; 30,000 btl

Philippe Glavier comes from a family of growers who belong to a cooperative; his wife Véronique comes from a wine-producing estate on the Côte des Blancs. They formed their own small domain in Cramant in 1995, starting by using the cellars of Veronique's father until they were able to get their own cuverie. They have a small press—the smallest press in Champagne, Véronique says—used for have a pocket handkerchief of 52 holdings spread over the Côte de Blancs. The range has about a dozen cuvées, divided into premier cru and grand cru in nonvintage, and village wines from Les Mesnil and Cramant for vintage. Everything is vinified in stainless steel except Folie de Cramant, a vintage wine made in oak. Malolactic fermentation is usual and dosage is low, typically 4-5 g/l.

Champagne Paul Goerg

30 rue du Général Leclerc, 51120 Vertus	📞 +33 3 26 52 15 31
@ *info@champagne-goerg.com*	👤 *Sébastien Petiteaux*
🌐 *www.champagne-goerg.com*	*[map p. 59]*
	118 ha; 300,000 btl

Paul Goerg is a high-end brand of the Goutte d'Or cooperative, started in 1984, and named for a negociant who was the mayor of Vertus. The heart of production is the Blanc de Blancs Brut; there are also Tradition (60% Chardonnay, 40% Pinot Noir) and Rosé (85% Chardonnay, 15% Pinot Noir). All have 8-9 g/l dosage. There is also a Blanc de Blancs without dosage, called Absolu. There are two vintage cuvées, the first with 85% Chardonnay to 15% Pinot Noir and dosage of 6 g/l, and the Lady cuvée, a Blanc de Blancs from the oldest vines, with only 4 g/l dosage, that spends nine years on the lees before release. The dosage tends to be a bit obtrusive, even though malolactic fermentation is blocked to maintain acidity; recently I've found the wines a little too obvious.

Champagne Gonet-Médeville

1 Chemin de la Cavotte, 51150 Bisseuil	📞 +33 3 26 57 75 60
@ *jx@gonet-medeville.com*	👤 *Xavier Gonet*
🌐 *www.gonet-medeville.com*	*[map p. 53]*
Owner: Vignobles Gonet-Médeville	*10 ha; 80,000 btl*

The Champagne house is part of Vignobles Gonet-Médeville resulting from the union of Julie Médeville and Xavier Gonet. The Médeville family come from Sauternes where they own Château Gilette, as well as other properties in Bordeaux, and the Gonet family have been growers in Mesnil-sur-Oger. When the 50 ha of Gonet vineyards in Mesnil were divided in

2000 as the result of inheritance, Xavier Gonet acquired a group of parcels in twelve villages, including Chardonnay in the grand cru of Mesnil-sur-Oger, Pinot Noir in the grand cru of Ambonnay and premier cru of Bisseuil, and Pinot Meunier in Mareuil. Most cuvées are fermented in used barriques. The nonvintage range includes Tradition and the Blanc de Noirs from Bisseuil. Both are Brut at the low end of the dosage range (6-7 g/l), and exclusively from premier crus. Each is about a third of production. The nonvintage rosé is Extra Brut. All the vintage cuvées are Extra Brut: Théophile is 60% Chardonnay and 40% Pinot Noir (2 g/l dosage), Grande Ruelle is Blanc de Noirs from Ambonnay (2 g/l dosage), and Champ d'Alouette is Blanc de Blancs from Mesnil-sur-Oger. Malolactic fermentation is usually blocked to keep freshness.

Champagne Michel Gonet et Fils

196 Avenue Jean Jaurès, 51190 Avize	📞 +33 3 26 57 50 56
@ *info@gonet.fr*	👤 *Sophie Signolle, Charles Henri Gonet, Antoine Gomérieux*
⊕ *www.gonet.fr*	*[map p. 59]*
🗓 €€ 🏭 🐌 ☁	*36 ha; 150,000 btl*

This is a relatively large house for a boutique grower and is only part of Vignobles Gonet, which also owns six châteaux in Bordeaux. The family has been involved in wine since 1802, and Michel Gonet established the Champagne house in 1973, with vineyards on the Côte des Blancs (in Avize, Oger, and Mesnil-sur-Oger), but also extending to the Côte de Sézanne (Vindey) and the Abe (Montgueux and Fravaux). The house is run today by Michel's children, Charles-Henri, Frédéric, and Sophie Signolle. Brut 6g (the name indicates the dosage) is Pinot Noir from Fravaux; the rosé is also 100% Pinot Noir from Fravaux. Les 3 Terroirs is an extra brut (5 g/l dosage) Blanc de Blancs sourced from all three areas. Grand Cru is a Blanc de Blancs from lieu-dit Les Hautes Mottes in Mesnil-sur-Oger, either zero dosage or extra brut with 2-3 g/l, aged for 7 years before disgorgement. Coeur de Mesnil is the vintage Blanc de Blancs from the same lieu-dit, but is labeled as Brut, with 4-6 g/l dosage depending on vintage. It ages for 10 years before disgorgement. The Champagne house is located in Avize, but the wines can also be tasted at Villa Signolle, which Sophie bought on the Avenue de Champagne in Epernay.

Champagne Philippe Gonet

1, rue Brèche-d'Oger, 51190 Le Mesnil-sur-Oger	📞 +33 3 26 57 53 47
@ *office@champagne-philippe-gonet.com*	👤 *Pierre Gonet*
⊕ *www.champagne-philippe-gonet.com*	*[map p. 59]*
🗓 🏭 🏠 ☁	*19 ha; 170,000 btl*

Founded in 1830, the house is now run by the seventh generation of brother and sister Pierre (winemaker) and Chantal (marketing), who took over after the death of their father Philippe. Vineyards are two thirds Chardonnay (mostly in Les Mesnil and Vertus) and one third Pinot Noir (extending into other parts of the region). "We are mostly Blanc de Blancs but we have a couple of blends," Pierre says. The style shows the focus on Blanc de Blancs in a generally citrus-driven, linear style. The Brut Réserve from Le Mesnil-sur-Oger is 60% Pinot Noir, 10% Pinot Meunier, and 10% Chardonnay with 7 g dosage; the palate is quite direct, and feels more Chardonnay-driven than it really is. The other blend is the rosé, 90% Chardonnay with 10% Pinot Noir, where the citric style is cut by faint red fruit impressions. The 3210 Blanc de Blancs from Le Mesnil is called Extra Brut, but is really zero dosage: the 3210 on the label stands for 3 years aging, 2 vineyards, 1 grape variety, and 0 dosage. The vintage Blanc de Blancs is very much Côte des Blancs in its linear focus on citrus fruits.

Champagne Grémillet

1 Rue Envers de Valeine, 10110 Balnot-sur-Laignes	📞 *+33 3 25 29 37 91*
@ *info@champagnegremillet.fr*	👤 *Anne Gremillet*
🌐 *www.champagne-gremillet.fr*	*[map p. 60]*
🗓 ⛏	*48 ha; 500,000 btl*

Jean-Michel Gremillet worked at the electricity company EDF before he established the house in 1979 with some vineyards from his mother. Today it is run by his children Anne and Jean-Christophe. One of the larger producers on the Côte des Bar, today grapes come about half from estate vineyards (all on the Côte des Bar with about 85% planted to Pinot Noir) and half from purchases from around 60 growers located on the Côte des Bar and elsewhere. The basic cuvée, Selection, is 70% Pinot Noir and 30% Chardonnay; there are also Blanc de Blancs, Blanc de Noirs, and Rosé d'Assemblage. All come from a blend of 4-5 recent vintages with 20% reserve wines, and dosage of 9g. A zero dosage cuvée is a blend of equal Pinot Noir and Chardonnay. Rosé Vrai is made by saignée from 100% Pinot Noir, and is extra brut, with 5g dosage. Evidence is a Blanc de Blanc with base wines aged in oak, and 7g dosage. The vintage is 100% Pinot Noir. The top cuvée is Clos Rocher, from a small plot of Pinot Noir at Les Riceys, given 7g dosage.

Champagne Guiborat Fils

99 Rue de La Garenne, 51530 Cramant	📞 *+33 3 26 57 54 08*
@ *champagne@guiborat.fr*	👤 *Richard Fouquet*
🌐 *champagne-guiborat.fr*	*[map p. 59]*
🗓 €€ ⛏ 🏠 ☺	*8 ha; 30,000 btl*

Richard and Karine Fouquet took over from Karine's parents in 1995 at this old family domain, where they are the fifth generation. The vineyards had been rented out but they started estate production with the 1996 vintage. Vineyards are mostly in the grand crus of Cramant and Chouilly on the Côte de Blancs, with some in Mareuil on the other side of Épernay. Half of the grapes used to be sold to Laurent Perrier until the vineyard of 4 ha of Pinot Meunier itself was sold to Laurent Perrier so the domain could focus more on Chardonnay. Cuvée Tradition is the nonvintage blend of 80% Chardonnay and 20% Pinot Meunier. The grand cru cuvées and vintage are 100% Chardonnay, and are extra brut or brut nature. Le Mont Aigu is a single vineyard vintage cuvée from vines planted in 1970. Nonvintage champagnes are made in stainless steel; some oak is used for the vintage.

Champagne Marc Hébrart

16 Quai du Moulin, 51160 Mareuil-sur-Aÿ	📞 *+33 3 26 52 60 75*
@ *champagne.hebrart@wanadoo.fr*	👤 *Jean-Paul Hébrart*
🧍 €€ ⛏ 🍇 ☺ *15 ha; 135,000 btl*	*[map p. 58]*

Hébrart is a bit unusual in splitting his vineyards between villages along the Aÿ (mostly Pinot Noir) and the Côte des Blancs (all Chardonnay). Marc Hébrart founded the domain in 1964, and his son Jean-Paul took over in 1997. The 65 parcels in 6 villages are vinified separately, and there are both wines from individual regions as well as blends across regions. Selection is a nonvintage blend of Pinot Noir from Mareuil-sur-Aÿ with Chardonnay from Chouilly, while Rive Gauche-Rive Droite is a vintage based on Pinot Noir from Aÿ and Chardonnay from the Côte des Blancs, vinified in barriques. This is his most distinctive wine. Hébrart is a member of the Trésors de Champagne and makes a Special Club cuvée that is a similar blend, but vinified in vat.

Champagne Olivier Horiot

25 rue de Bise, 10340 Les Riceys	📞 +33 3 25 29 32 16
@ *champagne@horiot.fr*	👤 *Olivier & Marie Horiot*
🌐 *www.horiot.fr*	*[map p. 60]*
📅 🏭 🍇 🎼	*9 ha; 40,000 btl*

"Vines have been in the Horiot family since the 1600's. I come from the side of the family that were innkeepers, but my grandfather replanted vines post-phylloxera, so you could say I am the third generation," says Olivier Horiot, who took over the family domain from his father Serge in 1999. Grapes were sent to the cooperative or sold to negociants, and the major part of production still is, but Olivier started focusing on producing cuvées from 2 ha single parcels and old grape varieties well before it became fashionable. He produces still wines as well as Champagne. "When I came home, I had a revelation," he says, "I realized that with just one grape (Pinot Noir), you could produce many different styles of wine and still have them be reflective of a place." Plantings are 75% Pinot Noir, the rest being 10% Chardonnay and small amounts of Pinot Meunier, Pinot Blanc, Pinot Gris, Arbanne, and Petit Meslier. All seven varieties go into the Solera cuvée. Métisse is a Pinot cuvée, with 80% Pinot Noir and 20% Pinot Blanc. Sève is a Blanc de Blancs Brut Nature from the parcel en Barmont. Arbane is a cuvée solely from this almost extinct variety. Dosage is always less than 2 g/l. More conventional cuvées, the Brut Tradition and Cuvée Prestige, which are blends from the usual varieties, are produced under the label of Serge Horiot. In addition to still wines, labeled as Coteaux Champenois, there's still rosé under the AOP Les Riceys (something of a throwback to production in the area before the Champagne era), with interest in terroir taken to the point of producing two cuvées, en Valingrain and en Barmont.

Champagne Hugues Godmé

9, rue de Verzy, 51360 Verzenay	📞 +33 3 26 49 41 66
@ *hugues.godme@wanadoo.fr*	👤 *Hugues Godmé*
🌐 *www.champagne-hugues-godme.com*	*[map p. 57]*
📅 🏭 🍇 🎼 ⊘	*8 ha; 45,000 btl*

Godmé Père et Fils was founded in Verzenay at the end of the nineteenth century, and started bottling all its production soon after the second world war. Hughes Godmé and his sister Sabine were the third generation, but separated in 2015, forming separate houses in adjacent premises, with Hughes operating under his own name, and his sister continuing under the name of Champagne Godmé. Hughes takes a more modern approach, with lower dosage, while his sister continues a more traditional approach. They divided the vineyards of the original Godmé house, and Hughes Godmé has 40 separate parcels (including 5.5 ha from the Godmé domain and some others from his wife), in four villages of the Montagne de Reims : Verzenay, Verzy, Villedommange, and Villers-Marmery. Parcels are vinified separately, using vats or oak depending on conditions, blends vary from year to year, and dosage ranges from zero to 7-8g. The range runs to 12 cuvées, separated into premier cru and grand cru, with blends, Blanc de Blancs, and Blanc de Noirs in both categories.

Champagne Huré Frères

2 Impasse Carnot, 51500 Ludes	📞 +33 3 26 61 11 20
@ *contact@champagne-hure-freres.com*	👤 *François Huré*
🌐 *www.champagne-hure-freres.com*	*[map p. 57]*
⊘ 🏭 🏠 ☙	*10 ha; 90,000 btl*

Georges Huré founded the domain at Ludes in the Montagne de Reims in 1960, and it took the name Huré Frères when he passed it on to his three sons in 1971. His grandsons, brother François and Pierre, have been running the estate since 2008, and have brought the house into a more modern, lighter style. The blends Invitation (brut) and Insouciance (rosé) have 6/g/l dosage. The Blanc de Blancs Inattendue, the undeclared vintage Instantanée (a blend made every year), and Terre Natale (a vintage blend from old vines) have 2.5-5 g/l depending on the year. Extra Brut Mémoire, with 2 g/l, comes from a solera started in 1982, and ages in foudre. The 4 Éléments range represents each of the single varieties from parcels, ferments and ages in demimuids, has malolactic fermentation blocked, and low dosage under 3g/l.

Champagne Jacquart

34 Boulevard Lundy, 51057 Reims	📞 +33 3 26 07 88 40
@ web@champagne-jacquart.com	👤 Gaëlle Demonceaux
🌐 www.jacquart-champagne.fr	[map p. 54]
🚫 ⧄ ▬	300 ha; 3,000,000 btl

This well regarded cooperative was founded in 1962 in Reims by a group of thirty growers. Vineyards extend over 60 villages. In 1998, Jacquart became part of Alliance Champagne, a group of cooperatives representing a couple of thousand growers with 2,500 ha, but the brand remains separate. A new winemaker, Florian Esznak, was hired in 2010 from Veuve Clicquot. Wines are made in a modern facility in the heart of Reims. The wines are well made and offer good value, although it's hard to find one that really stands out.

Champagne Jacquinet Dumez

26 Rue de Reims, 51370 Les Mesneux	📞 +33 3 26 36 25 25
@ contact@champagne-jacquinet-dumez.com	👤 Olivier & Aline Jacquinet
🌐 champagne-jacquinet-dumez.com	[map p. 55]
📅 €€ 🏭 🍇 🍷	7 ha; 45,000 btl

Established in 1935 when Henry Dumez planted 3 ha of Pinot Noir in Sacy, then run by his daughter Claudine and her husband Jean-Guy Jacquinet, the house has been run since 1992 by their son Olivier Jacquinet and his wife Aline. The daughters Diane and Agathe are now in the domain. Vineyards are in a group of premier cru villages in the Montagne de Reims near Reims. Base wines for most of the cuvées are aged mostly in stainless steel, with a small part, 10-20% in barriques or foudres. Dosage is usually low, with the Brut cuvées having a level at or just below the limit for Extra Brut (usually 4-6 g/l). Multimis is a classic blend of all three varieties, Blanc de Noirs Dialogie is 80% Pinot Meunier and 20% Pinot Noir, Sublimum is a rosé d'assemblage from the same blend, while Carmillon is a rosé de saignée from 100% Pinot Noir. Luministe is a premier cru Extra Brut, half Pinot Noir and half Chardonnay, with the proportion aged in oak bumped up to 50%. Vocabilis is 100% Pinot Meunier Extra Brut. In vintage cuvées, Vinographie is 60% Pinot Noir (aged in foudre) blended with 40% Chardonnay (aged in barriques), with dosage of only 3 g/l. Expression Libre No. 7 is Blanc de Blancs, from 40-year-old vines, vinified in barriques.

Champagne Jacquinot & Fils

34-36 rue Maurice Cerveaux, 51202 Épernay	📞 +33 3 26 54 36 81
@ contact@champagne-jacquinot.com	👤 Jean-Manuel Jacquinot
🌐 www.champagne-jacquinot.com	[map p. 58]
📅 €€ 🏭 🍇 🍷 17 ha	Private Cuvée

The Jacquinots started out as courtiers in wine in the seventeenth century, the vineyards were established after the first world war, they started to make wine in 1929, and the House was founded in 1947. Champagne is made from 7 ha and the base wine from the other 10 ha is sold to negociants. The vineyards are in two villages on the Côte des Bar, but the Maison is in Epernay. "When my grandfather set up the domain, all wine had to be made in Reims or Epernay," explains Jean-Manuel Jacquinot, who has been in charge since 1998. Only Pinot Noir and Chardonnay are used. There is no malolactic fermentation. The Private Cuvée releases are aged for at least four years before release. The wines are dense and flavorful, moving in a savory direction as they age.

Champagne Janisson-Baradon et Fils

9 place de la République, 51200 Épernay (tasting room)	📞 +33 3 26 54 45 85
2 rue des Vignerons, 51200 Épernay (cellars)	
@ *info@champagne-janisson.com*	👤 *Cyril Baradon*
⊕ *www.champagne-janisson.com*	*[map p. 58]*
🚶 € ⛰ 🏠 ☺	*9 ha; 80,000 btl*

The house was founded in 1922 by Georges Baradon (a riddler at Pol Roger) and his son-in-law (who worked at Moët). They bought vineyards close to Épernay which they could work at weekends; almost all of the vineyards are still in Épernay. Today the house is in its fifth generation under brothers Maxence and Cyril, who have taken over from their father Richard. Oak is used in vinification and aging. The most interesting wines are three single varietal, single vineyard cuvées, all made without malolactic fermentation with minimal (2 g/l) dosage: Toulette is Chardonnay from vines planted in 1947 on the chalkiest soil; Tue-Boeuf is Pinot Noir from vines planted in 1953; and Chemin des Congés is Pinot Meunier from vines planted on clay. The tasting room is in the heart of Épernay.

Champagne Jean Josselin

14 rue-des-Vannes, 10250 Gyé-sur-Seine	📞 +33 3 25 38 21 48
@ *champagne-josselin@wanadoo.fr*	👤 *Félix Josselin*
⊕ *www.champagnejeanjosselin.fr*	*[map p. 60]*
🚶 ⛰ 🍇	*12 ha; 85,000 btl*

The Josselins have been growers since 1854, and Félix is the third generation to produce Champagne. Vineyards are divided into 18 parcels in the village of Gyé, with Pinot Noir being 80% of plantings. Vinification and aging are in stainless steel, but the general model is Burgundy. "We vinify plot by plot," Félix says, "and we produce vintage wine every year." The philosophy is to use minimal dosage. "If the wine has good balance, you don't need to add sugar, we like to taste salinity in the glass. For vintage and rosé we focus on low dosage, but even our Brut is low, about 6 g. The wine decides the dosage." 'Saline' is a word that comes up often as Félix describes his wines. The Alliance Brut cuvée is 70% Pinot Noir and 30% Chardonnay, and represents a single year, although it's not labeled as vintage. It has a slight savory tang, but house style really comes into its own with the Blanc de Blancs, the more elegant of the pair, and Blanc de Noir, the more powerful, vintage cuvées, each with 4 g/l dosage, making a saline impression on the finish. "Cuvée des Jean is our only Champagne that is a blend of more than one year," Félix explains; typically two thirds of one year blended with a third of the previous year, it's a Blanc de Noirs showing the typical salinity of the house style, in fact the most marked of all. "Audace extra brut rosé is our driest wine at 3 g/l dosage." Grapes are harvested relatively late, and this shows in the sense of ripeness rising above the low dosage.

Champagne Jeeper

SA 8 Rue Georges Clémenceau, 51480 Damery	📞 +33 3 26 58 41 23
@ info@champagne-jeeper.com	👤 Nicolas Dubois
🌐 www.champagne-jeeper.com	[map p. 55]
🏃 🏭 🏠	40 ha

The family that founded the house had been growers since the eighteenth century when Victor Gourtorbe started to bottle his own Champagne in 1949, calling his house Jeeper to distinguish itself from the many other Gourtorbes. The Reybier group, who own Château Cos d'Estournel in Bordeaux, purchased the brand in 2013 and expanded it, so that estate vineyards now account for only 20% of production. The house style is creamy, although dosage is always around the border between Brut and Extra Brut. The Grand Assemblage Brut is 60% Chardonnay, 35% Pinot Noir, and 15% Pinot Meunier with 7 g dosage, and is quite round in a soft, forward, style. The Grande Réserve Brut is 100% Chardonnay (with Blanc de Blancs stated on the back label), with a touch more intensity, and staying in the creamy style. Moving down to 6 g dosage, Premier Cru Brut is fuller on the palate and more forceful, and Grand Cru Brut shows more intensity and sense of structure. Both premier cru and grand cru Bruts have some vinification in oak (40% for premier cru, 50% for grand cru). Vintage adds savory notes.

Champagne Labbé et Fils

5 Chemin du Hasat, 51500 Chamery	📞 +33 3 26 97 65 45
@ contact@champagnelabbe.com	👤 Damien & Jérôme Labbé
🌐 champagnelabbe.com	[map p. 55]
🏃 🏭 🍇 🍂	10 ha; 50,000 btl

The Labbe family has been growing grapes at Chamery in the Montagne de Reims since the end of the nineteenth century. Didier Labbe started to produce his own Champagne in 1975, and today his sons Damien and Jérôme are making wine. Brut Tradition reflects plantings in the vineyards, with 65% Pinot Noir, 20% Pinot Meunier, and 15% Chardonnay, coming from the youngest vines. The rosé, made by assemblage, has a similar blend. Réserve is intended to be fuller-bodied, with half Pinot Noir and a quarter each of Pinot Meunier and Chardonnay. Base wines for the Blanc de Blancs are vinified a quarter in oak. The Prestige cuvée is half Pinot Noir and half Chardonnay, and ages longer, for 4-5 years, before disgorgement. All the wines have dosage around 9 g/l.

Champagne JM Labruyère

1 place Carnot, 51360 Verzenay	📞 +33 3 26 49 40 63
@ info@champagne-labruyere.com	👤 Vincent Van Waesberghe
🌐 www.champagne-labruyere.com	[map p. 57]
📅 🏭 🍇 �′	7 ha; 40,000 btl

The Labruyère family started producing wine in Moulin-Ö-Vent in Beaujolais, and extended into Burgundy in 1988 when they purchased Domaine Jacques Prieur in Meursault, and into Bordeaux with the purchase of Château Rougeot in Pomerol in 1992. The property in Champagne was created by buying two estates in Verzenay in 2010 and 2012. (The grapes used to be sold to Moët for inclusion in Dom Pérignon.) The intention is to produce Champagne exclusively from grand cru vineyards. Most growers in Verzenay sell to the big houses; launching their house in 2017, Labruyère has joined a select group of boutique houses producing Champagne from estate vineyards. The first release, Prologue, is nominally nonvintage (although is so firmly based on 2012 that it could have been labeled as vintage); a typical blend of 70% Pinot Noir and 30% Chardonnay. Based on the same blend, Anthologie is the nonvintage rosé. Both are Extra Brut with 4-5 g/l dosage. Page Blanche is the Blanc de Blancs, with dosage only around 2 g/l.

Champagne Lacourte Godbillon

16 rue-des-Aillys, 51500 Écueil	📞 +33 3 26 49 74 75
@ contact@champagne-lacourte-godbillon.com	👤 Géraldine Lacourte
🌐 www.champagne-lacourte-godbillon.com	[map p. 55]
🚫 🌿 🍇 🍂 8 ha	🍾 Mi-Pentes, Blanc de Noirs

With origins in 1883, this is a relatively old house for a boutique grower, with the modern era dating from 1947, when Jean-Guy Lacourte and Claudine Godbillon started producing Champagne. The present marque was introduced when production from the estate vineyards started in 1968. Géraldine Lacourte and her husband Richard Desvignes changed careers in 2006 to take over the family estate. Plantings are 85% Pinot Noir and 15% Chardonnay in the premier cru village of Écueil. All the wines have low dosage. Terroirs d'Écueil represents the mix in the vineyards, goes through malolactic fermentation, spends 30 months on the lees, and has 5 g/l dosage. The vintage cuvée differs in that malolactic fermentation is blocked for Chardonnay, and of course aging is longer (5 years), and dosage is less (3.5 g/l). Chaillots is a Blanc de Noirs from vines planted in 1966 in the lieu-dit of the same name; it is vinified in 300-liter oak barrels, has no malolactic fermentation, ages for 48 months, and has dosage of only 2 g/l. Chaillots Hautes Vignes is a Blanc de Blancs, vinified in barriques, with malolactic fermentation blocked, 36 months aging, and dosage of 5 g/l. The rosé is made by assemblage, with 100% Pinot Noir. The house style is relatively full bodied, but dosage in the extra brut range, coupled with blocking MLF, allows the finish to be dominated by citric acidity.

Champagne Benoît Lahaye

33 rue Jeanne d'Arc, 51150 Bouzy	📞 +33 3 26 57 03 05
@ lahaye.benoit@orange.fr	👤 Valérie & Benoît Lahaye
📅 🍃 🍇 ▦ ◯ 🚫 5 ha; 38,000 btl	[map p. 57]

The Lahaye family has been making Champagne since the 1930s; Benoît took over his family estate in 1993, which he now works together with his wife Valérie and two sons. Committed to biodynamic viticulture, he works the vineyards with a horse. There are 3.2 ha in Bouzy, 1 ha in Ambonnay, and 0.6 ha in Tauxières. Pinot noir Is 90% of plantings. Wines are fermented in barrique, and a new barrel room was built in 2012. There are many old vines in the domain, and some unusual cuvées. Dosage is always low, with the main nonvintage blends in Extra Brut or Brut Nature. Rosé de Maceration is a varietal Pinot Noir made by direct pressing. Violaine is a sulfur-free, zero dosage blend of equal Pinot Noir and Chardonnay. Le Jardin de la Grosse Pierre is a field blend from a vineyard planted in 1923 by Benoît's grandfather; it has about 9 varieties, including some that are no longer allowed, and has been made as a separate cuvée since 2009. The flagship Pinot Noir is full-flavored, with a savory tinge that makes it a good wine to go with food.

Champagne Laherte Frères

3 rue des Jardins, 51530 Chavot	📞 +33 3 26 54 32 09
@ contact@champagne-laherte.com	👤 Thierry Laherte
🌐 www.champagne-laherte.com	[map p. 59]
📅 🍃 🏠 ◯	12 ha; 145,000 btl

The house started in Chavot in 1899; Aurélien took over from his father Thierry and uncle Christian in 2005. Vineyards are split between the neighborhood of the winery, just south of Épernay, and the Vallée de la Marne. Plantings focus on Pinot Meunier. Most of the wines are vinified in barrique. The Brut Blanc de Blancs mostly comes from near the winery, there is also a zero dosage Blanc de Blancs, Empreintes is a blend of Chardonnay from chalk terroir and Pinot Noir from the Vallée de la Marne, Les Vignes d'Autrefois comes from old (more than 50-year) Pinot Meunier, and Les 7 is made by cofermentation of grapes from a vineyard of all seven authorized varieties. There are two rosés from Pinot Meunier: Rosé de Meunier is made by assemblage, and Les Beaudiers is a single-vineyard wine made by saignée.

Champagne Jean Lallement et fils

1 rue Moët et Chandon, 51360 Verzenay	📞 +33 3 26 49 43 52
@ *alex.lallement@orange.fr*	👤 *Alexandra Lallement*
🌐 *www.champagne-jean-lallement.fr*	*[map p. 57]*
🗓 🏭 🍷 🍸	*5 ha; 20,000 btl*

With vineyards in 20 parcels split between the villages of Verzenay and Verzy, Lallement is one of the few producers to the north of Reims where the vineyards actually face north. Jen-Luc Lallement's grandfather started producing Champagne in the late 1940s. Plantings are 80% Pinot Noir. The domain is known for its powerful style. The Brut comes from the youngest vines; the Brut Réserve is the same blend, but from vines of 30-years ago or more. There is a varietal Pinot Noir rosé; and a vintage was released for the first time in 2006. Dosage is low, at around 4 g/l.

Champagne Lancelot Pienne

1 Place Pierre Rivière, 51530 Cramant	📞 +33 3 26 59 99 86
@ *contact@champagne-lancelot-pienne.fr*	👤 *Gilles Lancelot*
🌐 *www.champagne-lancelot-pienne.fr*	*[map p. 59]*
🗓 €€ 🏭 🍷 🍸	*9 ha; 70,000 btl*

The Lancelot domain was founded at the start of the twentieth century, when Jean-Baptiste Lancelot was in charge of Mumm's vineyards in Cramant. Its present name dates from a marriage in 1967, when the vineyards of the Lancelot and Pienne families were combined. Fourth generation Gilles Lancelot took over in 2005 and purchased the domain's present cuverie, the old Mumm property in the center of Cramant, with a view across the vineyards of the Côte des Blancs. Most of the vineyards are dispersed in small parcels on the Côtes de Blancs, with some in the Vallée de la Marne. The nonvintage blends are based on Pinot Meunier (70%). The nonvintage Blanc de Blancs cuvées are Instant Présent (Brut with 8 g/l dosage) and Ronde (Extra Brut with 3.5 g/l dosage). The nonvintage wines use 20% reserve wine drawn from a Réserve Perpétuelle maintained by a solera system, and are vinified in stainless steel. In vintage, Cuvée Perceval is an equal blend of Chardonnay and Pinot Noir, while the flagship Marie Lancelot is a Blanc de Blanc from old vines in Cramant.

Champagne J. Lassalle

21 rue Chataignier Fourchu, 51500 Chigny Les Roses	📞 +33 3 26 03 42 19
📠 +33 3 26 03 45 70	👤 *Angéline Templier*
🌐 *www.champagne-jlassalle.com*	*[map p. 57]*
🗓 €€ 🏭 🍷 🍸	*16 ha; 150,000 btl*

This has become a matriarchal house. It was founded in 1942 by Jules Lassalle, and when he died in 1982, his wife Olga took over, to be succeeded by her daughter Chantal, and then by her daughter Angéline Templier in 2006. There are two nonvintage Brut cuvées, Cachet d'Or, aged for 36 months, and Cuvée Préférence, aged for 48 months. Similarly there are two non-vintage rosés, the first aged for 36 months, and Cuvée Spéciale for 6 years. There is a vintage Brut and also a Special Club cuvée. The Cuvée Spéciale is made for the American market. All the grapes are from premier cru vineyards. There is always malolactic fermentation, and dosage is generally about 8 g/l.

Champagne Georges Laval

16 ruelle du Carrefour, 51480 Cumières	📞 *+33 3 26 51 73 66*
@ *champagne@georgeslaval.com*	👤 *Vincent Laval*
⊕ *georgeslaval.com*	*[map p. 58]*
🗓 ⛪ 🍇 ▦	*3 ha; 20,000 btl*

Georges Laval started to cultivate his tiny plots in Cumières by organic methods in 1971; his son Vincent has continued since 1996. Production is artisanal: no chaptalization, vinification in barriques, zero dosage (except for the Demi-Sec, Garennes, a recent addition to the range). Cumières Premier Cru is the largest cuvée, up to 7,000 bottles, Les Chênes is a Blanc de Blancs from a parcel east of the village, Les Hautes Chèvres comes from old vines of Pinot Meunier in a 1 ha plot above the village, and the vintage Les Longues Violes comes from a plot planted in 1947 that has been in the Laval family for generations. Even the nonvintage cuvées require time.

Champagne Le Brun de Neuville

Route de Chantemerle, 51260 Bethon	📞 *+33 3 26 80 48 43*
@ *commercial@lebrundeneuville.fr*	👤 *Damien Champy*
⊕ *www.lebrundeneuville.fr*	
🗓 ⛪ ▦ ☜	*152 ha*

The cooperative was founded in 1963 and today has 170 members. It takes its name from Madame le Brun, who owned the Château de Bethon, where it is located, in 1845. Located on the Côte de Sézanne, the majority of plantings (90%) are Chardonnay. The particularity here is that most wines have their second fermentation in a bottle under cork. Most cuvées have a small proportion of aging in barrique. The house style is flavorful and quite intense: these are wines to match food. The Blanc de Blancs, with 8 g dosage, has a soft, creamy style with stone fruits on the palate, Authentique Brut (75% Chardonnay and 25% Pinot Noir) has more sense of minerality, Authentique Blanc de Blancs increases that sense of minerality, and the Authentique Rosé (67% Chardonnay, 16% Pinot Noir, plus 17% red wine), is rounder with a greater sense of structure.

Champagne David Léclapart

8 rue Saint Vincent, 51380 Trépail	📞 *+33 3 26 57 05 01*
@ *david.leclapart@free.fr*	👤 *David Léclapart*
◎ ▦ 🍇 🍷 ∅ *3 ha; 12,000 btl*	*[map p. 57]*

Committed to biodynamics since he took over the family domain in 1996, to the extent of wanting to demonstrate the character of each vineyard and vintage, David Léclapart has the unusual policy of using no reserve wines (so there are only vintage wines), zero dosage, and minimal sulfur. This means there is more variation than usual from year to year. The 22 individual plots are planted 90% with Chardonnay. L'Amateur is Chardonnay fermented in enamel-coated tanks, l'Artiste comes from 30-50-year old Chardonnay half fermented in tank and half in old barriques, l'Apotre comes from a single plot of Chardonnay planted in 1946, and vinified in barriques, l'Astre is a Blanc de Noirs.

Champagne Leclerc Briant

67, rue Chaude Ruelle, 51200 Épernay (cellars)	☎ *+33 3 26 54 45 33*
25 Bis Avenue de Champagne, Épernay (boutique)	
@ *info@leclercbriant.com*	🧑 *Frédéric Zeimett*
🌐 *www.leclercbriant.com*	*[map p. 58]*
📅 ⛏ 🏠 🖼 🖋 🔵	*14 ha; 150,000 btl*

This house has had a complete change of scene since 2010. Funded as a grower by Lucien Leclerc in 1872, then converted to a negociant by Bertrand Leclerc in 1955, it moved to Épernay. Pascal Leclerc converted the vineyards to biodynamics in 1991, and in 2003 Leclerc Briant became one of the very few Champagne houses certified by Demeter. After Pascal died in 2010, the vineyards were sold off, and the brand was sold to an American couple, Denise Dupré and Mark Nunnelly. It continues the policy of biodynamics, managed by Frédéric Zeimett, who has reacquired 10 ha of vineyards; purchased grapes from another 8 ha come from organic or biodynamic vineyards. The home vineyard is a small plot (0.6 ha) that the house retained, adjacent to the Maison in Épernay, planted with Chardonnay in 1966, and never treated with herbicides or pesticides. Hervé Jestin has been the winemaker since 2008; previously he was Chef de Cave at Champagne Duval-Leroy for 24 years. The Sélections Parcellaires come from estate vineyards: there's a Blanc de Noirs from Hautvillers, and Blanc de Blancs from Le Mesnil-sur-Oger and from Vertus. There are 14 cuvées altogether. Most wines are vinified in vat, but the Réserve and some parcel selections age in barriques. Dosage is low, typically below 4 g/l. Hervé Jestin also started to produce his own cuvée in 2012 from a family plot at Cumières.

Champagne Emile Leclère

15 rue Victor Hugo, 51530 Mardeuil	☎ *+33 3 26 55 24 45*
@ *info@champagne-leclere.com*	🧑 *Marie Delouvin*
🌐 *www.champagne-leclere.com*	*[map p. 56]*
🚶 ⛏ 🍇	*12 ha; 120,000 btl*

Founded in 1832, just west of Epernay at the end of the Vallée de la Marne, this is a family domain, now under Vincent and Marie Delouvin. Marie is founder Emile's great-great granddaughter. Plantings have the usual balance of the Vallée, with Pinot Meunier predominant. Vincent produces one wine under the label of Champagne Vincent Delouvin, a 100% Meunier. Dosage is 9 g/l for most cuvées, but all taste drier than you would expect from the stated level. The style is mainstream, with the Brut Réserve nicely rounded, the Blanc de Blancs showing a touch more austerity and minerality, and the rosé showing the softer impression that comes from the assemblage with red wine, but even here there is a touch of saline austerity. Bicentaire is aged in oak for six months and is fuller bodied than the rest of the range; the increased sense of richness may also reflect the older age of the vines, about 35 years. This cuvée has 60% Chardonnay, 30% Pinot Meunier, and 10% Pinot Noir, and slightly lower dosage at 8 g/l. Generation 5 comes from older vines and ages half in oak and half in steel; it's full-bodied for a Blanc de Blancs.

Champagne Xavier Leconte

7 Rue Berceaux, 51700 Bouquigny	☎ *+33 3 26 52 73 59*
@ *contact@champagne-xavier-leconte.com*	🧑 *Alexis Leconte*

⊕ *champagne-xavier-leconte.com*

📅 🏭 🍇 ℰ *10 ha*

Xavier Leconte, who joined the domain in 1980, was the fifth generation at this family estate, and the first to produce his own wine. He handed over to his son Alexis in 2013. Vineyards are in many plots in the villages of Troissy, Dormans, Mareuil-le-Port, Vandières, and also in Aÿ. Vinification uses both stainless steel and wood. Coeur d'Histoire is named as historic cuvée of the house, an is 100% Pinot Meunier, vinified in stainless steel. Each release comes half from the current vintage and half from reserve wines stored in foudre. Signature du Hameau is an assemblage representing the mix in the vineyards, 80% Meunier, 15% Pinot Noir, and 5% Chardonnay, vinified in a mix of stainless steel and barriques, 60% from the current vintage, 40% from the reserve aged in foudre. There are several different blends in the brut category, which here means 7-8 g/l dosage. A range of wines from single parcels is all extra brut, including Pinot Noir from Le Clos de Poiloux, Pinot Meunier from La Croisette, and the blend of Pinot Noir and Chardonnay. Scellés 2 Terroirs, from two plots. These are vinified in barriques and have dosage of 3-3.5g/l.

Legras et Haas

9 Grande Rue, 51530 Chouilly	📞 *+33 3 26 54 92 90*
@ *info@legras-et-haas.com*	👤 *Jérôme Haas*
⊕ *www.legras-et-haas.com*	*[map p. 58]*
📅 🏭 🏠 ℰ	*38 ha; 160,000 btl*

This house was formally created in 1991 when François Legras left R & L Legras (an old house in Chouilly) and started Legras et Haas with his wife Brigitte, who had run her own house. The house may be young, but has substantial vineyards for a grower-producer, with 15 ha on the Côte des Blancs in Chouilly where it is located, another 10 ha of Chardonnay in Vitry to the far east, and 6 ha of Pinot Noir in Les Riceys on the Aube. Grapes are also purchased from Aÿ. Today it is run by three brothers of the second generation, Rémi, Olivier, and Jérôme. The approach is purist, you might say reductionist, with minimal exposure to oxygen, so there is no use of wood. Cuvées include Intuition (a blend of all three varieties), a rosé (a similar blend to Intuition), the Grand Cru Blanc de Blancs from Chouilly, the Exigence blend of equal Chardonnay and Pinot Noir, a vintage, and the vintage Les Sillons which is a Blanc de Blancs from a single plot.

Champagne Legret et fils

6 rue de Bannay, 51270 Talus Saint Prix	📞 *+33 6 07 97 29 14*
@ *contact@champagne-legret.fr*	👤 *Alain Legret*
⊕ *www.champagne-legret.fr*	*[map p. 53]*
📅 €€ 🏭 🍇 ▦ ◉	*5 ha; 21,000 btl*

This family estate turned to producing its own Champagne in the third generation when it was known as Champagne Jean-Pierre Legret, and then after Jean-Pierre's son Alain took over in 2006, the name became Champagne Legret et fils. Located south of the Côte de Blancs, the vineyards are around the Côte de Sézanne. It's a hands-on operation. "I'm the export manager," says Jennifer Frair, "but we are a small house and I also do the bottling." The house is not only organic (and moving towards biodynamic) but is certified vegan. The focus is on low dosage. "Our philosophy is that we work with Extra Brut and Nature, we want to taste the terroir, not sugar or other additives," Jennifer says. The nonvintage Equilibre comes from a blend of all three varieties with 5 g/l dosage and finishes with a saline impression. The Blanc de Blancs, Mineral, ages 20% in oak, and its dosage of 4 g/l moves the flavor spectrum further towards the savory tang of zero dosage. The only Brut is the rosé Corolle, which is the same blend of varieties as Equilibre. There is also a Rosé de Saignée, which comes exclusively from Pinot Meunier, and is Brut Nature to emphasize the saline tang on the finish. The vintage is also Brut Nature.

Champagne Lelarge-Pugeot

30 rue Saint Vincent, 51390 Vrigny	📞 +33 3 26 03 69 43
@ contact@champagnelelarge-pugeot.com	👤 Dominique Lelarge
🌐 champagnelelarge-pugeot.com	[map p. 55]
📅 🏭 🍇 🍷 ∅	9 ha; 65,000 btl

The Lelarge family began growing grapes in Vrigny at the start of the nineteenth century. Raymond Lelarge bottled the first wine under his own name in 1930. His son, Raymond, took over in 1950, and Raymond's son. Dominique studied oenology in Beaune, married his wife Dominique Pugeot (Dominique can be male or female in French), and when they took over the house, they renamed it as Lelarge Pugeot. Their daughter Clémence joined in 2012. Vineyards are mostly north-facing, and Pinot Meunier is predominant. Clémence has had a modernizing effect on the domain. Cuvée Tradition has been made since the mid 1980s as a blend of 65% Pinot Meunier with 20% Pinot Noir and 15% Chardonnay, but at Clémence's instigation, dosage has dropped from its original 12 g/l to the present 5 g/l. The rosé Extra Brut is 100% Pinot Noir and has the same 5 g/l dosage. Other cuvées have lower dosage. The Blanc de Blancs has 3 g/l. Nature is a zero dosage blend of half Pinot Meunier with a quarter each of Pinot Noir and Chardonnay. Les Charmes de Vrigny is a similar blend based on a single base year plus a solera, with 4 g/l dosage, and ages for 6 years before disgorgement. The Rosé de Saignée comes from 50-year-old vines of 60% Pinot Meunier and 40% Pinot Noir; it has zero dosage. The first 100% Pinot Meunier, Les Meuniers de Clémence, was produced in 2010—"Meunier is the ancestral grape of the terroir of Vrigny." In vintage cuvées, Quintessence has 70% Chardonnay, 20% Pinot Noir, and 10% Pinot Meunier, vinified in foudres, then aged for 7 years before disgorgement, with dosage of 5 g/l. There is also an Extra Brut with a third of each variety and only 3 g/l dosage. For a while, the Lelarge-Pugeots used honey to provide the dosage in their Bises Champagne—"we are beekeepers, the honey comes from our land"—but the authorities have made them return to more conventional sugar.

Champagne Claude Lemaire

9 Croix Saint Jean, 51480 Boursault	📞 +33 6 72 45 93 14
@ champagne.lemaire@wanadoo.fr	👤 Patrice Lemaire
🌐 www.champagne-claude-lemaire.fr	[map p. 56]
📅 🏭 🍇 ☕	7 ha

Louis Lemaire started producing Champagne in the 1920s. His son Claude took over in 1950, and the house was called Claude Lemaire. Claude's son Patrice took over in 1987 and is now helped by his son Aurélian. The house is know variously known as Claude Lemaire or Patrice Lemaire, and bottles can be found under both names. Located near the river Marne, vineyards are dispersed into 18 separate parcels. Cuvée Tradition has a third of each grape variety and comes as either as Brut (6 g/l dosage) or demi-sec (13 g/l dosage). Blanc de Noirs comes from Pinot Noir only, and has 3 g/l dosage. The oldest vines here are Pinot Meunier, 50 years old, and the cuvée Vieilles Vignes is 100% Meunier, with dosage of 5 g/l. Dosage is increased to 8 g/l for the rosé, made by assemblage, from 100% Pinot Noir. The Blanc de Blancs comes from the village of Boursault, and here the base wine is vinified in barriques; dosage is 4 g/l. The vintage also is Chardonnay; dosage 6 g/l.

Champagne Lemaire Père & Fils

8 rue du Mont d'Hor, 51220 Saint Thierry	📞 +33 3 26 03 12 42
@ *info@mhchampagne.com*	👤 *Nicolas Lemaire*
⊕ *www.mhchampagne.com*	*[map p. 53]*
🗓 🏭 🖼 🏠 🍇	*14 ha; 140,000 btl*

Dating from 1885, the house recently changed its name from Domaine du Mont d'Hor to Lemaire Père & Fils, and is now run by brothers Nicolas and Antoine. Located northeast of Reims, plantings are about a half of Pinot Noir and a quarter each of Pinot Meunier and Chardonnay. There are only 56 ha of vines in the commune, and Veuve Clicquot owns 30 ha, leaving Lemaire as the second largest grower. The style is nicely restrained but ripe. The Extra Brut (dosage 3 g/l) gives an impression of ripeness, so the low dosage is not punishing, and the wine seems quite round and fruity. When I ask Nicolas if it's from a selection of specially ripe grapes, he says, "Usually we do Extra Brut when we have a good harvest." The Brut is the same wine as the Extra Brut, but has higher dosage (9 g/l); the wine is carried more by the fruits than the dosage and tastes only a fraction sweeter. The rosé is the same blend again, but with 13% red wine (dosage is a gram lower to compensate for the extra roundness of the red wine). "We used to make a rosé saignée but it was too spicy," Nicolas says, so Lemaire switched to this more accessible rosé d'assemblage. The Blanc de Blancs comes from silex terroir, so is more linear than one from the Côte des Blancs. Nicolas has switched to fermenting the base wine in oak as of 2014, so it may become softer. Vintage varies from Extra Brut to Brut. "A vintage has to be something different," Nicolas says. "The 2004 was Extra Brut but the 2008 is Brut—it was more linear and needed a little more sugar." Nicolas also makes a Ratafia (a mix of grape juice and brandy) of which he is proud—I was not allowed to leave the tasting without trying it. "The right process is to extract only from the first run of the press." It ages for three years in new oak, and is a little spicy, but not too sweet.

Champagne Lilbert Fils

223 rue du Moutier, 51530 Cramant	📞 +33 3 26 57 50 16
@ *info@champagne-lilbert.com*	👤 *Bertrand Lilbert*
⊕ *www.champagne-lilbert.com*	*[map p. 59]*
🗓 🏭 🍇 🍇	*4 ha; 27,000 btl*

This small domain is tightly focused on Blanc de Blancs, growing only Chardonnay from grand cru sites in Cramant (60%), Chouilly (30%), and Oiry (10%). The family has been growing vines in Cramant since 1746, and making Champagne since the start of the twentieth century. Oenologist Bertrand Lilbert took over from his father in 2003. The nonvintage Blanc de Blanc is a blend from all three villages and amounts to 80% of production. The vintage comes only from the Les Buissons vineyard in Cramant. Perle is an unusual cuvée in an old style—it used to be called Crémant de Cramant—in which pressure is only 4 atmospheres instead of the usual 6 bars. It comes from 80-year-old vines and ages for 1-2 years longer than the nonvintage Brut before release. To maintain lightness of style, there is no use of wood, no battonage, and dosage is light at 7 g/l.

Champagne Nicolas Maillart

5 Rue de Villers aux Noeuds, 51500 Écueil	📞 +33 3 26 49 77 89
@ *contact@champagne-maillart.fr*	👤 *Nicolas Maillart*
⊕ *champagne-maillart.fr*	*[map p. 55]*
🗓 € 🏭 🏠 🍇	*8 ha; 130,000 btl*

The first trace of the Maillart family in the region dates from 1533 at the Abbaye de Saint Nicaise; by 1753 they were vignerons in Chamery. Nicolas Maillart is the ninth generation, and took over in 2003, after working at other domains in France. Because the estate had been reduced by inheritance issues, he changed from RM status to NM in 2008 in order to have a larger supply of grapes, but he still functions like a grower, as the purchased grapes come only from other members of the family. The estate plantings are 75% Pinot Noir and 25% Chardonnay, in the premier cru village of Ecueil and in grand cru Bouzy. One unusual feature of the holdings are the ungrafted vines of Pinot Noir that his father planted in 1973 in a plot in Ecueil where the usual grafted vines had not been doing well. The relatively sandy soil may be responsible. The cuvées are divided into premier cru and grand cru. Fermentation takes place in wood, and the reserve wines are kept in oak. The Platine Brut and the Extra Brut premier cru cuvées are actually blends from premier cru villages Ecueil and Villers Allerand with some lots from Bouzy grand cru. There is also a Platine Late Disgorgement, a blend of four vintage released about ten years later. Dosage is low for all cuvées, with the Brut at 6 g/l and the Extra Brut at 4 g/l. Mont Martin premier cru comes from 1.8 ha of Pinot Meunier exclusively in Villers Allerand and has zero dosage. Franc de Pied is the cuvée made in some vintages only from the ungrafted vines. It's also zero dosage to focus on the fruits. The other premier cru vintage is a blend of Pinot Noir and Chardonnay with 4 g/l dosage. Although the house is focused on Pinot Noir, there is a Blanc de Blancs, Les Chaillot Gillis. The vintage grand cru from Bouzy is a Blanc de Noirs called Jolivettes, and with only 1 g/l dosage is close to the Brut Nature style. The Grand Cru Rosé comes from 60% Pinot Noir in Bouzy, blended with 40% Chardonnay and has the highest dosage used in the house, 6 g/l, the same as the Brut. There's significant variation in style among the cuvées, so it's hard to pin down a house style, but Platine is relatively weighty, the Millésime vintage is more textured, Montchenot premier cru is the most elegant, and the Platine Late Disgorgement has noticeably higher dosage than the other cuvées.

Champagne Michel Mailliard

11, Boulevard Jean Brion, 51130 Vertus	☎ +33 7 60 39 83 11
@ reservations@champagne-michel-mailliard.com	👤 Jacqueline Mailliard
🌐 www.champagne-michel-mailliard.com	[map p. 59]
🗓 👪 🍇 🗘	23 ha; 36,000 btl

Michel Mailliard is well known in Vertus where he created what is basically a custom crush facility so small growers could produce their own Champagne. (Because multiple growers use the facility, where he also makes how own wines, he has to label his wines as RC (récoltant-coopérateur) although in all other respects he is a boutique grower (RM or récoltant-manipulant). The domain dates from 1894, but it was Michel, the third generation, who really established the marque, initially in France, and now with Gregory's help, exporting elsewhere. The focus is on Chardonnay. Cuvée Gregory premier cru is 95% Chardonnay and 5% Pinot Noir, in aperitif style.

Champagne Mailly

28 rue de la Libération, 51500 Mailly Champagne	☎ +33 3 26 49 44 44
@ contact@champagne-mailly.com	👤 Xavier Millard
🌐 www.champagne-mailly.com	[map p. 57]
🧍 € 👪 ▬ 🗘	75 ha; 500,000 btl

Relatively small for a cooperative, this house exclusively represents Mailly. It was founded in 1929 by a group of 24 growers. Today it represents 80 growers and is headquartered in a modern glass building on the edge of the village. Plantings are 85% Pinot Noir and 15%

142

Chardonnay, and amount to about a quarter of the vineyards in Mailly. There is a wide range of cuvées. Most are 75% Pinot Noir with 25% Chardonnay, with dosage for the Bruts between 6-9 g/l. Rosé Alexia is 90% Chardonnay with 10% Pinot Noir. The vintage wines are Blanc de Blancs, with Cuvée Prestige (a blend from various plots), Mont Vergon (from a single parcel), and grand cru l'Oger (from the village). The house keeps a supply of older wines, not just vintage but including also the assemblage of Cuvée Gregory from various base years.

Champagne Mandois

66 rue Charles de Gaulle, 51530 Pierry	☎ +33 3 26 54 03 18
@ info@champagne-mandois.fr	👤 Joséphine Barnier
🌐 www.champagne-mandois.fr	[map p. 58]
🗓 🇪🇪🇪 ⛏ 🏠 ▦	35 ha; 500,000 btl

Jean Mandois bought the family's first vineyards in Champagne in 1753. His great grandson Victor founded the house and started bottling wine in 1860. His son bought the cellars in Pierry, under the old church where Frère Oudard (a contemporary of Dom Pérignon) is buried. Ninth generation Claude Mandois is in charge today. Vineyards are around Epernay and on the Côte des Blancs and Côte de Sézanne, planted with 70% Chardonnay and 15% of each Pinot. The nonvintage range include Brut and Rosé (both 7 g/l dosage) and Brut Zero; the base are vinified 90% in stainless steel and 10% in demi-muids. The vintage range has both Blanc de Blancs (vinified 20% in demi-muids) and Blanc de Noirs (vinified in stainless steel), both abele extra brut, with 6 g/l dosage right at the border between brut and extra brut. The prestige cuvées all have 5 g/l dosage. Victor Mandois Brut is a Blanc de Blancs from 50-year-old vines, Victor Mandois Rosé is 90% Chardonnay; base wines for both are vinified 30% in demi-muids. Clos Mandois comes from a 1.5 ha enclosed plot of Pinot Meunier Clos Mandois and ages entirely in barrels.

Champagne Gilles Mansard

4 rue de Tirvet, 51700 Cerseuil	☎ +33 6 86 04 26 99
@ contact@champagne-mansard-gilles.com	👤 Maxime Mansard
🌐 www.champagne-mansard-gilles.com	[map p. 56]
🗓 ⛏ 🍇	24 ha

The house dates from 1901 when Benoni Mansard produced the first wine. His son Gaston bought the first estate vineyards in 1926. Gaston's grandson Gilles took over in 1986, and added a negociant activity that increased production from 100,000 to 1.8 million bottles. The house is located in the Vallée de la Marne, but Gilles bought some eighteenth century cellars in Epernay. In 1997 he stopped and sold off some parcels. Today's vineyards are divided into 71 separate parcels. Today his son Maxime runs the house. Under the name of Champagne Achille Princier, there are three cuvées: Grand Tradition (with more or less equal proportions of each variety), a rosé d'assemblage, and Grand Art (equal Chardonnay and Pinot Noir), all with dosage around 8 g/l. Under the name of Champagne Gilles Mansard, cuvées are produced from 1.7 ha of the best plots: Brut Ancestral and Ancestral Rosé, both with Chardonnay as the most important variety and more or less equal proportions of Pinot Noir and Meunier, and a Blanc de Blancs (actually labeled as 100% Chardonnay). All are vinified in barriques and have dosage of 7 g/l.

Champagne Margaine

| 3 Avenue Champagne, 51380 Villers Marmery | ☎ +33 3 26 97 92 13 |
| @ contact@champagnemargaine.com | 👤 Arnaud Margaine |

champagnemargaine.com · [map p. 57]

8 ha; 70,000 btl

The house dates from 1910 and has been in the hands of the fourth generation under Arnaud Margaine since 1989. Vineyards are mostly around the village, virtually all Chardonnay. There is some Pinot Noir at Verzy. The Brut is 90% Chardonnay with 8 g/l dosage, while the Extra Brut is a Blanc de Blancs with 4.5 g/l dosage. There are two rosés, the rosé d'assemblage with 9 g/l dosage, and the rosé de saignée, which is tighter at 4 g/l dosage. The vintage is a Blanc de Blancs, as is the Special Club cuvée, which is a selection from the best parcels. Cuvée M is 95% Chardonnay and made on the solera principle, with 25% of the current vintage added to the mix every year. Some cuvées have partial malolactic, others are described as "malolactique non recherchée," which is to say that malolactic fermentation does not usually occur, but this is not a fixed rule.

Champagne Marguet Père & Fils

1 place Barancourt, 51150 Ambonnay	+33 3 26 53 78 61
@ info@champagne-marguet.fr	Benoît Marguet
www.champagne-marguet.fr	[map p. 57]
	8 ha; 80,000 btl

Benoît Marguet took over from his father Christian in 2005 at Champagne Marguet-Bonnerave, a grower house in Ambonnay with a 13 ha estate. As a result of a family split in 2008, Marguet-Bonnerave became dormant, and Benoit established his own house. He now has 7 ha in Ambonnay and 1 ha in Bouzy, and also buys some grapes. He is married to Séverine of the Launois family, and is also involved with the viticulture at Champagne Launois. Committed to biodynamics, he has built a stable for two horses, who plough the vineyards. Wines are vinified in oak, either in barriques or in egg-shaped foudres. Cuvées are zero dosage or extra brut, with no or minimal sulfur. The Cru Selections represent individual villages, and there are also single-vineyard wines in top years. Cuvée Sapience was created in 2006 as a high-end biodynamic cuvée with grapes sourced from the estate and from David Léclapart, Georges Laval, and Benoît Lahaye.

Champagne Marie Courtin

8, rue de Tonnerre, 10110 Polisot	+33 3 25 38 57 45
@ contact@piollot.com	Dominique Moreau
	[map p. 60]
3 ha; 15,000 btl	Efflorescence

This domain is one half of a husband and wife team. Roland Piollot has an 8.5 ha domain in Polisot (called Champagne Piollot Père et Fils), while his wife Dominique Moreau has adjacent vineyards (in fact, Dominique's vineyards are part of a 3 ha plot facing east-southeast, with Roland owning the other 0.5 ha). They share viticultural practices, including production of biodynamic preparations, but produce wines under separate labels. (Practices go beyond biodynamics into the spiritual, using pendulums, supposed to reflect energy, to assess the state of grapes and wines.) Dominique's label is called Marie Courtin after her grandmother. Plantings are mostly Pinot Noir. Since 2005, Dominique has been producing single vineyard (well, single plots within the vineyard), single variety (well, mostly Pinot Noir), single vintage, zero dosage Champagne. The major cuvées are the Blanc de Noirs, Résonance (from the top of the slope, aged in stainless steel) and Efflorescence (from 40-year old vines, lower down, more powerful, aged in oak). Concordance is a Blanc de Noirs from 50-year-old vines with less sulfur. The style is rich and full-bodies, with increasing intensity, perhaps from increasing vine age, going along the series of Blanc de Noirs, sometimes bringing with it a faint bitterness to cut the fruits on the finish. There are also very small amounts of Blanc de Blancs and rosé.

Champagne Serge Mathieu

6 rue des vignes, 10340 Avirey Lingey	📞 +33 3 25 29 32 58
@ *information@champagne-serge-mathieu.fr*	👤 *Isabelle & Michel Jacob*
🌐 *www.champagne-serge-mathieu.fr*	*[map p. 60]*
📋 *lutte* 🍇	*11 ha; 90,000 btl*

The Mathieus have been growing grapes on the Côte des Bar since the eighteenth century. Serge Mathieu started estate bottling in 1970. The estate is run today by his daughter, Isabelle, and Michel Jacob. All the vineyards are in the commune of Avirey-Lingey, 20 miles south of Troyes, planted with 80% Pinot Noir and 20% Chardonnay. The vineyard around the cellar is a 3 ha block, on steep slopes, planted exclusively with Pinot Noir. Vinification occurs in a mix of enamel and stainless vats, and there is complete malolactic fermentation. Blanc de Noirs comes in Brut (8.6 g/l dosage) and Extra Brut (5 g/l dosage); The Brut Prestige is two thirds Pinot Noir, and the Brut Select reverses the composition to have 80% Chardonnay, both at 8.6 g/l dosage. The vintage is a Blanc de Noirs, labeled Brut but on the edge of Extra Brut with 6 g/l dosage, and the rosé comes from assemblage, with dosage on the high side at 9.5 g/l.

Champagne Le Mesnil

19 rue Charpentier, 51190 Le Mesnil-sur-Oger	📞 +33 3 26 57 53 23
@ *lemesnil@upr.coop*	👤 *Gilles Marguet & Marie Laure Romagny*
🌐 *www.champagnelemesnil.com*	*[map p. 59]*
🚫 🏭 ▬	*320 ha; 150,000 btl*

Founded in 1937, the cooperative now represents 500 growers, but production under its own label is relatively small, as it sells most of the vin clair to the large houses. All cuvées are Blanc de Blancs except for the rosé. In addition to the nonvintage range of Extra Brut, Brut (9g/l dosage), and Demi-Sec, the Cuvée Prestige is a vintage coming from older vines (average age 38 years), and the top cuvée is Sublime, made in Blanc de Blancs (with 10.4 g/l dosage). The Sublime Rosé is a nonvintage, again with dosage on the high side at 10 g/l.

Champagne Paul Michel

20 Grande Rue, 51530 Cuis	📞 +33 3 26 59 79 77
@ *champagne-p.michel@orange.fr*	👤 *Geoffroy Michel*
🌐 *www.champagne-paul-michel.fr*	*[map p. 59]*
🏃 🏭 🍇	*20 ha*

This is quite a sizeable domain for a grower. The family has been growing grapes since 1847, and started producing Champagne when Paul Michel set up in Cuis, at the northern end of the Côte des Blancs, in 1952. His sons Philippe and Denis took over in due course, joined by the next generation, Geoffroy, in 2014. Vineyards are mostly in Cuis and Pierry (both premier cru) with some also in grand cru Chouilly. Plantings are almost entirely Chardonnay. There are three cuvées: Blanc de Blancs premier cru nonvintage, Blanc de Blancs grand cru vintage, and rosé premier cru (Chardonnay except for the 5-10% of red wine). Dosage is average at 8g/l.

Champagne Christophe Mignon

La Boulonnerie, 51700 Festigny	☎ +33 3 26 58 34 24
@ contact@champagne-christophe-mignon.com	▲ Laurence & Christophe Mignon
⊕ www.champagne-christophe-mignon.com	[map p. 56]
⊡ ⛏ 🍇	7 ha; 45,000 btl

"I come from an old line of vignerons, starting in 1870," says Christophe Mignon, who is the fifth generation at this family domain. Christophe works by what he calls "ancestral methods," but although he is not certified as organic or biodynamic, you can get a good idea of the approach from his comment that "disgorgement is according to the phase of the moon." Located in the Vallée de la Marne, his focus is on Pinot Meunier, which is almost 90% of plantings. All cuvées have very low dosage. Under the name of Pur Meunier, it comes as Brut Nature, Extra Brut (3 g/l), or Brut (only 6 g/l); as vintage there is both Brut Nature and Extra Brut (5 g/l). There are two rosé cuvées, both 100% Pinot Meunier; the Rosé de Saignée (Extra Brut or Brut) and the Rosé d'Assemblage (Brut but only 6 g/l dosage). There is also a Blanc de Blancs. His wines are regarded as a definitive expression of Pinot Meunier.

Champagne Pierre Mignon

5 rue des Grappes d'Or, 51210 Le Breuil	☎ +33 3 26 59 22 03
@ info@pierre-mignon.com	▲ Jean-Charles & Céline Mignon
⊕ www.pierre-mignon.com	
🏃 ⛏ 🏠 🍃	18 ha; 500,000 btl

The house is located in the sub valley of Surmelin, south of the Vallée de la Marne, but has vineyards in the Marne, around Epernay, and on the Côte des Blancs. Pierre and Yveline Mignon took over the family estate in 1970, and their children Jean-Charles (now the winemaker) and Céline joined in 2000. Vineyards are 60% Pinot Meunier, 30% Chardonnay, and 10% Pinot Noir. The Grande Réserve, Rosé, and Blanc de Noirs reflect the vineyards, with a majority of Pinot Meunier. The Prestige Brut add Rosé (made by saignée) have less Meunier. The Blancs de Blancs Grand Cru comes from the Côte des Blancs. All have dosage of 8 g/l. Cuvée Pure is a zero dosage. Vintage cuvées include Année de Madame (both Brut and rosé have a majority of Chardonnay), Harmonie is a Blanc de Blancs from grand cru villages on the Côte des Blancs, and Clos des Gravières comes from a single plot of 50% Chardonnay, 40% Pinot Noir, and 10% Pinot Meunier, vinified in barriques before aging for 9 lees on the lees.

Champagne Jean Milan

8 rue Avize, 51190 Oger	☎ +33 3 26 57 50 09
@ info@champagne-milan.com	▲ Jean-Charles Milan
⊕ www.champagne-milan.com	[map p. 59]
🏃 € ⛏ 🏠	6 ha; 70,000 btl

This family estate dates from 1864 and is run today by Caroline and her brother Jean-Charles. Vineyards are in 42 parcels all around Oger, and all the cuvées except the rosé are Blanc de Blancs from the village, starting with the non vintage Brut and Extra Brut. In vintage, Transparence comes from Oger, Symphorine is a selection from four parcels with an average age of 45-years, and Terres de Noël comes from vines of over 75-years old in a single plot just behind the winery. All are aged in vat, except for Grand Réserve, which is aged in barriques.

146

Champagne Robert Moncuit

2, place de la Gare, 51190 Le Mesnil-sur-Oger	📞 +33 3 26 57 52 71
@ contact@champagnerobertmoncuit.com	👤 Pierre Amillet
🌐 www.champagnerobertmoncuit.com	[map p. 59]
📅 🏭 🎺 🍷	8 ha; 70,000 btl

The Moncuits have owned vineyards in Le Mesnil-sur-Oger since 1889, Robert Moncuit started estate bottling in 1928, and his grandson Pierre Amillet has been the winemaker since 2000. Vineyards are in Les Mesnil. All the cuvées are Blanc de Blancs, with Brut (5 g/l dosage) and Extra Brut in nonvintage; the Extra Brut has become the Réserve Perpetuelle, a blend of reserve wines from around six recent vintages with 2 g/l dosage. Les Chetillons is a Brut Nature from a 2 ha parcel planted in 1956, and was introduced with the 2008 vintage. The vintage Brut has 6 g/l dosage.

Champagne Monmarthe

38 Rue Victor Hugo, 51500 Ludes	📞 +33 3 26 61 10 99
@ contact@champagne-monmarthe.com	👤 Jean-Guy & Sandrine Monmarthe
🌐 www.champagne-monmarthe.com	[map p. 57]
📅 🏭 🎺 🍷	17 ha; 130,000 btl

The family history in Ludes dates from 1737. Champagne production began with Ernest Monmarthe in 1930, under the name of Champagne Ernest Monmarthe. Sixth generation Jean-Guy joined his father at the estate in 1990 and runs it today. Most of the vineyards (15 ha) are in Ludes. classified premier cru. in the Montagne de Reims. The range starts with Secret de Famille and the Rosé de Ludes (both blends of all three varieties), and Privilège (equal Pinot Noir and Chardonnay), all with malolactic fermentation performed and 8 g/l dosage. The vintage blend has slightly more Pinot Noir (60%) and slightly less dosage (7 g/l). Les Grimpants is a Blanc de Noirs from a single parcel, with base wines aged for six months in barriques, and 8 g/l dosage, Le Clos A. Doré is Blanc de Blancs from an enclosed plot. Coup de Coeur is the only extra brut, an equal blend of Pinot Noir and Chardonnay, with 3 g/l dosage. In 2014, Jean-Guy took over a neighboring house, Gérard Doré, with 4 ha in Ludes, and makes the Doré wines under its separate label.

Champagne Moussé Fils

5 Rue Jonquery, 51700 Cuisles	📞 +33 3 26 58 10 80
@ contact@champagnemoussefils.com	👤 Cedric Moussé
🌐 champagnemoussefils.com	[map p. 56]
📅 🔬 🏠 🍷	16 ha; 92,000 btl

The family has been growing grapes in the Marne Valley since the seventeenth century, and making wine since 1923. Jean-Marc Moussé took over in 1990, and in 2009 constructed a new eco-winery using solar panels and geothermal energy. His son Cédric took over in 2013. Vineyards are in a side-valley running off the Marne, spread over three villages including Cuisles, but all on the same south-facing slope with unusual terroir that includes green clay and schist. Plantings are 80% Pinot Meunier. Malolactic fermentation is done for all cuvées. The house is a member of the prestige association of smaller growers of Club Trésors de Champagne. Their Spécial Club cuvées are 100% Pinot Meunier both as extra brut (1 g/l dosage) and rosé de saignée. Cuvées are mostly Blanc de Noirs, all with minimal dosage: 3.5 g/l for L'Or d'Eugène (80% Pinot Meunier, from a 'perpetual reserve'), 1.5 g/ for Rosé Effusion (92% Pinot Meunier), zero dosage for the late disgorgement of L'Extra Or (80% Pinot Meunier from the perpetual reserve) and Les Vignes de Mon Village (100% Pinot Meunier from Cuisles, aged in bottles under corks instead of screw caps), and 1.5 g/l for the vintage Terre d'Illite (95% Pinot Meunier)—Illite is the name of the special soil. The only non-Meunier cuvée is Anecdote, Blanc de Blancs with 1.5 g/l dosage from a single parcel where the soil is deeper and not suitable for Meunier.

Champagne Mouzon-Leroux et fils

16 rue Basse des Carrières, 51380 Verzy	📞 +33 3 26 97 96 68
@ *champagnemouzon@gmail.com*	👤 *Sébastien Mouzon*
🌐 *www.champagne-mouzon-leroux.com*	*[map p. 57]*
📅 ⚒ 🍇 🌑 ⊘	*8 ha; 60,000 btl*

Sébastien Mouzon gave new life to this old family domain, which dates from 1776, when he took over in 2008. Vineyards are dispersed in 50 plots mostly around Verzy, with 60% Pinot Noir; almost all the rest is Chardonnay. Vinification includes the use of barriques (some cuvées use a mix of vat and barriques, some use only barriques), performing malolactic fermentation, and using minimal dosage. Atavique is a conventional blend for the area, 70% Pinot Noir with 30% Chardonnay; Incandescent is a rosé de saignée from 100% Pinot Noir; Ascendant is a blend based on a perpetual reserve started in 2010. All are Extra Brut, with very low dosage. The vintage cuvées are all zero dosage.

Champagne Nowack

10 rue Bailly, 51700 Vandières	📞 +33 3 26 58 02 69
@ *champagne@nowack.fr*	👤 *Flavien Nowack*
🌐 *www.champagne-nowack.com*	*[map p. 56]*
📅 ⚒ 🍇 ▦	*10 ha; 45,000 btl*

This is presently somewhat of a bifurcated house, producing both its traditional range of blends and also a new line of terroir-specific cuvées. Estate production started in 1919, and the domain continued to be passed from father to son. Vineyards are mostly in Vandières and Châtillon-sur-Marne; plantings are about 75% Pinot Meunier, typical for the Vallée de la Marne. Labeled Champagne Novack, the traditional range is made by Frédéric Novack; labeled Domaine Novack, the new range comes from his son Flavien, who began focusing on single vintage, single parcel cuvées in 2011. Each year Flavien adds another parcel to convert to organic farming and add to the list. The single-parcel wines are extra brut, including Les Bauchets (Pinot Noir planted in the 1980s), La Fontinette (Pinot Meunier planted around 1966), and La Tuilerie (Chardonnay planted around 1999). The base wines ferment and then age in barriques for 30-36 months. Usually there is no malolactic fermentation. They are not labeled as vintage wines, but each release comes from a single wine, indicated on the back label. They are labeled with the variety rather than traditional terms such as Blanc de Blancs. Flavien also has another range, Cru d'Origine, in which each release features a single village. The first releases come from Vandières and Châtillon-sur-Marne; these are real micro-cuvées, under 500 bottles each, also with very low dosage, under 3 g/l.

Champagne Francis Orban

23 Rue de Gaulle, 51700 Leuvrigny	📞 +33 3 26 58 84 41
@ *francis.orban@free.fr*	👤 *Francis Orban*
🌐 *www.champagne-francis-orban.fr*	*[map p. 56]*
📅 ⚒ 🍇 ⌇	*8 ha; 70,000 btl*

This family domain is now in its fourth generation under Francis Orban. Located on the sand and clay terroirs of the Vallée de la Marne, plantings are 90% Pinot Meunier. Francis joined the domain in 1999 after completing studies in viticulture and oenology, and created the marque Franc Orban in 2007. Nonvintage cuvées come 50% from the current year and 50% from the reserve. Everything is vinified in stainless steel, and malolactic fermentation is performed for all cuvées except the top nonvintage, l'Orbane. The brut cuvées usually have 9 g/l dosage, while the extra brut have 3 g/l. The cuvées are all effectively Blanc de Noir from Pinot Meunier, except the Brut Prestige, which has some Chardonnay.

Champagne Pierre Paillard

2 Rue 20ème Siecle, 51150 Bouzy	📞 +33 3 26 57 08 04
@ contact@champagne-pierre-paillard.fr	👤 Antoine & Quentin Paillard
🌐 www.champagne-pierre-paillard.fr	[map p. 57]
🚫🔪🍂🍷	11 ha; 90,000 btl

Brothers Antoine and Quentin Paillard are the eighth generation at this small grower-producer, which started in Bouzy in 1768, and has been producing estate Champagne for four generations. Vineyards are entirely in Bouzy, but unusually for the village, include a substantial (40%) proportion of Chardonnay (planted by Antoine's grandfather). There are five cuvées, with Brut and Brut Rosé in nonvintage, usually around two thirds Pinot Noir and one third Chardonnay. In vintage, addition to the general cuvée, there are two single-vineyard wines, Les Maillerettes Blanc de Noirs and Les Mottelettes Blanc de Blancs.

Champagne Palmer & Co

67, rue Jacquart, 51100 Reims	📞 +33 3 26 07 35 07
@ contact@champagne-palmer.fr	👤 Rémi Vervier
🌐 www.champagne-palmer.fr	[map p. 54]
📅 €€ 🏭 🍷	430 ha; 1,000,000 btl

The cooperative was founded by seven growers in Avize in 1947, with vineyards on the Côte des Blanc and Montagne de Reims. It moved to Reims in 1959, and then expanded to include all the other areas of Champagne (although the Montagne de Reims remains the main source of grapes). The expansion created a need for more space, and it acquired its present premises in 1997. There is a large range, with six nonvintage cuvées, vintage, and the prestige cuvée Amazone de Palmer. The style is warm with a diffuse flavor spectrum and often some nutty impressions on the finish. Vintage wines have a more refined, more linear impression. The rosé has more character than the Brut. There's also a policy of holding back some of each declared vintage for late disgorgement. Moving into oenotourism, the coop has opened a hotel and restaurant at Chigny-les-Roses, just south of Reims.

Champagne Franck Pascal

1 Bis Rue Valentine Régnier, 51700 Baslieux-sous-Châtillon	📞 +33 3 26 51 89 80
@ franck.pascal@wanadoo.fr	👤 Franck Pascal
🌐 deschampagnespourlavie.net	[map p. 56]
📅 €€ 🏭 🍂 🌾 🚫	8 ha; 55,000 btl

Franck Pascal was going to become an engineer, but changed career to take over the family estate when his younger brother died in 1994. The estate started with 20 parcels of vineyards extending over five villages, but doubled in size in 2014-2015. Franck made an early commitment to biodynamics, but had to abandon it (temporarily) in the extreme conditions of 2016.

Plantings are 70% Pinot Meunier and 30% Pinot Noir. The cuvées are all blends: Reliance is a Brut Nature, Tolerance is a rosé with low dosage of 4 g/l, Pacifiance is made on the solera principle, Harmonie is the vintage, and Sérénité is made without any added sulfur.

Champagne Paul-Etienne Saint Germain

51 Avenue de Champagne, 51200 Épernay	📞 +33 3 26 32 31 12
@ contact@pauletiennesaintgermain.com	👤 Agnès & Jean-Michel Lagneau
🌐 www.pauletiennesaintgermain.fr	[map p. 58]
🉐 €€ ⛏ 🏠 ☘	4 ha; 40,000 btl

After a career working at grand marque Maisons, Jean-Michel Lagneau and his wife created their own negociant house, purchasing Pinot Noir and Chardonnay exclusively from grand cru villages. All cuvées are nonvintage. The Tradition Blanc de Blancs comes from the Côte des Blancs, the Exception Blanc de Noirs comes from Verzenay in the Montagne de Reims, Charme and Divine are blends of Pinot Noir from the Montagne de Reims with Chardonnay from the Côte des Blancs, and the rosé is 90% Pinot Noir and 10% Chardonnay sourced from the Montagne de Reims. The style is fresh and elegant.

Penet-Chardonnet

La Maison Penet, 12 rue Gambetta, 51380 Verzy	📞 +33 3 51 00 28 80
@ contact@lamaisonpenet.com	👤 Alexandre Penet
🌐 www.lamaisonpenet.com	
🉐 ⛏ 🍇	🍾 Terroir et Sens, Blanc de Blancs
Owner: La Maison Penet	

Alexandre Penet trained as an engineer before he took over the family estate in 2008. The estate wines are labeled as Penet-Chardonnet, and there is a separate label, Alexandre Penet, for a negociant activity that was started in 2011 Alexandre is also involved in making Crémant in Alsace, at the estate of his wife, Martine Penet-Grimm. All three houses, together with the Eclat sparking wine producer in Mendoza, Argentina, are now grouped under the rubric La Maison Penet. The nonvintage cuvees are labeled Terroir et Sens, and come from Verzy and Verzenay. The Extra Brut, which has no MLF, is a little austere; the Blanc de Blancs is broader, although dosage is a touch lower. There are five cuvées from single parcels in Verzy or Verzenay. There are three vintage cuvées from lieu-dits in Verzy: the Les Fervins blend of Pinot Noir and Chardonnay, Les Epinettes Blanc de Noirs, and Les Blanches Voies Blanc de Blancs. Overall the house style shows a touch of austerity, even for cuvées with typical dosage around 5g. They may need a little time to develop after release. The Alexandre Penet wines are mostly sourced from the Montagne de Reims.

Champagne Pertois-Lebrun

399 Rue de La Libération, 51530 Cramant	📞 +33 3 26 57 54 25
@ contact@champagne-pertoislebrun.com	👤 Clément & Antoine Bouret
🌐 www.champagne-pertoislebrun.com	[map p. 59]
🎴 ⛏ 🍇 ▦	10 ha; 40,000 btl

The house takes its name from the marriage in 1955 of Paul Pertois from Cramant with Françoise Lebrun from Le Mesnil-sur-Oger, both from winegrowing families. Their daughter Odile took over in due course, and then her nephews Clément and Antoine Bouret joined in 2007 and 2013. They have 44 plots in five different grand cru villages on the Côte des Blancs. Each parcel is vinified separately. All Blanc de Blancs, the range includes extra brut and brut (all with low dosage), typically with some aging of base wines in oak, and a longer than usual period in bottle before disgorgement. Nuances is a cuvée with lower pressure than usual (increasing creaminess). There are some single-vineyard wines from Chouilly, including Le Fond du Bateau and Derrière de Mont Aigu, not identified as vintage but carrying a number that refers to the year.

Champagne Roger Pouillon & Fils

3 rue de La 17 rue d'Aÿ, 51160 Mareuil-sur-Aÿ	📞 +33 3 26 52 63 62
@ contact@champagne-pouillon.com	👤 Fabrice Pouillon
🌐 www.champagne-pouillon.com	[map p. 58]
🗓 🏭 🍇 🐌	7 ha; 55,000 btl

Established in 1947 when Roger Pouillon decided to start bottling wine from the family vineyards, the house has been run since 1998 by Fabrice, Roger's grandson. Vineyards are mostly in Aÿ and Mareuil-sur-Aÿ, but extend along the Vallée de la Marne farther west. Located in a small house on the main road through Mareuil-sur-Aÿ, this very much gives the impression of a boutique house, with a small cellar stuffed with wood containers of various sizes, which are used for 80% of winemaking. Wines are vinified in a mix of vats and barriques, and the reserve wines are aged in old oak tonneaux and foudres. The winery is here, and there's another facility elsewhere for bottling. The elegant, light style is reinforced by low dosage. The major cuvée (half of production) is the Brut Réserve, 65% Pinot Noir, 20% Pinot Meunier, and 15% Chardonnay, with dosage of 5 g/l. It has a very fine texture. "This represents the domain as it has grapes from all our plots," Fabrice says. There are several single-vineyard wines: Les Terres Froides is a Blanc de Blancs from Tauxières in the Montagne de Reims; a new cuvée, this has a little more weight to the palate and greater aromatic lift. Les Blanchiens is an equal blend of Pinot Noir and Chardonnay from Mareuil and has zero dosage. It's aged under cork instead of crown caps. Although it's zero dosage, it's the richest of the cuvées, moving in the direction of salinity. Les Valnons is a Blanc de Blancs from Aÿ, and Chemin du Bois is a Blanc de Noirs from Mareuil; they are Extra Brut. Solera is an Extra Brut with 3 g dosage and comes from withdrawing 30% of the wine from a solera with half Pinot Noir and half Chardonnay that was established twenty years ago. The rosé is a Pinot Noir made by saignée; a faint sense of red berry fruits cuts the austerity of the style.

Champagne Prévoteau-Perrier

15 Rue André Maginot, 51480 Damery	📞 +33 3 26 58 41 56
@ champagneprevoteau-perrier@orange.fr	👤 Christophe & Delphine Boudard-Prévoteau
🌐 www.champagne-prevoteau-perrier.fr	[map p. 56]
🗓 €€ 🏭 🏠 🐌	24 ha; 300,000 btl

The house was founded in 1946 as the result of marriage between two families of growers, and was really built up by the next generation, Patrice Prévoteau. Third generation Delphine Prévoteau and her husband Christophe Boudard (who comes from Brittany) now run the domain. The estate vineyards are around Damery in the Vallée la Marne, but grapes are also sourced from the Côte des Blancs. Most cuvées are an assemblage from all sources. La Vallée and the rosé brut are based on Pinot Meunier with some Pinot Noir and Chardonnay; dosage is on the high side for brut at 10-11 g/l. Equilibre is a brut (dosage 9-10 g/l) with a third of each variety. Extra brut hast he same blend but lowers dosage to 2-4 g/l. Blanc de Noirs comes two thirds from Pinot Noir and a third from Pinot Meunier and lowers the dosage a touch to 8-9 g/l. Blanc de Blancs comes from sources extending from the Vallée to south of Epernay to the

Côte des Blancs, with dosage of 7-8 g/l. Cuvée Adrienne Lecouvreur is a step up, with equal Chardonnay and Pinot Noir, aged a year longer before disgorgement, with dosage of 6-7 g/l. Edition Limitée is a prestige cuvée aged for 6 years before disgorgement, with dosage of 6 g/l. The vintage Cuvée l'Historique was introduced only with 2012, and is 70% Chardonnay with 30% Pinot Noir, aged for 7 years, with dosage of 6 g/l. All the cuvées are vinified in stainless steel and go through malolactic fermentation. Fût de Chêne is an exception, a Blanc de Noirs from 50-year-old vines of Pinot Meunier with 30% aged in tonneaux for 18 months; dosage is 6 g/l.

Champagne Rémy Massin et Fils

34 Grande Rue, 10110 Ville-sur-Arce	📞 +33 3 25 38 74 09
@ contact@champagne-massin.com	👤 Cédric Massin
🌐 www.champagne-massin.com	[map p. 60]
📅 € 🏭 🍇 ☕	22 ha; 110,000 btl

Located in the Aube, in the heart of the village of Ville-sur-Arce, the family has been growing grapes since 1865 for five generations. The house was founded in 1974 when Rémy Massin and his son Sylvère decided to produce their own Champagne. Rémy managed the vineyards and Sylvain became the winemaker; Sylvère's son, Cédric, also an oenologist, joined in 2002. Vineyards are close to the river Arce, planted with 75% Pinot Noir, 5% Pinot Blanc, and 20% Chardonnay. The Brut Tradition is in fact 100% Pinot Noir, L'Intégrale is an Extra Brut Blanc de Noirs, and the rosé is 85% Pinot Noir. The top cuvées are Louis Aristide, a Blanc de Noir based on a solera of 18 vintages, and the Spécial Club vintage cuvées, which include a 100% Pinot Blanc.

Champagne de la Renaissance

2, rue d'Avize, 51190 Oger	📞 +33 3 26 57 53 90
@ champagne.renaissance@orange.fr	👤 Michel Bernard
🌐 www.champagne-de-la-renaissance.com	[map p. 59]
📅 🏭 🍇	9 ha; 30,000 btl

Nelly Dhondt created the domain in 1974 and handed over to her son Michel Bernard in 2015. Vineyard parcels are quite dispersed in Oger and other villages of the Côte des Blancs, the Côte de Sézanne, and Aÿ. Brut Plus comes only from the Côte des Blancs, fermented in stainless steel, but with 30% aged in barriques for a year. Dosage is 4 g/l. Origine Plus comes from both the Côte des Blancs and the Côte de Sézanne, and is 100R Chardonnay, with dosage of 6 g/l. Rosé des Blancs is 95% Chardonnay from grand cru villages on the Côte des Blancs and 5% Pinot Noir red wine from Aÿ, with dosage of 6 g/l. Sauvage is a zero dosage Blanc de Blancs from Oger and Avize. Fleuron is Blanc de Blancs with only two successive vintages from Oger, dosage at 7 g/l. The vintage is Blanc de Blancs with varying dosage—"each vintage is unique."

Champagne Roses de Jeanne

4 rue du Creux Michel, 10110 Celles-sur-Ource	📞 +33 3 25 29 69 78
@ rdj@orange.fr	👤 Cédric Bouchard
🚫 ⚗ 🍇 🍂 3 ha; 14,000 btl	[map p. 60]

This is a real boutique winery. After leaving home and working as a sommelier in Paris, Cédric Bouchard returned to start his own domain in 2000—Roses de Jeanne is named for his Polish grandmother—producing a single cuvée from a mere hectare of vines, the Les Ursules plot which came from his father. Subsequently he increased the domain by working the rest of his father's vines, which he bottled under a separate label, Inflorescence; but since he took over completely in 2012, all the wines have been labeled as Roses de Jeanne. Cédric's philosophy is somewhat counter to the conventional wisdom of blending, focusing on single-vineyard wines from single varieties in single vintages (although the wines may not be vintage-labeled as they do not age long enough on the lees to meet the requirement for vintage). Yields are about a third of the norm for the region. The major cuvées (if the term major can be used here) are three Blanc de Noirs, Val Vilaine, Côte de Bachelin, and Les Ursules, each from plots of 1-1.5 ha. From much smaller plots, there are La Haut-Lemblée (Chardonnay), Bolorée (very old Pinot Blanc), and Le Creux d'Enfer rosé (made by saignée from Pinot Noir). Wines are aged in stainless steel and dosage is zero; pressure is lower than the norm, at 4.5 bars instead of the usual 6 bars. Going along with the distaste for high pressure, Cédric recommends that his Champagnes should be decanted for an hour before consuming. Cédric also makes some still wines from the same vineyards under the Coteaux Champenois appellation, with Chardonnay, a white from Pinot Noir, and (red) Pinot Noir.

Champagne Ruppert-Leroy

La Bergerie, 10360 Essoyes	📞 *+33 3 25 29 81 31*
@ *ruppertleroy@orange.fr*	👤 *Bénédicte & Emmanuel Leroy*
🌐 *champagne-ruppert-leroy.com*	*[map p. 60]*
🗓 ✂ 🍇 🍷	*4 ha; 275,000 btl*

Bénédicte Leroy's parents started with a small sheep farm in Essoyes on the Côte des Bar. In the 1980s they planted vines and sold the grapes to the cooperative. When her father retired in 2009, Bénédicte changed career from teaching to winemaking. They divide the domain into three plots and make separate cuvées from each. (In addition, there are 20 ha used for cows, sheep, and horses.) Fermentation and aging are in a mix of barriques and demi-muids. Malolactic fermentation occurs naturally. The wines are all Brut Nature (no dosage), and no sulfur is added except for Cuvée 11,12,13, which comes from a 'perpetual reserve' (a sort of solera), and is an assemblage of Pinot Noir and Chardonnay from all the parcels. Cuvée Fosse-Grely has equal Pinot Noir and Chardonnay, and the other cuvées are monovarietals. Les Cognaux is Chardonnay, Martin Fontaine and Papillon (from different parcels) are Pinot Noir, and the rose (made by saignée) is Pinot Noir. The labels use varietal names rather than Blanc de Blancs or Blanc de Noirs.

Champagne Louis de Sacy

6 rue de Verzenay, BP 2, 51380 Verzy	📞 *+33 3 26 97 91 13*
@ *contact@champagnelouisdesacy.com*	👤 *Alain, Jonathan , or Yaël Sacy*
🌐 *www.champagnelouisdesacy.com*	*[map p. 57]*
🗓 € 🏭 🍇 ⚘	*18 ha; 150,000 btl*

The family has been involved with Champagne since the seventeenth century. Champagne Sacy Père et Fils was formed in 1962, changing its name in 1986 to Champagne Louis de Sacy (after the notable author of the early eighteenth century). Vineyards are divided into 23 plots in the villages of Verzy, Cernay, Trellon, and Bligny. Plantings are 65% Pinot Noir, 30% Chardonnay, and 5% Meunier. The composition of the Brut, cuvée Originel, has a little less Pinot Noir and more Chardonnay compared to plantings, with 6 g/l dosage. Cuvée Nue is the zero dosage. The nonvintage range also includes two Kosher wines, one a Brut and the other a rosé. There are also nonvintage wines specifically from grand crus, including a Brut (4g/l dosage), Rosé de Saignée (4 g/l) and Blanc de Blancs (6 g/l). The vintage cuvée, Les Courtisols, is 75% Pinot Noir with 25% Chardonnay, and has 3 g/l dosage.

Champagne de Saint-Gall

7 rue Pasteur, 51190 Avize	☎ +33 3 26 57 94 22
@ info@de-saint-gall.com	👤 Dominique Babé or Pierre Desanlis
🌐 www.de-saint-gall.com	[map p. 59]
🗓 🏭 ▬	1400 ha

The name Champagne de Saint Gall is used by the Union Champagne group of cooperatives, and is restricted to cuvées coming from plots in premier and grand crus on the Côte des Blancs. Production takes place in a facility constructed in Avize in 2013. In nonvintage, Blanc de Blancs comes from premier cru vineyards, and the Blanc de Blancs Extra Brut comes from grand cru vineyards. Other cuvées include Le Selection (a blend from all three varieties) and Le Tradition (a blend of Chardonnay and Pinot Noir), and a demi-sec. There is a vintage Blanc de Blancs from grand cru vineyards, and there are also some prestige cuvées.

Champagne Salmon

21 Rue Cap Chesnais, 51170 Chaumuzy	☎ +33 3 26 61 82 36
@ info@champagnesalmon.com	👤 Alexandre Salmon
🌐 champagnesalmon.com	[map p. 55]
🗓 🏭 🍇 🍷	10 ha; 80,000 btl

Michel Salmon bought his first plot and produced his first vintage, only 500 bottles, in 1958. His son Olivier and grand son Alexandre run the house today, describing themselves as specialists in Pinot Meunier, which comprises 85% of plantings. In addition, there is 1 ha each of Pinot Noir and Chardonnay. An interest in hot air balloons is the basis for naming the regular range Montgolfière., It includes Selection (50% Pinot Meunier, 25% each of Pinot Noir and Chardonnay), Rosé (the selection blend plus 15% red wine), Prestige (50%Chardonnay and 25% of each Pinot), all with 9 g/l dosage. The dosage is slightly lower, at 7 g/l for the vintage cuvée (a third of each variety) and for the prestige cuvée A.S., which has equal amounts of Chardonnay and Pinot Noir, aged in barriques. There is also a demi-sec. The house is one of the 28 members of the Special Club, under which it produces zero dosage (60% Chardonnay, 40% Pinot Noir), and a zero dosage rosé from saignée of 100% Pinot Meunier. In the Meunier range, it also produces a Brut and Brut Rosé (both 7g/l dosage), and both red and white still wine.

Champagne Savart

1, 51500 rue du Chemin de Sacy, Écueil	☎ +33 3 26 84 91 60
@ fred@champagne-savart.com	👤 Frédéric Savart
🌐 champagne-savart.com	[map p. 55]
🚫 🔪 🏠 🍷	6 ha; 40,000 btl

"The aim is to make wines with their own identity, avoiding the standardization of taste," says Frédéric Savart, who took over this small domain of 4 ha from his father, Daniel. The estate was founded by René Savart when he purchased the first vineyards in 1947. Vineyards are all around the village of Ecueil. His son Daniel took over in the 1970s. Frédéric had planned to be a footballer, but returned to help Daniel with the domain, and took over in 2005. The focus is on Pinot Noir, with a small amount of Chardonnay. Most of the cuvées are zero dosage or extra brut; even the Brut cuvées are on the margin, with only 6-7 g/l dosage. Most wines are handled in stainless steel, but there is some use of oak, with wood coming from the forest near Ecueil, especially for the Expression Brut Nature. The vintage cuvée, L'Année, comes from cofermentation of roughly equal amounts of Pinot Noir and Chardonnay.

Champagne François Secondé

6 Rue Galipes, 51500 Sillery	📞 +33 3 26 49 16 67
@ *francois.seconde@wanadoo.fr*	👤 Jérôme Groslambert
🌐 *www.champagnefrancoisseconde.com*	[map p. 57]
🏠 €€ 🏭 🍷 🍂	6 ha; 45,000 btl

François Secondé left school at 14, became a vineyard worker, bought a small parcel in 1972, and then leased more vineyards in 1976. He built the domain up to its present size, with 3 ha in Sillery, where he was the only grower in the village and the only house to produce dedicated cuvées from the Cru. Plantings are two thirds Pinot Noir and a third Chardonnay. François died prematurely in 2018 as the result of an accidental fall, and his wife, Anne-Marie is continuing the domain with the help of chef de cave Jérôme Groslambert. There is quite a large range for a small domain. The Brut is about half of production, with a grape mix reflecting plantings. Cuvée Clavier is essentially the same with slightly longer aging. La Loge is a Blanc de Noirs exclusively from Sillery, with dosage into the Brut range at 8g. The rosé is 100% Pinot Noir. The Blanc de Blancs vintage release comes only from Sillery. All the cuvées have dosage of 8 g/l, except for the single parcel release Les Petites Vignes, which comes from grand cru Puisieux and is half Pinot Noir and half Chardonnay, with 6 g/l, and the zero dosage Intégral. These wines give a solid impression, enhanced by the dosage.

Champagne J-M Sélèque

9 Allée de la Vieille Ferme, 51530 Pierry	📞 +33 3 26 55 27 15
@ *contact@jmseleque.fr*	👤 Jean-Marc Sélèque
🌐 *www.jmseleque.fr*	[map p. 58]
🗓 🍷 🍷 🍂	9 ha; 80,000 btl

The house was founded in 1965 by Henri Sélèque. His sons Richard and Jean joined in 1974. The estate was split in 2008, with half going to Richard's son, Jean-Marc, who set up his own domain in Pierry, and the other half to Jean's daughter (whose wine is made by the local coop, and should not be confused with J-M Sélèque, although the labels and vineyard names are similar). Vineyards consist of around 40 dispersed plots, in seven villages extending from Dizy just north of Épernay, to villages just south of Épernay, along the Vallée de la Marne, and to Boursault and Vertus at the south of the Côte des Blancs. Chardonnay is the predominant grape with 60% of plantings, together with 30% Pinot Meunier and 10% Pinot Noir. Wines are aged about two thirds in steel and one third in wood. The nonvintage Solessence is blended from all the holdings, and comes as Brut, Extra Brut. and Brut Nature. Blanc de Blancs Quintette comes from five of the villages (including the extremes of Dizy and Vertus). Les Solistes is a Pinot Meunier from 70-year-old vines in a single vineyard in Pierry. Dosage is always low; with the exception of the nonvintage Brut, all the wines are Extra Brut (usually 2-3 g/l dosage) or Brut Nature.

Champagne Suenen

53 Rue de La Garenne, 51530 Cramant	📞 +33 3 26 57 54 94
@ *aurelien@champagne-suenen.fr*	👤 Aurélien Suenen
🌐 *www.champagne-suenen.fr*	[map p. 59]
🗓 🍷 🍷	3 ha; 28,000 btl

Aurélien Suenen took over the estate when his father died in 2009. Aurélien produces Blanc de Blancs from 3 ha of Chardonnay, in three grand cru villages on the Côte des Blancs: Cramant, Chouilly, and Oiry. From 2 ha of Pinots Noir and Meunier elsewhere, he sells the grapes, except for one plot of old ungrafted Meunier. Originally there were Blanc de Blancs nonvintage and vintage assembled from all three villages, but in 2013 Aurélien replaced them with cuvées from separate terroirs, Oiry and C+C (Cramant plus Chouilly). Aurélien views the Oiry terroir, with less clay and harder chalk, as producing greater tension than Chouilly and Cramant. The next new cuvée was Les Robarts, a vintage release from a 40-year old single vineyard in Cramant (first release was the 2012 vintage in 2017). He followed the next year with the single vineyard La Cocluette in Oiry, where the vines are close to 100-years old, and Montaigu from Chouilly. Breaking away from Blanc de Blancs, La Grande Vigne comes from the ungrafted Meunier at Montigny-sur-Vesle. With the focus on expressing terroirs, dosage is always low; cuvées are extra brut, with dosage usually 1-2 g/l, occasionally 4 g/l, decided on the basis of blind tasting. Aurélien describes his approach: "Most important for me is to extract the DNA of these grapes. Without mask, extraction, chemical. Just the DNA."

Champagne Eric Taillet

37, rue Valentine Regnier, 51700 Baslieux-sous-Châtillon	📞 +33 3 26 58 11 42
@ *champagneerictaillet@gmail.com*	👤 *Eric Taillet*
🌐 *www.champagne-eric-taillet.fr*	*[map p. 56]*
📅 €€ ⛪ 🏠 ☺	*6 ha; 40,000 btl*

Eric Taillet has a passion for Pinot Meunier, to the point of starting the Meunier Institute, a group of producers focusing on Meunier. The fourth generation since the family planted its first vines in 1900, he has been in charge of the family house since 1995. Located in the Vallée de la Marne, with soils of clay, marl, and sand, Pinot Meunier is his dominant variety, with 80% of plantings, and several of the cuvées are monovarietal or almost so. Excusiv'T Brut is a Blanc de Meunier, and Bansionensi Extra Brut is 100% Meunier from the Vallée du Belval. Sur le Grand Marais is 90% Pinot Meunier and 10% Chardonnay from intermingled plantings, and the rosé Luminosi'T is 92% Pinot Meunier with 8% of still Pinot Noir. The blended cuvées are Egali'T, which is a third of each variety, and Décennie Extra Brut is a vintage blend of 50% Pinot Meunier aged in barriques with 50% Chardonnay aged in cuve.

Champagne Alain Thiénot

14 rue des Moissons, 51100 Reims	📞 +33 3 26 77 50 10
@ *infos@champagne-thienot.com*	👤 *Garance Thiénot*
🌐 *www.champagne-thienot.com*	*[map p. 54]*
🚫 ✒ 🏠 ☺ *Owner: Champagne Joseph Perrier*	*30 ha; 400,000 btl*

This house is not quite the simple family domain it might appear to be superficially. It was founded 1985 by Alain Thiénot, formerly a broker in Champagne, who subsequently handed it on to his children Stanislas and Garance. Alain also owns properties in Bordeaux, and under the rubric of Thiénot Bordeaux-Champagnes owns or has stakes in the Dourthe-Kressmann negociant in Bordeaux, and Champagnes Joseph Perrier and Canard-Duchêne, and other properties. Total production of the group is around 30 million bottles. In champagne the collection of houses owns 720 ha. The address of Champagne Alain Thiénot is in Reims, but the wines are produced at a cuverie in Taissy, just to the south. About half of the estate vineyards on the Côte de Blancs or Montagne de Reims are premier or grand cru. There's a full range of both nonvintage and vintage Champagnes, with style generally in the direction of aperitifs.

Champagne Trousset-Guillemart

Rue de Villedommange RD 6, 51370 Les Mesneux	📞 +33 6 16 70 32 66
@ *contact@champagnetrousset.fr*	👤 *Karine Diot Trousset*

🌐 *champagnetroussetguillemart.fr*   [map p. 55]

📅 €€ ⛏ 🍇 🍷   8 ha; 52,000 btl

The Guillemart family has been growing grapes since 1697, and the name of domaine became Trousset-Guillemart when France Guillemart married Jackie Trousset in 1958. Their son Jean-Philippe joined the domain in 1988 and has run the house since 2008. Vineyards are in the premier cru villages of Les Mesneux, Sacy, and Villedommange in the Montagne de Reims. In addition to the usual trio of varieties, there are plantings of the old varieties Arbanne and Petit Meslier. The wines are vinified in 85% stainless steel and 15% barriques, and go through malolactic fermentation. The first wine comes as Brut or Brut Nature from 50% Pinot Noir, 31% Pinot Meunier, and 19% Chardonnay. The Blanc de Blancs (actually labeled 'Pure Chardonnay') has zero dosage, and the Blanc de Noirs is very low at 1.15 g/l. The vintage release has equal Chardonnay and Pinot Noir, is vinified in stainless s steel, and has zero dosage. Les Croisettes is the cuvée with old varieties, 51% Petit Meslier, 46% Chardonnay, and 3% Arbanne.

Champagne Varnier-Fannière

23 Rempart du Midi, 51190 Avize	📞 +33 3 26 57 53 36
@ varnier-fanniere@orange.fr	👤 Valérie Varnier
🌐 www.varnier-fanniere.com	[map p. 59]
📅 ⛏ 🍇 🍷	4 ha; 36,000 btl

The Fannière family have been growing grapes since 1860, but it was only in 1950 that Jean Fannière started estate bottling. His grandson, Dennis Varnier, took over the vineyards in 1989. Dennis died unexpectedly in 2017 and his wife Valérie continues to run the domain. Vineyards are mostly split between Cramant and Avize, with a small holding in Oiry. The style shows as quite rich, because there is always full malolactic fermentation, and the wines are bottled at slightly lower pressure (about 5 bars instead of the usual 6 bars). There are many cuvées for such a small domain. Most of the nonvintage blends are made as both Extra Brut and zero dosage. There is a single vintage wine.

Champagne Jean-Louis Vergnon

1 Grande Rue, 51190 Le Mesnil-sur-Oger	📞 +33 3 26 57 53 86
@ contact@champagne-jl-vergnon.com	👤 Clément Vergnon
🌐 www.champagne-jl-vergnon.com	[map p. 59]
📅 ⛏ 🏠 🍷	5 ha; 60,000 btl

The Regnault family started as a negociant in the nineteenth century, and then Elizabeth Regnault's son, Jean-Louis Vergnon, acquired vineyards and became a member of the cooperative in 1950. Estate bottling started in 1985. The present reputation of the house owes much to cellarmaster Christophe Constant, who has recently been succeeded by Julian Goût. Estate vineyards are mostly in Le Mesnil-sur-Oger; all the cuvées are Blancs de Blanc. The policy is to harvest grapes at high ripeness and to avoid malolactic fermentation. The nonvintage Brut Conversation, Extra Brut Éloquence, and zero dosage Murmure are aged in cuve, as is the vintage Brut Résonance; the vintage Extra Brut Confidence is aged in barriques.

Champagne Georges Vesselle

16 Rue Postes, 51150 Bouzy	📞 +33 3 26 57 00 15
@ contact@champagne-vesselle.fr	👤 Éric & Bruno Vesselle

| ⊕ *www.champagne-vesselle.fr* | *[map p. 57]* |
| 🕴 ⛏ 🍇 ☕ | *18 ha; 250,000 btl* |

The Vesselle family has been in Bouzy for a long time, and Georges established the house in 1954. He was mayor of the village and vineyard manager for Perrier-Jouët, Mumm, and Heidsieck Monopole. His sons Éric and Bruno joined him in 1993 and are now in charge. Pinot Noir is 90% of plantings. In addition to Champagne, the house produces Bouzy rouge, for which Georges was a great advocate. The blend of the Brut, both nonvintage and vintage, the Brut Nature, and the rosé reflects the vineyards. Cuvée Juline, which is a special selection, changes to 80% Pinot Noir and 20% Chardonnay. Cuvée Hélènais is 60% Pinot Noir and 40% Chardonnay, and ages for 7 years before disgorgement. All the cuvées are Brut except for the Blanc de Noirs and Blanc de Blancs, which are Extra Brut.

Champagne Maurice Vesselle

3 Rue Gambetta, 51150 Bouzy	📞 +33 3 26 57 00 81
@ *champagne.vesselle@wanadoo.fr*	👤 *Didier & Thierry Vesselle*
⊕ *www.champagnemauricevesselle.com*	*[map p. 57]*
🕴 ⛏ 🍇 ☕	*8 ha; 60,000 btl*

There are five Vesselle family domains in Bouzy; Maurice Vesselle was founded in 1955, and his sons Didier and Thierry run the house today. As well as at Bouzy, they have vines in Tours-sur-Marne. They describe their house as '100% Côte des Noirs, 100% Gran Cru.' Wines are vinified in stainless steel, and malolactic fermentation is blocked. The Brut is 80% Pinot Noir and 20% Chardonnay with 9 g/l dosage, aged for 5 years before disgorgement. The vintage is 85% Pinot Noir and 15% Chardonnay with 5 g/l dosage. Les Haut Chemins is a single-parcel vintage, 100% Pinot Noir, dosage 3 g/l, aged for 10 years before disgorgement.

Domaine Vincey

6 Rue du Mesnil 4 et, 51190 Blancs-Coteaux	📞 +33 6 76 40 99 63
@ *marine@domainevincey.com*	👤 *Marine & Quentin Vincey*
⊕ *www.domainevincey.com*	*[map p. 59]*
📅 ⛏ 🍇 ☕	*7 ha; 16,000 btl*

Quentin Vincey is the eighth generation at this small family domain, which until recently functioned under the RC category, with grapes sent to the cooperative, which produced the Champagne for the domain. Quentin took over in 2010, and in 2014 he and his wife Marine started to produce their own Champagne. The first vintage was only 4,000 bottles. The 5 ha of vineyards used for production of Blanc de Blancs are closest to the domain, all grand cru and classified as biodynamic; the other 2 ha are organic, and the grapes are sold off. Committed to representing both terroir and vintage, the domain follows an unusual model of producing only vintage Champagne. "We have at heart the idea of reflecting the terroirs of the three grand cru villages, Oger, Le Mesnil sur Oger, and Chouilly," Marine says, "and we want to present the wine's expression through each vintage." The policy is to harvest relatively late to get good maturity, vinification uses gravity feed to avoid pumping, use of sulfur is minimal (sometimes there is none), and the wines ferment and age in old (5-6-year) barriques, with regular battonage to maintain a more reductive rather than oxidative environment. Wines age in bottles under cork for a minimum of five years before disgorgement. Dosage is always low, from zero to 3 g/l. Production started with cuvées from Oger: La Première comes from several plots around the village, and Grand Jardin from a single parcel. After 2016, cuvées were added from Le Mesnil sur Oger village and two single parcels, Auge and Chemin de Chèlons. Modum Q.V. is a cuvée using a variation on the usual production method in which the must from one year is used to start the second fermentation for the previous year.

Domaine Vouette & Sorbée

8 rue de Vaux, 10110 Buxières-sur-Arce	📞 *+33 3 25 38 79 73*
@ *vouette-et-sorbee@orange.fr*	👤 *Bertrand Gautherot*
🌐 *www.vouette-et-sorbee.com*	*[map p. 60]*
🚫 ⚒ 🍇 ▣ ◯ ∅	*5 ha; 25,000 btl*

Like most houses on the Côte des Bar, this started as a grower selling grapes to the grand Maisons in the north. Bertrand Gauthier started estate bottling in 2004. His vineyards fall into six lieu-dits, most around the village, on Kimmeridgian soils, with some on Portlandian limestone. The domain is named for two of the lieu-dits. Committed to biodynamics, the focus is on natural production, so chaptalization is done only in exceptional circumstances, sulfur is used only at harvest, and all the cuvées are zero dosage. Fidèle is a Blanc de Noirs from several sites, Blanc d'Argile is a Blanc de Blancs, and the rosé, Saignée de Sorbée, comes from Pinot Blanc in the warmest site. The newest cuvée is unusual: Textures comes from Pinot Blanc, and the base wine is aged in both barriques and amphorae. In 2017, Champagne Clandestin started as a project between Bertrand and his chef de cave, Benoît Doussot. Operating on a negociant basis, Clandestin's name refers to its purchase of grapes from hidden vineyards, those not used in the past because of exposure or soil type. Les Sembables is a Blanc de Noirs from Pinot Noir west-facing parcels of Kimmeridgian terroir (not favored in the past when the objective was to capture the most sunlight). Les Grandes Lignes is Blanc de Blancs from Chardonnay in a south-facing vineyard planted on Portlandian clay. The base wines age in 300- and 500-liter barrels of neutral oak, and they are bottled with zero dosage.

Champagne J. Vignier

427 rue de la Libération, 51530 Cramant	📞 *+33 6 84 77 33 32*
@ *contact@champagnevignier.fr*	👤 *Sebastian Nickel*
🌐 *www.champagnevignier.fr*	*[map p. 59]*
🚫 ⚒ 🍇 ☙	*4 ha; 28,000 btl*

This is effectively a new Champagne house in an old setting, or perhaps more accurately a specialized offshoot of an existing house. Paul Lebrun started with 2 ha in 1902 and founded the house with his name in the 1930s. The champagne is still called Paul Lebrun, but the nameplate at the domain says Vignier-Lebrun, reflecting marriage into the Vignier family. Nathalie Vignier and her brother Jean took over in 2006. Nathalie's husband Hubert Soreau is the chef de cave at Le Clos l'Abbé in Epernay. Nathalie works with Sébastian Nickel (whose uncle was a close friend of Paul Lebrun), and in 2007 and 2008 they picked and fermented some parcels separately as an experiment. These became single-vineyard cuvées, which are bottled under the name of J. Vignier. The focus here is on purity, so the base wine is fermented, goes through malolactic fermentation, and ages in stainless steel; all the these cuvées have 5 g/l dosage and are labeled as Extra Brut. Lees aging is much longer than usual for non-vintage, varying from 4 to 8 years. Plantings are exclusively Chardonnay (the oldest dating from 1950), so all the wines are Blanc de Blancs. Ora Alba comes from three villages, Cramant, Chouilly, and Oiry. Les Longues Verges comes from a single parcel with part in Cramant and part in Chouilly. Until 2019 there was a vintage release, but now it carries a name like the other cuvées: Deux Terres does not declare a vintage on the label, but effectively it is the vintage release, is made only in top years. The 2008 is the current release, and is a blend between a parcel in Cramant and a parcel on the Côte de Sézanne. All these come from chalk-based terroirs, but Silexus Sézannensis comes from siliceous parcels on the Côte de Sézanne. In another style, there are experimental cuvées made in tiny amounts, labeled as QVFMR (Cuvée Éphémère), blends of two years or undeclared vintages, that change each year, with base wines aged in oak, dosage very low at 3 g/l, and malolactic fermentation blocked.

Champagne Waris-Hubert

14 Rue d'Oger, 51190 Avize	📞 +33 3 26 58 29 93
@ contact@champagne-waris-hubert.fr	👤 Stéphanie & Olivier Waris-Hubert
🌐 champagne-waris-hubert.fr	[map p. 59]
🉐 ⛏ 🍇 🍷	13 ha; 70,000 btl

The name reflects the joining of two estates in 1997 by Stéphanie Hubert and Olivier Waris, both from Avize. Most of the plots are on the Côte des Blancs, but they also have plots on the Côte de Sézanne, Côte de Bars, and Aÿ, making an unusually broad range for a producer on the Côte des Blancs. There's a rosé made by maceration, and a demi-sec. Premier crus are rosé made by saignée, and Brut Estence from 60% Chardonnay and 40% Pinot Noir. The range of grand crus starts with nonvintage Blanc de Blancs blends across villages: Albsecent is Brut and Lilyale is Extra Brut. Vintage cuvées are Extra Brut from Avize: Blanches base wines age in stainless steel, while Eminence spends 6 months in barriques. Annexä is a Blanc de Noirs from Aÿ.

Index of Houses by Rating

Index of Organic and Biodynamic Houses

Champagne Allouchery-Perseval
Champagne Aspasie
Champagne Barrat-Masson
Champagne Françoise Bedel
Champagne Bérêche et Fils
Champagne Maxime Blin
Champagne Francis Boulard & Fille
Champagne Bourgeois-Diaz
Champagne Vincent Charlot
Champagne Coessens
Champagne Marie Copinet
Champagne Vincent Couche
Champagne Benoît Déhu
Champagne Paul Déthune
Champagne Pascal Doquet
Champagne Didier Doué
Champagne Drappier
Champagne R. Dumont et Fils
Champagne Émilien Feneuil
Champagne Alexandre Filaine
Champagne Fleury
Champagne Olivier Horiot
Champagne Hugues Godmé
Champagne Labbé et Fils
Champagne Lacourte Godbillon
Champagne Benoît Lahaye
Champagne Laherte Frères
Champagne Larmandier-Bernier
Champagne Georges Laval
Champagne David Léclapart
Champagne Leclerc Briant
Champagne Lelarge-Pugeot
Champagne Lombard
Champagne Nicolas Maillart
Champagne Mandois
Champagne Marguet Père & Fils
Champagne Marie Courtin
Champagne Moussé Fils
Champagne Mouzon-Leroux et fils
Champagne Nowack
Champagne Franck Pascal
Champagne Éric Rodez
Champagne Louis Roederer
Champagne Roses de Jeanne
Champagne Ruppert-Leroy
Champagne Salmon

Champagne Savart
Champagne Jacques Selosse
Champagne De Sousa
Champagne Tarlant
Champagne Vazart-Coquart
Domaine Vincey
Domaine Vouette & Sorbée
Champagne Waris-Hubert

Producers Making Natural Wines or Wines With No Sulfur

Champagne Aspasie
Champagne Francis Boulard & Fille
Champagne Marie Copinet
Champagne Vincent Couche
Champagne Drappier
Champagne Émilien Feneuil
Champagne Fleury
Champagne Hugues Godmé
Champagne Benoît Lahaye
Champagne Larmandier-Bernier
Champagne David Léclapart
Champagne Leclerc Briant
Champagne Legret et fils
Champagne Lelarge-Pugeot
Champagne Marguet Père & Fils
Champagne Marie Courtin
Champagne Mouzon-Leroux et fils
Champagne Franck Pascal
Champagne Jacques Selosse
Domaine Vouette & Sorbée

Index of Houses by Area

Champagne Alfred Gratien
Champagne Marc Hébrart
Champagne Jacquinot & Fils
Champagne Janisson-Baradon et Fils
Champagne Lallier
Champagne Leclerc Briant
Champagne Emile Leclère
Champagne Lombard
Champagne Mandois
Champagne Moët et Chandon
Champagne Paul-Etienne Saint Germain
Champagne Joseph Perrier
Champagne Perrier-Jouët
Champagne Philipponnat
Champagne Pol Roger
Champagne Roger Pouillon & Fils
Champagne J-M Sélèque

Montagne de Reims

Champagne Yann Alexandre
Champagne Allouchery-Perseval
Champagne André Chemin
Champagne Michel Arnould et Fils
Champagne Aspasie
Champagne Aubry Fils
Jean Baillette-Prudhomme
Champagne Paul Bara
Champagne Edmond Barnaut
Champagne Phal B de Beaufort
Champagne Bérêche et Fils
Champagne H.Billiot & Fils
Champagne Maxime Blin
Champagne Francis Boulard & Fille
Champagne Louis Brochet
Champagne Canard-Duchêne
Champagne Cattier
Champagne Chartogne-Taillet
Champagne La Closerie
Champagne André Clouet
Champagne Paul Clouet
Champagne R.h. Coutier
Champagne Paul Déthune
Champagne Duménil
Champagne Egly Ouriet
Champagne Émilien Feneuil
Champagne Feneuil Pointillart
Champagne Forget Chemin
Champagne Gonet-Médeville
Champagne Charles Heidsieck
Champagne Piper-Heidsieck
Champagne Henriot

Champagne Hugues Godmé
Champagne Huré Frères
Champagne Jacquart
Champagne Jacquinet Dumez
Champagne Krug
Champagne Labbé et Fils
Champagne JM Labruyère
Champagne Lacourte Godbillon
Champagne Benoît Lahaye
Champagne Jean Lallement et fils
Champagne Lanson
Champagne J. Lassalle
Groupe Laurent-Perrier
Champagne David Léclapart
Champagne Lelarge-Pugeot
Champagne Lemaire Père & Fils
Champagne Nicolas Maillart
Champagne Mailly
Champagne Margaine
Champagne Marguet Père & Fils
Champagne Pierre Mignon
Champagne Monmarthe
Champagne Mouzon-Leroux et fils
Maison G. H. Mumm
Champagne Bruno Paillard
Champagne Pierre Paillard
Champagne Palmer & Co
Penet-Chardonnet
Champagne Pommery
Champagne Éric Rodez
Champagne Louis Roederer
Maison Ruinart
Champagne Louis de Sacy
Champagne Salmon
Champagne Savart
Champagne François Secondé
Champagne Taittinger
Champagne Alain Thiénot
Champagne Trousset-Guillemart
Champagne Georges Vesselle
Champagne Maurice Vesselle
Champagne Veuve Clicquot
Champagne Vilmart et Cie
Domaine Vincey

Vallée de la Marne

Champagne Apollonis
Champagne Françoise Bedel
Champagne Bourgeois-Diaz
Champagne Château de Boursault
Champagne Roland Champion

Champagne Dehours & Fils
Champagne Benoît Déhu
Champagne Maurice Delabaye et Fils
Champagne A. & J. Demière
Champagne Fallet Dart
Champagne Faÿ Michel
Champagne Alexandre Filaine
Champagne Gaston Chiquet
Champagne Jacquesson
Champagne Jeeper
Champagne Laherte Frères
Champagne Georges Laval
Champagne Xavier Leconte
Legras et Haas

Champagne Claude Lemaire
Champagne A. R. Lenoble
Champagne Gilles Mansard
Champagne Christophe Mignon
Champagne Moussé Fils
Champagne Nicolas Feuillatte
Champagne Nowack
Champagne Francis Orban
Champagne Franck Pascal
Champagne Prévoteau-Perrier
Champagne Eric Taillet
Champagne Tarlant
Champagne Vazart-Coquart

Index of Houses by Name

Made in the USA
Las Vegas, NV
22 December 2023